Powhatan Lords of Life and Death

Powhatan Lords
of Life and Death

Command and Consent in
Seventeenth-Century Virginia

MARGARET HOLMES WILLIAMSON

UNIVERSITY OF NEBRASKA PRESS · LINCOLN & LONDON

⊗

Library of Congress Cataloging-in-Publication Data

Williamson, Margaret Holmes.
Powhatan lords of life and death : command and
consent in seventeenth-century Virginia /
Margaret Holmes Williamson.
p. cm.
Includes bibliographical references and index.
ISBN 0-8032-4798-2 (cloth : alk. paper)
ISBN 978-0-8032-6037-5 (paper : alk. paper)
1. Powhatan Indians—Politics and government.
2. Powhatan, ca. 1550–1618. 3. Powhatan Indians—
Religion.   I. Title.
E99.P85.W55   2003
975.5004'973—dc21
2002028523

In memory of my parents,
Eleanor and Harry Williamson,
and of my uncle,
Richard Beale Davis

Contents

Illustrations

Map

Figures

Preface

The topic of this book was originally the subject of my B. Litt. thesis at the University of Oxford. I returned to a study of the Powhatan after spending 15 months among the Kwoma of Papua New Guinea, finding that the insights provided by fieldwork made a difference to my approach to this old material. This work treats the documents about the Powhatan as ethnographic reports. Rather than writing ethnohistory or archaeology, I have aimed to produce the equivalent of a modern ethnographic study of the Powhatan by reconstructing their culture as it was in about 1607, the year Jamestown was founded.

The reader may think that I have quoted too extensively from original sources, and perhaps I have done so. But much of my argument rests on textual analysis, and so my choices were either to present the texts I refer to immediately for the reader's assessment or to send the reader off to find a copy of the texts for comparison. It seemed to me that the former was preferable. Likewise, the degree of citation may strike some as overscrupulous. But again, because this is a work of interpretation, and but one of many based on the same texts, and because I have found certain of these interpretations frustrating for their lack of citation, I have thought it best to let readers know exactly on what I based any claims I made. Many of my sources were published, or at least written, early in the seventeenth century and have been republished recently. I have put the original date of publication or writing, where this is known, in square brackets following the publication date of the modern edition.

In writing this book, I have received encouragement and assistance from many sources. That original analysis, on which this one is based, benefited greatly from the advice of Peter Rivière and Rodney Needham; the latter read a draft of this book, also, and offered most helpful suggestions. Discussion with Jeffrey Hantman, particularly about trade between the Powhatan and Monacan, I have found most productive. I am especially grateful to Allyson Poska, of the Department of History at Mary Washington College, who willingly recommended most of the sources about Renaissance England on which I have relied; and to David Wood, also of that department, for reading a draft of the book and providing critical advice about empire and monarchy in early modern Europe. I must also thank Mary Beth Culley for advice on sources for the Powhatan language and Henry S. Sharp for his comments on power and political process. For the shortcomings of this analysis, none of them is responsible. I am grateful to Thomas Barnes for more than once rescuing electronic versions of this work from annihilation and to Robert Burchfield for his sympathetic copyediting. Mary Washington College has been generous with grants, including a semester sabbatical, which have materially assisted the completion of this work; and the staff of Simpson Library, especially Carla Bailey and Beth Perkins, have been most helpful at every turn. I am grateful also to the staffs of the British Library, the Department of Prints and Drawings at the British Museum, the Bodleian Library, the State Library of Virginia, the Firestone Library at Princeton University, and the Alderman Library at the University of Virginia.

My greatest debt of gratitude is, as always, to Peter Birkett Huber, without whom this work would not exist.

An offence . . . is punished by contempt, by exclusion from society, or, where the case is serious, . . . by the individuals whom it concerns. Imperfect as this species of coercion may seem, crimes are very rare among them; insomuch that were it made a question, whether no law, as among the savage Americans, or too much law, as among the civilized Europeans, submits man to the greatest evil; one who has seen both conditions of existence would pronounce it to be the last: and that the sheep are happier of themselves, than under the care of the wolves. It will be said, that great societies cannot exist without government. The savages therefore break them into small ones.

Thomas Jefferson, *Notes on the State of Virginia*

Introduction

In 1612 William Strachey, secretary to the nascent English colony at Jamestown in Virginia, wrote in his *Historie of Travell into Virginia Britania,* "The severall territoryes and provinces which are in chief commaunded by their great king Powhatan, are Comprehended vnder the denomynation of *Tsenacommacoh*" (1953 [1612]:37), "a nearby dwelling-place" (Geary 1953:211). The area Strachey refers to includes what today we call Tidewater Virginia, not the whole of the modern commonwealth. This area was, at the time Jamestown was founded, pretty much under the leadership of one man, known today as Powhatan; the people are known as the Powhatan Indians.

The political organization of the Powhatan in the early 17th century has attracted more attention from modern anthropologists and ethnohistorians than any other aspect of their culture. Using archaeological data from the area and comparative ethnographic material from around the world, modern scholars have been able to relate the Powhatan to contemporary indigenous political forms and forces along the entire Atlantic seaboard. This is certainly an advance on our understanding of the Powhatan even 50 years ago.

The work of these writers is essentially positivist and typologically oriented. Its goals are to determine into what category this polity falls, how it must have come into being, and thus the practical causes and consequences of chiefly status and economic control.[1] I have wondered, though, whether the colonial documents might not tell us more about Powhatan culture if analyzed in a structuralist mode. This monograph presents the results of that investigation. It rests on three fundamental points that, while they are pertinent to a study of the Powhatan, may have wider implications for anthropology as well.

One point is that understanding the cultural descriptions in the colonial documents is impossible without an understanding of contemporary European culture (see Kupperman 1980; Gleach 1997). This is particularly true of political and theological ideas (which are largely the same) current in England during the late 16th and early 17th centuries. In this regard, the present study represents a departure from most other contemporary works, which take what the colonial sources say to be pretty much literally true. They make minor translations—"chief" instead of "king," "shaman" rather than "priest," and the like—but they treat these Renaissance documents as if they were written by modern anthropologists who share their professional and cultural assumptions.

This is a questionable method. Darnton's caution that "nothing is easier than to slip into the comfortable assumption that Europeans thought and felt two centuries ago just as we do today" (1984:4) must be even more pertinent to documents and events by now four centuries old. Vigorous political argument, specifically about the theoretical relations between ruler and ruled, characterized Europe at that time (Pocock 1967:16). The English explorers who observed and reported on chiefs and their actions among the Powhatan and their Algonkian neighbors interpreted these experiences in terms of such arguments. Whether these were consonant with Powhatan Indian ideas or practices must be demonstrated rather than assumed. It is certain that in their particulars they had little in common with modern American political custom or modern political anthropology. Theological debate waxed ferocious during this time as well. Protestants and Catholics were still fighting—verbally and physically—and the Protestant groups formed internal factions that split yet again (Elliott 2000:15–20). English attitudes to the relation of the Crown to the Church and to ecclesiastical hierarchy find expression in the descriptions the colonists provide of Powhatan religious persons and their relationship to chiefs. The study of Powhatan culture at the time of contact must thus also be a study of contemporary English culture: we must, as it were, translate into our own anthropological terms the English translations of Powhatan culture. As a result, we study the Powhatan, not the Renaissance English version of the Powhatan.[2]

Descrying the Powhatan, or indeed any culture, in the mist of Renaissance prose benefits, moreover, from an ethnographic imagination, whose value in understanding historical texts Evans-Pritchard urged (1962:184–185). Today, nearly 50 years later, historians are not so oblivious to the bread-and-butter topics of anthropology: kinship and family and household, magic and witchcraft, modes of subsistence and forms of exchange, rituals of birth and death. Even so, his observation that historians—and, by implication, anthropologists who deal only with historical texts—do not ask the same sorts of questions of their material as an ethnographer remains true. In particular, there are few attempts to synthesize the whole of a culture and present it in terms of its principles. This arises, I suspect, from the fact that in history we already know how it comes out. The contingent events take on the character of necessary happenings—necessary not just to us but also to those who experienced them and indeed brought them about (see Wolf 1997:5–7). But although structure produces events (Sahlins 1981), it does not produce them predictably; alternatives are always possible, and few if any events are necessary. In an ethnographic field situation, one is always aware of the contingent, contested, ambiguous nature of people's lives even as one tries to understand the continuities and similarities so apparent to one's informants. This is in part what I mean by the ethnographic imagination: to be able to see the contingent and ambiguous aspects of 17th-century Powhatan and colonial life through the fixed forms in which we find it recorded.

My second point is about the nature of the anthropological terms the English accounts should be translated into or, more generally, the anthropological method that would best reveal aboriginal Powhatan culture. Rather than cast the Powhatan into a typology, which in the end tells us only that as a political system this was similar to some and different from others—and as Leach points out, "the typology makers never explain why they choose one frame of reference rather than another" (1961:3; see Balandier 1970:14–15) or offer a reconstruction of the origins of the polity, which is both inconclusive and unnecessary to understanding how it worked—I have thought it more productive to try to find out what sense Powhatan governance made to the Powhatan. I take such an institution as an expression of fundamental cultural ideas rather than as something existing sui generis, without (culturally speaking) reference to, or influence from, anything but itself (see Mackenzie 1969:222; Gledhill 1994:131; Clastres 1994). In order to make sense of Powhatan chiefs, I have had to analyze the culture as a whole, or anyway what we know of it from the colonial documents. The association between Powhatan chiefs and priests or shamans is an example of dual sovereignty (see Coomaraswamy 1942; Balandier 1970:37; Hocart 1970a; Dumont 1972:111; Needham 1980; Dumézil 1988), in this case a reciprocal complementary relationship between a religious authority and a secular power. (I discuss this relationship in greater detail below.) It is related to other aspects of Powhatan culture such as gender, subsistence, long-distance and local exchange, seasonal transhumance, culinary practices, and funeral customs in the sense that these all express the same cultural principles.

It may be objected that dual sovereignty is itself a type and that this analysis has done no more than to substitute one kind of typology for another. But although there is a superficial resemblance, in that both operations seem to result in a label and that the label refers to categorical social relationships, the operations are not the same, nor have they the same consequences for our understanding of the phenomena they are meant to identify.

Classifying a culture, or a cultural form, as one thing or another is supposed to be an efficient way of conveying ethnographic information: given the characteristics of the type, much about the culture can be assumed, and so one is spared the necessity of spelling out (or reading) all the details. Consequently, when we read that a polity is a redistributive chiefdom we think we know a great deal about its political forms and processes and about its economy, and perhaps we do. But difficulties remain. The ethnographer really must show in what regards this example differs from others so classified, not simply because interest in yet another example of the same thing is likely to be minimal but because there are certain to be differences, some of them possibly significant. Because this is so, it is impossible to leave the details to even the knowledgeable imagination of anyone else. It is also unwise, because it seems to justify the unwarrantable assumptions that all the cases ever adduced are exactly alike, and that therefore certain political and economic forms are necessarily bound to occur together. The category would find justification in the great similarity of the cases that make it up. But, being circular, none of it proves anything.

Moreover, to classify in such terms is open to criticism. It may, for instance, be argued that the identification of activities as "political" or "economic" involves the imposition of a Western classification on a non-Western culture (e.g., Clastres 1994:87; Gledhill 1994:13); the difficulty anthropologists have in defining "politics" suggests that this may indeed be a false category. But even if we accept that these terms may have some heuristic value, to classify a culture as a re-distributive chiefdom is to divorce the political and the economic from the rest of the culture, a proceeding whose value is debatable. True that a chief may engross to himself some of the products of his chiefdom and afterward give them back again in the form of feasts, social welfare, or payments for specialized labor. But these activi-ties do not occur—and so cannot be understood—without a cul-tural context that includes not only all the forms of production and exchange and all the hierarchical relations in that culture but also what are conventionally called social relations (kinship, affinity, co-residence), religious ideas and customs, gender relations, and so on, and, above all, the ideas that inform, make intelligible, and mutually relate these facets of social life.

The fact of relationship is one critical difference between iden-tifying a polity as a dual sovereignty and relating it to a typological scheme. It is also what makes the two seem superficially similar. To characterize a polity in terms of whether it is or is not a redistributive chiefdom is, indeed, to imply some type of relationship between the chief and his supporters. Any sort of relational understanding stops there, though, as we do not know from such a classification how that relationship is itself related to anything else in that culture. It is quite otherwise with dual sovereignty. As Needham observes, this is preeminently relational: "Complementary governance is not peculiar to any particular tradition . . . but is a fundamental and global instance of an elementary classification of powers. . . . Structurally, dual sovereignty is characterized by bipartition, opposition, and complementarity" (1980:88–89). Thus the relation between authority and power, however that may be construed locally, is necessarily related to other complementary oppositions in the culture: they may include, for example, light and dark, active and passive, male and female, hunting and agriculture, warfare and peace, health and sickness, life and death. Nonetheless, the associations among these categories are by no means necessary or predictable. Each case must be worked out on its own.

A dual sovereignty is, then, an exemplar of a particular set of cultural categories. It is what Mauss calls a "total social phenomenon" (1990:78; see Feeley-Harnick 1985:300). Typology, on the contrary, classifies cultures rather than recognizing cultural classifications. The latter method of analysis must tell us more about the people we are trying to understand than the former and is thus to be preferred.

This method of analyzing Powhatan culture, or indeed any culture, assumes that people establish a mutual relevance among most, if not all, of the disparate kinds of things they do (e.g., identifying, or insisting on, a resemblance between the treatment of a dead person and the treatment of dead game) and that therefore no aspect of the culture can be understood properly without reference to everything else. It assumes also that "we are significance-seeking organisms" (Frayn 1974:[§6]). Consequently, it follows that nothing a people recognize is without signification (see Lévi-Strauss 1966). Such an approach has the virtue of making us attend to even the most seemingly trivial aspects of the culture (for instance, how the Powhatan cut their hair), in order both to sort out the principal relationships we are trying to understand (in this case, that between shaman and chief) and then to confirm any hypotheses we formulate about those relationships (see Medawar 1967:155–156). The expectation is that we shall by this means be able to formulate explanations of any type of collective activity, whether humdrum or bizarre, in terms that make native sense.

Analyzing the bizarre in a culture—funeral customs, for instance—in structuralist terms seems acceptable because we can convincingly show that such activity is culture-specific; moreover, it is obvious that it might be done in a variety of other ways even in that particular environment, and so the custom is a matter of choice, not necessity. The elucidation of the humdrum—horticulture, for example—by such means is a different matter. Horticulture is too common in the world to seem to require comment beyond reporting any culturally specific symbolic associations; such symbolism is itself often considered humdrum, no more than what one would expect from a people whose livelihood is achieved in the garden. Anthropologists usually regard growing food for a living as the most desirable means of subsistence, and success in the endeavor certainly depends on knowing what plants need in order to grow. The humdrum, then, would seem to be equivalent to the necessary, and since such activities cannot be susceptible to structural analysis we can safely leave them out of our consideration.

This assumes, though, that people living in land suitable to horticulture will adopt the practice as soon as they can and allow it ultimately to supercede any other sort of subsistence activity, because it is either more productive or more efficient or both. But the productivity of agriculture is not obvious in its early stages, and that a people value efficiency above any other consideration must be demonstrated rather than assumed. So although we cannot know at this point what exactly motivated the Powhatan, or anyone else, to develop or to adopt horticulture, or any seemingly practical adjustment to the environment, we have to assume that they did so because it agreed with ideas about how they thought the world worked or ought to work. Consequently, we can argue that horticulture among the Powhatan was a product of and a source for cultural ideas and subject it to the same methods of analysis as we use for understanding rituals of kingship or the form of a sacred house.

A common objection to this sort of analysis is that it represents nothing more than the imaginative acrobatics of the (Western-trained) analyst, which while they may be impressive do not get us much further in understanding why a group of people act as they do. It may be objected also that the really die-hard structuralist is so handy with an answer to any possible objection to a proposed structure, or to the method of structuralism, that disproving the validity of either is impossible. Indeed, the matter of proof raises a serious question. How is anyone to know whether what is proposed is "true" or not, particularly when, as in this case, we cannot even ask informants their opinion of any hypothetical structure? The answer is that we cannot know. But we can make a case that all the available evidence supports one interpretation more strongly than it does the alternatives (Darnton 1984:257–259). This is no more than an application of the law of parsimony: the most economical explanation of the phenomena we are trying to understand. Thus I assume that my analysis of the Powhatan is probably correct because it provides an explanation for everything that we know that they did, and moreover it establishes logical kinds of relationships among all those things.

My third point is about the nature of power and of hierarchy. The Jamestown colonists describe an hierarchical society in which the paramount, Powhatan, and his lesser chiefs enjoyed absolute power over their subjects. Until very recently, students of Powhatan culture interpreted this "power" to mean willful, coercive power; the colonists' statements were unchallenged even though they are so inconsistent with what is reported everywhere else in the Americas as to raise profound doubts about whether this was the case, quite apart from why it might have been. Some more recent analyses (e.g., Rountree 1989; Gleach 1997) do question the reliability of these statements, although they do not, I think, go far enough. Settling this problem is a necessary first step in understanding the real nature of Powhatan sovereignty. Briefly, "power" in this analysis means "efficacy," and no more; as an aspect of Powhatan hierarchy, it belongs to those of lesser, not greater, status.

These propositions differ radically from commonly held ideas about political organization and process. Indeed, the phrase "political power" appears redundant: power is political, politics means power; and power is understood to mean force, whether legitimate or not. Radcliffe-Brown's summary agenda for the study of political organization makes this point explicitly (1940:xiv; see Fortes and Evans-Pritchard 1940:14; Dumont 1972:197; de Heusch 1987:217). While his position has been criticized on various grounds (e.g., Barth 1965; Mackenzie 1969; Gledhill 1994:13), nevertheless most discourse on political organization and process argues that power is universal and necessary to the maintenance of social order and that "a conscious or unconscious wish to gain power is a very general motive in human affairs" (Leach 1965:10; see Mackenzie 1969:215; Wolf 1999).

"Power," like Saint Augustine's "time," is a slippery concept, though. Like the term "political," it is difficult to define, and its sources are notoriously baffling. Wolf, for instance, writes that "conceptualizing power presents difficulties of its own. Power is often spoken of as if it were a unitary and independent force, sometimes incarnated in the image of a giant monster such as Leviathan or Behemoth, or else as a machine that grows in capacity and ferocity by accumulating and generating more powers, more entities like itself. Yet it is best understood neither as an anthropomorphic force nor as a giant machine but as an aspect of all relations among people" (1999:4). Because power is relational, he argues that it will differ in different kinds of relationships, of which he identifies four principal modalities: efficacy, control over persons, control over contexts, and control over resources, especially labor (Wolf 1999:4). (According to the argument advanced here, though, these last three are evidence of efficacy.)

One may thus look for power in the family or in gender relations as well as within a village or a kingdom, even if the relations between political leaders and followers are usually taken as the paradigm for a relationship of power. Two related assumptions need to be made explicit in this context. One is the equivalence of hierarchy and power: the superior is powerful (whether the status is cause or consequence is immaterial), and the inferior is powerless. The other is that the power of the superior is "power over others," that is, coercive. And while not everyone goes so far, still it is common to find the assumption that such power is inherently selfish, the powerful using their power for their own benefit rather than for the benefit of the whole society. By "benefit" is understood not only material gain but the preservation, if not the increase, of that power (e.g., Barker and Pauketat 1992; Barker 1992; Wolf 1999). The conflict theory of the origin of the state, for example, takes coercive power for granted and assumes that the appearance of centralization and hierarchy spells doom for the autonomy of the majority (e.g., Carniero 1970; Earle 1997; Fried 1967, 1978; Haas 1982; Cohen and Service 1978; Earle 1991).

All these assumptions may be criticized both on theoretical and empirical grounds. Balandier, for instance, regrets the identification of the political with coercion because this is "more a concept of delimitation than a concept of definition" (1970:28). Mackenzie, going further, would prefer "to set the word 'power' aside . . . ; to use 'influence' as the most general word, with 'inducement', 'authority' and 'dominance' as its elements; to know the relation between influence and manipulation" (1969:225, see 220). Clastres is even more vigorous in his objection, arguing (1977, 1994:87) that "primitive" societies "are societies whose bodies do not possess separate organs of political power" (1994:88). In his view, there is no logical compulsion to assume that power is coercive, nor do the ethnographic data support such an assumption.

If we confine ourselves only to native North America, we find that coercive power does not appear as a property or characteristic of rulers or leaders, or rather of the relations between such persons and those they rule or lead (Lowie 1967; Clastres 1977). Ethnographic accounts repeatedly include statements from the informants and from the ethnographers alike that political action depends on consensus, not coercion, both in theory and in practice. Descriptions of chiefs and of the processes of decision-making in the Southeast are no exception (e.g., Hudson 1976:205; Swanton 1987:652; Anonymous 1931:243; Gibson 1971:22). The importance of autonomy in native North American cultures and the corresponding etiquette that avoids any suggestion of command are commonplaces of anthropology. Even chiefs are reported to ask or suggest or persuade rather than to command. The notion that power or authority might be imposed by the higher on the lower—apart from the requirements of the spirits over human persons—seems thus to be alien to native American social relations.

It would appear, then, that the assumption that power is coercive, that it means "control over others" and nothing else, is fallacious. Two other common assumptions about power are likewise fallacious: that power is limited, so that the more there is for one the less there is for others, and that it is the same as, or conjoined with, authority.

A consequence of regarding "power" as "control over others," or coercive, is that "power" is treated as a measurable "thing" and regarded in the same light that Western economics regards "things," or "goods," in general—that is, in terms of scarcity. If power is, as it were, a limited good, it follows that great power in the hands of one or a few necessarily means less or none for others: the power another has over me necessarily diminishes my power over the other as well as my autonomy, that is my control of myself. In other words, it is a zero-sum game. This understanding of the matter entails the conclusion that everyone must, to paraphrase Leach, seek power or do without. The apparent accommodation, in a stratified society, of the less powerful to their deprivation is variously explained: for instance, they have willingly ceded power to the authorities for the benefit of society (e.g., Cohen and Service 1978:1) or they accept the propagandic symbolism created by the powerful to the effect that hierarchy is divinely ordained or otherwise absolutely necessary (e.g., Earle 1997; for a brief survey, see Demarest 1992:8).

The assumption that scarcity, whether of "power" or of "goods," forms a part of other people's thinking about resources is questionable, however (see, e.g., Sahlins 1972:2–3). Cross-culturally, we find that people regard power as *un*limited, often because it is understood to be an endowment of the spiritual world on the human.[3] As such, it is potentially available to everyone no matter how powerful anyone may become. That not everyone is equally endowed with it is due to the difficulties of acquiring it rather than to its being scarce because concentrated in a few hands. One such difficulty, if we may call it that, can be variable access to different sources of power, such that, for instance, only the highest-ranking may enter places of greatest power or expect a vision of the highest divinity. Even this need not imply a zero-sum, however, since lesser persons have their own access to power points and to spiritual help and protection.

Moreover, in these cultures, the idea of power means simply the ability to get things done, to be effective, rather than having control over others. Taken this way, it is obvious that any one person's increased power cannot entail a diminution of anyone else's. Success in seeking spiritual power allows one to become a more efficacious actor—hunter, warrior, shaman, chief—than before. Ultimately, this change may improve one's social influence (although it may equally lead to charges of sorcery or witchcraft), but achieving direct control over them is not a stated immediate intention of such quests.

Nevertheless, some people do appear to comply with the requests or commands of others. Observing acquiescence, one may easily conflate authority and power and endow a single person or body with both. A request seems to have the force of a command with implied sanctions of force for failure to comply. Closer or more prolonged study would show that the request has such a force only when the agent agrees that it should; failing such agreement, the request might as well be made into a vacuum for all the effect it has. Willingness to acquiesce to the request of another reflects a recognition of his or her right to make it, not fear of reprisals.

Force, then, is not the simple equivalent of power. Force that causes compliance is power; force that fails to do so is not (see Mackenzie 1969:197). Likewise, we may call an American Indian chief "powerful" if, by charisma or example or rhetoric, he persuades his followers to accept his leadership. We must understand the causal relationship here. He is not followed because he is powerful; he is powerful because he is followed. We say that he is powerful because we see that he is effective. In this sense, what is commonly called political power is the same as any other kind: the ability to bring about a desired consequence, whether it is unanimity or a good dinner.

But if force and power are not synonymous, neither are power and authority. This fact is critical for understanding the nature of hierarchy. Authority, which may ordain, and power, which can effect, are quite different; they are most commonly distinguished as complementary opposites vested in different persons or bodies who together constitute a dual sovereignty.

Such a relationship can be recognized in numerous cultures. Needham mentions in the course of what he calls a "rapid examination" nine separate cases from around the world as well as the Indo-European examples adduced by Dumézil (Needham 1980).[4] Coomaraswamy (1942), Hocart (1970a), and Dumont (1972) make the same point regarding sovereignty in India specifically. Consistently, we find sovereignty separated into an authority, variously called religious, priestly, or mystical, and a complementary secular, kingly, or material power. So, for instance, Needham reworks Evans-Pritchard's analysis of the divine kingdom of the Shilluk to show the "complementarity between the practical government exercised by the settlement chiefs and the ritual unification provided by the sacerdotal office of the king" (1980:70). Coomaraswamy, writing about the theory of governance in India, demonstrates a congruence between the relationship of the gods Mitra, or Counsel, and Varuna, or Power, on the one hand, and the Brahmin priest and the king in the earthly kingdom, on the other hand. "'The Counsel and the Power' are the equivalents of Plato's essentials of good government, *philosophia* and *dúnamis*, of the Islamic 'Mercy and Majesty' (*jalal* and *halal*), in Christian theology of the spirit that giveth life and the letter that killeth (II Cor. III.6), and of our 'Right and Might'" (Coomaraswamy 1942:7–11). These relations are analogous also to *gravitas* and *celeritas*, which Dumézil shows to have been fundamental qualities in ancient Indo-European culture. As a pair, they are analogous to static and dynamic, regulated and free, calm and violent, this ("social") world and the "other" world, *seniores* and *iuniores*, conservation and creation (Dumézil 1988:33–45).

A distinction between authority and power, as exemplified in dual sovereignty, may be necessary and therefore universal. How it is realized in any given culture and at any given period is a contingent matter, but the complementarity of the relationship, as Needham (1980:88) has observed, remains constant. In every case, the authority has the right to say what shall be done but cannot do it; the power has the ability, but no independent right, to act and executes what is authorized. It is a reciprocal relationship in the sense not that one is equal to the other but that each is dependent on—causes or supports—the other (Coomaraswamy 1942:69).

This means that "power," or efficacy, because it is not the attribute of the authority, is necessarily the attribute of authority's complement. If the authority is supreme, nevertheless it depends for its support on the efficacy of the lower ranks. Pursued logically, this idea must mean that those with the lowest status must be the most powerful, always in the sense of "efficacious." Even if, in their case, "power" takes the form of sorcery or witchcraft, still this completely overturns the common notion that hierarchy results in (if it is not caused by) unequal access to life's desiderata.

This conclusion conforms to Dumont's argument that hierarchy has no necessary relationship to power or to politics; that "hierarchy," in other words, is not the same as "stratification." Hierarchy, in his view, is purely a matter of valuation (Dumont 1972:54–55). He defines it as "the *principle by which the elements of a whole are ranked in relation to the whole*" (Dumont 1972:104–105). Such ranking may have as a consequence differential access to power or the expectation that rank has positive or negative associations with efficacy. But such consequences must be demonstrated, not assumed.

The argument that Powhatan chiefs were not "powerful" in any modern sense depends, in short, on the demonstration that the English who wrote in these terms had a notion of their meaning very different from the modern one and on the supposition that much anthropological writing about power is at odds with what non-Western peoples think about it and its relation to hierarchy. Subsequent chapters address these matters in detail. It will be useful first, however, to provide some general background information on both the English colonists at Jamestown and on the native peoples they encountered there.

Background

The Jamestown colony was founded in 1607, at which time James I of England, who was also James VI of Scotland, had been on the English throne for four years. His decision to colonize Virginia came after a lapse of some 20 years since the previous attempts, under Elizabeth I, to colonize what is now Tidewater North Carolina. The continued domination of Spain in Europe, despite the defeat of the Armada in 1588, and Spain's consequent threat to England and to Protestantism constituted the primary motivations for English colonizing in North America.

Conflict between Spain and the Hapsburgs, and many other European states, was also conflict between Catholics and Protestants. Since the Act of Supremacy of Henry VIII in 1533-1534, England was both officially and factually Protestant. Henry VIII established the monarch as the head of the Church of England, a counterpart to papal authority (Figgis 1965:93), a responsibility James I accepted despite the Scottish Presbyterian insistence that the Church must be superior to the Crown because the king was subject to God (Willson 1956:37–38). Indeed, in most ways James I favored the established Church of England against both Presbyterians and Puritans (Willson 1956:197).

As a Protestant nation, England expected to oppose, with force if necessary, Spain and its allies and to support other Protestant governments. King James, however, preferred peace to war, recognizing that the situation in Europe was such that war anywhere would mean war everywhere—and that war dreary and inconclusive, as religious wars are apt to be (Davies 1938:46; Smuts 1987:31). By this time, "war was becoming a financial disaster" (Hill 1980:39; see MacCaffrey 1992) because of the expense of gunpowder and firearms and of the corresponding defenses required. Preferring compromise and reconciliation to any show of force, James allowed Spain's ambassadors increasing influence at court (Davies 1938:16, 51–52; Smuts 1987:31) and tried to arrange a marriage between the Prince of Wales and the infanta (Willson 1956:222). At the same time, he joined the Protestant Union (Davies 1938:51) and sent covert support to the Dutch (Willson 1956:278). The marriage of his daughter, Elizabeth, to the Protestant Elector Palatine, Frederick V, in 1613 was "a diplomatic event of the first importance," not least for the king, whose aim was "to balance the marriage of his daughter to a German Protestant prince with the marriage of his son, Charles . . . , to a Spanish Catholic princess, and so, at all costs, to avoid war with the Hapsburg powers, his great dread" (Yates 1972:1, 6).

The king's decision to establish—or, rather, to reestablish—an English Protestant colony on the eastern seaboard of North America was another strategy for containing Spanish Catholic influence and, incidentally, the influence of France, then a presence in Canada, as well. In organizing this effort, he revived the earlier colonizing effort at Roanoke in what is now North Carolina. The result of this plan was the Jamestown colony, the first permanent English settlement in the New World, to the founders of which we owe our knowledge of the Powhatan in the early 17th century. An understanding of the colonists' motivations, expectations, and frame of reference is one adjunct to recovering the culture of the Virginia Indians.

The motivations for establishing the Jamestown colony were, for the most part, those that motivated the attempt some 25 years before to settle at Roanoke. These are best known from the younger Richard Hakluyt's *Discourse of Western Planting*, written in 1584 (Hakluyt 1935 [1584]:214–326). But his work was hardly idiosyncratic; as Taylor observes, "the main arguments for colonizing America had already been formulated in the public and private statements issued by Gilbert, the elder Hakluyt, Anthony Parkhurst, Sir George Peckham and Carlisle, all members of a group of men with common aims to which the younger Hakluyt had for a decade been attached" (1935:34). Rather, Hakluyt's work is significant because it summed up a body of opinion in a "persuasive and logical" argument intended for the consideration of Elizabeth I and Lord Walsingham (Taylor 1935:33; Andrews 1984:203) in order to convince them that the state ought to undertake an enterprise not only desirable but necessary for the welfare of England. Hakluyt proposed at one fell swoop to glorify God and England; relieve England's economic and demographic problems; and make England the means of bringing Spain to its knees, for which the rest of Europe, as well as the American natives, would be grateful.

Viewed objectively, these are independent ambitions. Nevertheless, as Hakluyt and his contemporaries saw them, these intentions were functionally interrelated, the conversion arising from commercial arrangements and in turn affecting the political relations of Europe. Spain was the crux: Spanish Catholicism, including the Inquisition; Spanish wealth; Spanish commodities, necessary to English cloth manufacture; Spanish political domination in Europe and overseas (see Elliott 2000:10). "Many and unmistakable are the evidences that English settlement in its genesis was based partly on a desire to challenge the power of Spain" (Craven 1970:33; see Quinn 1991:6; Kupperman 1984:2).

The choice of the Outer Banks for colonizing was an attempt to realize this desire. The English had been exploring the Atlantic coast of North America since the late 15th century. Both the northern coast, what is now New England, and areas farther south, such as modern South Carolina, were mooted as possible colonial sites. The Protestant French colony established at the latter in the middle 1560s was destroyed by the Spanish in short order. The Spanish claimed the Outer Banks in the same year, and in 1570 they set up a short-lived mission in the Chesapeake, probably on the York River, with the help of a captured Powhatan chief (Quinn 1985:12–13, 1991:4–6; Lewis and Loomie 1953). But by the middle 1580s, peace between England and Spain, instituted in 1574, was no more than a fiction (Quinn 1985:13), and the Outer Banks seemed an excellent place from which the English could harass Spanish ports and shipping in the New World, seizing prizes to enrich England and its sailors at the same time (Quinn 1991:6).

Although modern scholarly opinion regarding the sincerity of English interest in conversion is mixed (Zuckerman 1995:147; Andrews 1984:320; McFarlane 1994:43; Pagden 1995:35; Kupperman 1980:64–66; Oberg 1999:48), Craven is correct to urge rejection of "the modern tendency to interpret the talk of missionary undertakings in contemporary promotional tracts as nothing more than a promotional device" (1970:77–78). More important, one must challenge the inclination to distinguish absolutely the spiritual from the commercial at this period (see Tawney 1987:20–22; Pagden 1995:34–36). In 1608 the Quiyoughcohannock chief in Virginia is reported to have observed to the Jamestown colonists that his people thought the Christian god "as much exceeded theirs, as our Gunnes did their Bowes and Arrows" (Smith 1986 [1612]:172), suggesting that neither the Powhatan nor the English made such a distinction. Contemporary theory argued, indeed, that the best means to accomplish conversion was to plant colonies among the indigenous people so that the colonists might learn their customs and language and, in the process, gradually impart Christian truths to their hosts (see McFarlane 1994:28; Pagden 1995:33; James I 1918 [1599]:22). In the *Discourse,* Hakluyt observes that using the Irish ports that the English then controlled as a base for establishing and maintaining American colonies would "drawe the Irishe by little and little to more civilitie" (1935 [1584]:267). It was enough that these "barbarians" or "savages" had the example of civilization, which necessarily included Christianity, before them to make them wish to emulate it in its entirety.

The modern reluctance to take seriously the religious promises of the proponents of colonizing is hardly surprising considering that they devote much more attention in their writings to commerce than to religion. But in the opinion of the younger Hakluyt, the work of colonizing must necessarily precede that of conversion (1935 [1584]:274). In turn, the success of any colony depended on its economic viability. The elder Hakluyt states the principle in his "Notes on Colonisation":

> The people there to plant and to continue are eyther to live without trafficke, or by trafficke and by trade of marchandize. If they shall live without sea trafficke, at the first they become naked by want of linen and wollen, and very miserable by infinite wantes that will otherwise ensue, and so will they be forced of them selves to depart, or els easely they will bee consumed by the Sps. by the Fr. or by the naturall inhabitantes of the countrey, and so the interprice becomes reprochfull to our nation, and a lett to many other good purposes that may be taken in hande.
>
> And by trade of marchandize they can not live, excepte the sea or the lande there may yeelde commoditie for commoditie.

> And therefore you ought to have most speciall regarde of that
> point. (1935 [1578]:117)

We must therefore regard this minute attention to commerce as the
practical means to the more desirable end of conversion rather than
an end in itself. And in fact, Hakluyt's *Discourse* shows concern not
just with the heathens of America but also with the religious state of
English sailors. His first point in arguing for colonization is "That
this Western Discoverie will be greately for thinlargemente of the
gospell of Christe" (Hakluyt 1935 [1584]:214, 274; see Hakluyt 1935
[1585]:327, 332). In the chapter immediately following, he enumer-
ates the difficulties of trade with Spain, observing "that all other
englishe trades are growen beggerly or daungerous especially daungerous in all the kinge of Spayne his domynions, where our men
are dryven to flynge their bibles and prayer bookes into the sea, and
to forsweare and renounce their Relligion and conscience, and consequently their obedience to her Matie" (Hakluyt 1935 [1584]:218).
English ships arrived in Spain in the course of ordinary trade, but
they also found themselves driven to the Spanish coast while sailing to or from the north coast of Africa. The Spanish authorities
routinely seized the sailors and handed them over to the Inquisition, where, Hakluyt complains, they had three recourses: to become
Catholics, to be hypocrites, or to be executed by the Inquisition (1935
[1584]:218–219, 221). An alternative to dealing with Spain and its
neighbors was desirable from the point of view of English religious
well-being, if for no one else's.

But savage souls also concerned the colonists. The *Discourse* offers
several justifications for "thinlargemente of the gospell of Christe":
that the title "Defender of the Faith," borne by English monarchs,
obliged them to spread the true (i.e., Protestant) religion as well as
to support established Protestant endeavor; that the considerable
missionary success of the Spanish and Portuguese in the Americas in preaching a false religion shows how much more successful
a mission to spread the true religion there must be; that introducing the Catholic converts in America to the true religion is to do

them an enormous favor, since to convert from heathen practice to Catholicism is to go "from one error into another"; and that sending English divines to America will lessen their number at home and diminish the religious dissension that troubles the church and the kingdom (Hakluyt 1935 [1584]:214–217).

When Hakluyt urges conversion to Protestantism rather than Catholicism, we may understand him to mean "Spanish Catholicism," since at the time Spain was regarded as the most dangerous defender of Catholicism in Europe (see Sandys 1605:§40). That he equated "Protestantism" with "England" is neither so clear nor so justifiable an inference, but there is no question that England and its queen were highly significant in opposing Catholic Spanish influence. The younger Hakluyt states that "her Matie [Elizabeth I] ys principall" among the "Princes of the refourmed Relligion" (1935 [1584]:214), and he does not exaggerate her importance. All Protestant states were under attack, primarily from the Hapsburgs; hence her title, "Defender of the Faith." Even before the defeat of the Spanish Armada, Protestants regarded the queen as their sheet anchor. In order to counter and contain the domination of Spain and the Catholic Church, she established political alliances with Protestants in the Netherlands, Germany, and France, and she sent covert support to the Dutch rebels (Yates 1975:1; Neale 1971:292; MacCaffrey 1992). Of these allies, England was the strongest: comparatively inaccessible to attack, relatively large and unified, with Catholics in the minority and lacking official standing in the kingdom. By contrast, the States General was fairly vulnerable; the Germans were neither unified nor immune to attack; and the Huguenots had the entire weight of the French government and Church to resist. Although these polities were agreed in principle on religious verities, Sir Edwin Sandys in 1599 bemoans the lack of unity among them as a weakness in the face of united Roman opposition. He mentions in particular the lack of a Protestant head of the Church analogous to—and to counter—the Roman pope. The queen, he suggests, is the closest thing to such a person in contemporary Europe (even this late in her reign this was true); but she cannot be the pope's equivalent if only because England is physically separated from the rest of Europe (Sandys 1605:§47).[5] Sandys's estimation of her importance is the same as Hakluyt's written 15 years before.

If the English wish to spread the Protestant religion in America was so bound up with their intention to at least curb Spanish expansion, still more were their economic concerns. Hakluyt's second point is indeed that the Spanish posed a threat to English crews, body and soul together; but trade with other countries had serious drawbacks, too: trade in Turkey and Malta was expensive because of the need to placate (i.e., bribe) the people there, and there was also the constant threat from Venice; trade with France was difficult because the French were capricious; war for 18 years had spoiled trade into the Low Countries; the Danes were bad-tempered (1935 [1584]:218–221).

The solution to this problem was to find some new place to trade, with fewer hazards and greater returns: in other words, the New World, where indigenes and colonists alike could provide a market for English products and, in return—this is Hakluyt's third point— provide "all the commodities of Europe, Affrica and Asia, as far as wee were wonte to travell, and supplye the wantes of all our decayed trades" (1935 [1584]:222). The area in which Jamestown was finally established was thought to be so much like the Mediterranean in climate and soil that everyone confidently expected the colonists to be able to grow all sorts of Mediterranean crops without difficulty: "vines, sugar, olives, hemp, prunes, currants, tobacco, cotton, saffron, woad, hops" (Craven 1970:70–71; Andrews 1984:201; McFarlane 1994:43).[6] The forests of North America were equally coveted, England having nearly exhausted its own resources of wood (see Cronon 1983:20; Stone 1965:345–346).

In short, whether as a source of raw materials that could be resold domestically or abroad or as a market for English commodities, the New World looked like a sure thing. But it promised a further economic advantage, which was also a social one: providing employment for the many people in England who were out of work and on the tramp, who were perceived to be a threat to social order (Hakluyt 1935 [1584]:233; see Amussen 1988:7–8, 123; Fincham 1993:18–19; Underdown 1985:18, 34–37). Citing the successful examples of Spain and Portugal, who had pursued a similar policy with regard to their unemployed, Hakluyt suggested that removing them from England would diminish the crime rate at the same time as it increased the supply of commodities for England (1935 [1584]:233–234). And as their wealth increased, these people would be increasingly ready to marry and not "abstaine from mariage as nowe they doe" (Hakluyt 1935 [1584]:238–239), contributing to the bastardy rate and to the breakdown of social order (Amussen 1988:102; Gowing 1996:10, 56). As with his assessment of the New World as an economic resource, Hakluyt sees multiple social benefits resulting from the transportation of those out of work: the individuals involved will be better off, and so will the country as a whole.

Colonization would improve England's economy in other ways as well. Hakluyt reckons the length of the voyage at five to six weeks; since it could be undertaken at any time of the year, from Irish ports, he calculates that merchants may have "twoo returnes every yere in the selfe same shippes" (1935 [1584]:265).[7] In addition, the queen would see additional income from the various taxes and customs duties levied on the increased commerce, both in imports and exports. Hakluyt suggests that the English could impose tolls on non-English fishers, trappers, and traders on the coast of Newfoundland, just as they would tax English merchants coming to trade with the natives (1935 [1584]:268–270). He argues, too, that by the act of establishing even one colony, England would be obliged to increase support of the navy and of shipping, which he says are "the strength of our realme" (Hakluyt 1935 [1584]:270). (In this, as we know from hindsight, he was perfectly correct.) And as usual, he sees a reciprocal relation between the cost of improving and maintaining a fleet—he complains that the existing fleet is in serious decline—and the benefits that would result in the form of ships' timbers and naval stores from the forests of North America. The work of improving shipping would, moreover, give work to many people, which could only be a blessing for the kingdom (Hakluyt 1935 [1584]:270–273; see Craven 1970:102).

But England's benefits were, or should be, Spain's discomforts also, and Hakluyt enlarges on this point in several different contexts besides his concern for limiting, if not reversing, the spread of Spanish religious domination. Thus he urges colonization because it "will be a greate bridle to the Indes of the King of Spaine" (Hakluyt 1935 [1584]:239). England would be able to detain Spanish fishing ships off the coast of Newfoundland, as well as any ships coming along the coast (as they must, he thought, because of the current); it could use the colony as a base for harrying Spanish treasure ships and thus enrich Elizabeth I at Philip II's expense while at the same time balking his plans to rewrite the map of Europe with American silver, as his father Charles V had done (Hakluyt 1935 [1584]:45–52; see Pagden 1995:70–71). (Taylor observes, however, that "in point of fact, Virginia proved too far north for a base, although Hakluyt's statements are correct" [1935:240n].) As a result, Hakluyt argues, Philip II may be displaced from the exalted status he has assumed over the rest of Europe and become "equall to the princes his neighboures" (1935 [1584]:246). Hakluyt is not slow, either, to draw attention to the fact that "the Spaniardes have exercised most outragious and more then Turkishe cruelties in all the west Indies," with the result that they found themselves deeply resented among the natives (1935 [1584]:257). If England allied itself with those natives and supplied them with arms and armor, together they could bring about the expulsion of the Spanish from the Americas (Hakluyt 1935 [1584]:240–241, 257). Although he expects that English colonies would, as we have seen, exercise control over those natives and ultimately bring them to civilized life, nevertheless it is clear that he considers this a fate preferable either to Spanish enslavement or to native ignorance.

Most of Hakluyt's proposals were carried out first in the colonial enterprise at Roanoke, in the Outer Banks, under the aegis of Sir Walter Raleigh. That Raleigh, and not the state, sponsored the effort was contrary to Hakluyt's recommendation. "Hakluyt envisaged large-scale planting from Newfoundland to the borders of Florida, only possible with State support" (Taylor 1935:237n; Hakluyt 1935 [1584]:331). An initial reconnaissance by Captains Arthur Barlowe and Philip Amidas identified this as a suitable place for making contact with the natives, extracting commodities from the surrounding territory, and raiding Spanish settlements and shipping (Craven 1970:40-41; Quinn 1991:ix). Although the plan ultimately failed, it had important consequences for the Jamestown colony. The company of Englishmen who lived at Roanoke from 1585 to 1586 explored inland and as far north as the Chesapeake Bay, where a part of the group spent the winter. Among the Roanoke colonists was Thomas Harriot, a mathematician and intimate friend of Raleigh and Hakluyt (as well as of others, such as John Dee and Walsingham, interested in establishing English colonies in the New World), whose presence on the voyage was due to his great interest in improving instruments of navigation (Stevens 1900:51; Hulton 1972:viii–ix). He set himself to learn the local language (Salmon 1992) and to record as much as he could of the country, including the appearance and customs of the people. His *Report of the New Found Land of Virginia* is the earliest and most extensive ethnographic account we have of the Algonkians of this area. It was well known to the Jamestown colonists, who quickly recognized that the Powhatan were culturally very similar to the people Harriot describes. That familiarity must have had a positive effect on how they viewed the Powhatan as well as making it easier to understand them and their actions.

For a number of reasons, the English attempted no colonizing after the collapse of the Roanoke venture until 1606, two years after the conclusion of a peace with Spain (Dietz 1973:107; McFarlane 1994:31). The Chesapeake was chosen because it offered the same advantages as the Outer Banks without the disadvantages. It was close to Spanish colonies without being a threat to them; the local Algonkian Indian culture and language were familiar; the climate was agreeable. On the other hand, the Chesapeake is deeper than Pamlico and Albemarle Sounds; the entrance is easier to find from the sea and easier to navigate once found; and it offers more protection against marauders and the weather than the islands of the Outer Banks.

This time, though, the enterprise was not the work of an individual, as Roanoke had been, nor of the state, as Hakluyt had urged, but of a joint-stock company, a form of enterprise that, according to Rabb, "was first widely used in England in this period. The distinctive structure of a joint-stock company allowed large numbers of investors to pool their resources and finance ventures as expensive as voyages to India on a scale which no single promoter or small group of partners would have been able to support alone" (1962:3). The organization was in essence democratic: anyone with the cash could participate. It was modeled on several predecessors of which the most significant was probably the Muscovy Company, chartered under Mary Tudor in 1555 for the purpose of acquiring spices and gold from lands in Asia (Brenner 1972:363). The Muscovy Company had the rights of exploration—"that is, those of conquest, of acquiring lands, and of seizing the ships of any who should infringe on their monopoly of trade" (Kingsbury 1906:13). By 1583 they had developed a policy of devoting one year to exploration in order to provide a sense of the land and its commodities. Using this information, they would establish trade relations to exploit the local resources, which could be transported to England for sale there (Brenner 1972:363). This policy influenced Raleigh's own plans for his Roanoke colony and "hence foreshadowed companies of the seventeenth century" (Kingsbury 1906:13). Also like the later Virginia companies, the Muscovy Company recognized two sorts of participants, "adventurers" and "enterprisers." Only the former could trade with the peoples encountered, but all would share land equally. Their plan discussed monopoly but not government: in other words, the Muscovy adventurers were interested in trade rather than colonizing. "This plan of the Muscovy Company stands as a connecting link between the ideas of the explorer and those of the trader and planter, a plan which may be said to have been carried out by the Virginia Company" (Kingsbury 1906:13–14).

Following the establishment of the Muscovy Company, other similar enterprises, such as the East India Company and the Levant Company, were established; "significantly overlapping groups of merchants were behind all of these trades, and their operations may be seen to represent successive connected phases in a unified process of development" (Brenner 1972:366, 1993:14). These same men supported westward expansion when that became a desirable option—following, that is, the peace with Spain in 1604—and they took on the direction of the new trading companies as well (Brenner 1972:366). But their avowed interest was primarily commercial, not colonial (Brenner 1972:376), although in the end colonial control was seen to be necessary to commercial success (Kingsbury 1906:15).

The Virginia Company, then, grew out of a tradition of English overseas expansion, founded and directed by a group of merchants and gentry with experience in eastern markets and now ready to apply that experience in the Americas. The arguments that the Hakluyts and their circle had advanced regarding the advantages to the kingdom of western expansion motivated investment in this new enterprise just as much as did the possibility of strong economic returns for that investment: conversion of the heathen, expansion of the kingdom, increased revenues to the king and the adventurers, employment for the vagrant poor, a market for English manufactures. Containing Spain was still a concern, if not in the same way as it had been in the early 1580s. Spain was by no means impotent, and it seemed indeed too interested and too powerful in the affairs of England (Smuts 1987:33). The interests of the Virginia Company were, in short, national—it took on a task that the state might have taken on, and later would take on, but chose not to at that time— though it was not an office of the state (Craven 1970:60–61).[8]

Following the recommendations of the Hakluyts and the experiences of the Roanoke explorers, the settlement at Jamestown was initially intended to be for purposes of reconnaissance. The "Instructions by way of advice" (London Company of Virginia 1910 [1606]:xxxii–xxxvii) issued by the London Virginia Council to the first expedition recommend, as the elder Hakluyt had done 20 years before, the discovery of a safe harbor preferably on a large river running well inland; the establishment of a base easily defended against the local people as against marauding Spanish and French; the early building of a fort and clearing of the surrounding area both to remove cover from an attacking party and to make planting possible; and the exploration of the surrounding countryside in search of minerals (i.e., gold, silver, and copper) and other commodities. They advise, too, on the proper relations to establish with "the naturals": to establish and maintain cordial relations with them since the colonists' own food supplies are, and may continue to be, limited; to avoid inflating the prices of the local commodities; to conceal from them the intention to settle permanently in the land; to use them as guides and take their advice about the country; never to let them carry or handle the weapons; never to let them see that English soldiers are anything but perfect marksmen. Finally, the colonists are urged to "make yourselves all of one mind for the good of your country and your own, and to serve and fear God the Giver of all Goodness, for every plantation which our Heavenly Father hath not planted shall be rooted out" (London Company of Virginia 1910 [1606]:xxxvii).

The London Virginia Council, which issued these recommendations, was the official governing body of the Virginia Company as originally constituted.[9] Its membership was appointed by the king, to whose service they were sworn. It remained in London, receiving information and suggestions (and criticism) from the council in Virginia and returning orders and advice. The organization of the colony itself called for a council of seven men, with a president to be elected from among them by the others of the council (Smith 1986

[1612]:205, 207). These were to have governing powers over the rest of the colonists.

Although the present book is not in any sense a history either of the Jamestown colony or of the Powhatan, still the sequence of events during the first two years contributes to an understanding of Powhatan culture at that time; incidentally, the sequence of these events reflects something of the continued importance of the Hakluyts' ideas concerning colonizing. The three ships, *Susan Constant*, *Godspeed*, and *Discovery*, arrived at the mouth of the Chesapeake Bay on 26 April 1607 (see map). They proceeded to the mouth of the James, the southernmost river emptying into the bay, and went up it a little distance to "a very fit place for the erecting of a great cittie," namely, Jamestown Island (Smith 1986 [1608]:29; Percy 1910 [1607]:lxi; see Hakluyt 1935 [1578]:116-120). Here they began to build a fort, and on 22 May they began the exploration of the river, which the Indians called the Powhatan but the English renamed the James. They went as far as the falls, that is, the modern site of Richmond, at which point they realized that this waterway was not going to take them to the Pacific. (Finding a northwest passage from the Atlantic to the Pacific was something some of the adventurers set great store by; Hakluyt's *Discourse* (1935 [1584]:283) includes it as a desirable consequence of colonization but relegates it to a minor position in the entire list.)

Preliminary battle lines were in effect drawn up during this period. According to Archer (1910 [1607]), the explorers made the acquaintance of several friendly chiefs during this voyage. But on their return at the end of May, they discovered that the fort had been attacked (probably by the Paspahegh, on whose territory they were unwittingly camped) and that two of the colonists were dead. On or about 14 June, after attempted ambushes of the colonists and desultory skirmishes between them and the Paspahegh, a first embassy came from Powhatan to let them know who among the various Tidewater tribes were amicable and who were not to be trusted (Archer 1910 [1607]:liv–lv; Wingfield 1910 [1608]:lxxv; Smith 1986

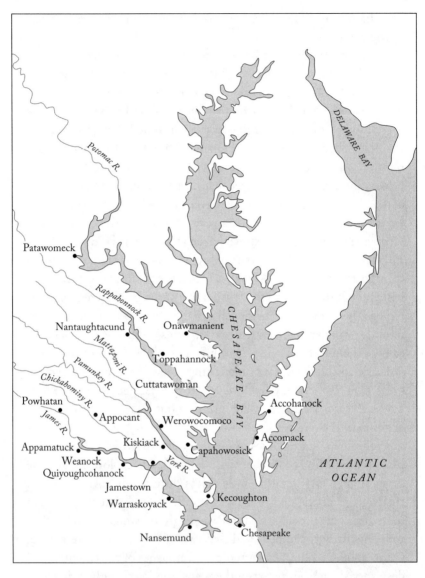

Major Powhatan villages in 1607

[1608]:33).[10] But the cautious optimism of the colonists was to suffer another serious check.

Even today, with industrial pollution, the site of Jamestown in late May and early June is a delightful place. The air is comparatively dry, the days are warm and the nights cool, and insects are not yet a nuisance. In 1607 it must have seemed indeed the paradise the colonists called it (e.g., Percy 1910 [1607]:lxi). And, of course, one need not today rely on the waters of the James for washing, cooking, or answering calls of nature. In 1607 it was otherwise. Captain Christopher Newport, who had led the voyage out, left for England at about the same time as the embassy came from Powhatan, and then "it fortuned that within tenne daies scarse ten amongst us coulde either goe, or well stand, such extreame weaknes and sicknes oppressed us" (Smith 1986 [1612]:209; Wingfield 1910 [1608]:lxxvi). "Our men were destroyed with cruell diseases, as Swellings, Flixes, Burning Feuers, and by warres; and some departed suddenly: but for the most part, they died of meere famine" (Percy 1910 [1607]:lxxii). George Percy was not alone in blaming their ills on a severely diminished diet due to the greed of their president, Wingfield (Smith 1986 [1612]:210), but modern analyses conclude that the causes were more likely microbial than nutritional or political. Carville Earle (1979) makes the convincing argument that the water of the James, polluted by human waste, infected many with typhoid and dysentery and, in addition, afflicted everyone with salt poisoning, the symptoms of which are edema, lassitude, and irritability. "The idle, lazy, and factious behavior of early Virginians was, in part, the result of a steady summer diet of salty water" (Earle 1979:103).

Captain John Ratcliffe was elected president on 10 September to replace the unpopular Wingfield; he appointed John Smith cape merchant of the colony (Smith 1986 [1608]:35), with responsibility for trading with the local people and for distributing commodities within the colony. Smith's efforts were quickly rewarded, and in addition several Powhatan Indian groups brought green corn and other food as gifts to the colonists (Smith 1986 [1608]:35).

The next important events in the colony were the capture of Smith in December 1607 and his release about a month later. Among other significant happenings during his captivity, Smith met the paramount chief, the *mamanatowick*, Powhatan, of whom the English had so far only heard reports. Although modern opinion differs on whether Smith owed his release to the spectacular intervention of Pocahontas, Powhatan's daughter, it is almost certain that during his capture he was initiated as a Powhatan *werowance*, or chief (Williamson 1992). Certainly relations between the Powhatan and the English improved following this meeting, the Indians coming frequently and freely to the fort (Smith 1986 [1612]:215). Smith and his companions were making acquaintance with the "naturals," as encouraged by the Hakluyts and, following their direction, the London Virginia Council—possibly a closer acquaintance than either had anticipated or thought advisable—with the predicted result that a brisk exchange of commodities developed. Only one of these tribes is reported to have gone further and welcomed Christianity (Smith 1986 [1612]:172), but there is some hint that others began to regard it with respect (Smith 1986 [1624]:154). The introduction to Powhatan of Captain Newport, who returned to the colony in January 1608 with the first supply, contributed to the improved relations.

Relations soured again by late March following the colonists' refusal to make a return gift for a present of turkeys sent them by Powhatan; there were attacks and counterattacks, captures and retaliatory captures. Nevertheless, in June 1608 Smith decided to explore the Chesapeake Bay. Among other results of his explorations was his well-known and invaluable map of Virginia, on which he marks all the rivers, the towns, the "king's houses," and tribal territories.[11] He also marks, with a Maltese cross, the point at which he abandoned exploration of each of the westward rivers. These points correspond to the fall line, where the rivers cease to be tidal and navigable. Smith's voyage was intended in part to discover whether there was a passage from the Chesapeake to the Pacific. He abandoned his quest at each river in turn, as soon as he reached the falls. At the head of the Chesapeake Bay, having gone up the Susquehanna and neighboring rivers and realized that they were just that, and not inlets of the ocean, he decided (correctly, as we know now) that this colony, at any rate, was not going to discover the passage.

A modern eye, informed with modern knowledge of North American geography, may see Smith's endeavor as so futile as to amount to a junket: surely it would have been obvious from the start that no one could cross the continent by going up these rivers. That is to reckon without either the terrain of the Chesapeake or the experiences of Tudor explorers. The Chesapeake is an estuary bounded in its southern reaches by low, flat land. From the deck of a small boat it is difficult, and at some points impossible, to make out one side of the bay from the other. From the Eastern Shore side, at about the modern towns of Cambridge or Easton, one might well mistake the expanse of water for an arm of the Pacific. The mouths of most of the western rivers are very broad, so that even from a short distance away they, too, give the impression that they must lead into another sea. The falls that Smith and his party encountered showed them their mistake every time.

The English may have been ignorant of the true breadth of North America, but they knew that it was a continent (Quinn 1985:12). They knew also, from explorations in the 16th century, that one could traverse the whole of Russia, from the Arctic Ocean to the Caspian Sea, almost entirely by water (Hakluyt 1962 [1589]:438–464; Craven 1957:10). They expected to find a similar situation in Virginia, and the physiography of the Chesapeake Bay gave them no reason to think otherwise. Indeed, at the conclusion of this first expedition they had "good hope . . . (by the Salvages relation) our Bay had stretched to the South-sea [i.e., the Pacific]" (Smith 1986 [1612]:229).

The expedition exhausted its food supply after exploring no farther north than the Anacostia River, and it turned back at that point. By now it was July, and they returned to find that the ailments of the previous summer again afflicted the colonists so that they were "al unable to do anything" (Smith 1986 [1612]:229). The president, Ratcliffe, was in particular so unpopular that he was deposed and Smith elected in his place. Putting his friend Matthew Scrivener in command at the fort, Smith set out again to finish his exploration of the Chesapeake.

On this second trip, they proceeded much more directly up the bay. At its head they discovered, to their disappointment, that it was fed by four rivers, none of which led to the Pacific as they had hoped. Up one of these rivers—the writer does not specify which —they met a group of unfamiliar Indians whom they call Massawomecke.[12] Continuing down the Eastern Shore, the English met a people they identify as the Tockwogh—possibly the Nanticoke—an Algonkian-speaking people with whom they achieved a modicum of communication and with whom they got on very well. With their help, the English made contact with another Iroquoian people, the Susquehannock, whom Smith describes as "giantlike-people" and with whom the English again enjoyed a friendly exchange of gifts. All these people were enemies of the Massawomecke, as were the Patuxent, whom they encountered on their voyage to Jamestown; Smith engaged their alliance by promising to return the next year to attack the Massawomecke on their behalf (Smith 1986 [1612]:231–232). In fact, he did not, nor did he again travel up the bay. What the Tockwogh Indians made of this no one knows.

Smith was sworn in as president on 10 September, and some three weeks later Captain Newport arrived again with the second supply. Smith comments sourly, and with some justice, on Newport's commissions to find gold, the south sea, and some survivors from the Lost Colony at Roanoke; his bringing a barge in sections for exploring beyond the mountains; and his orders to crown Powhatan king of Virginia (Smith 1986 [1612]:234).

The coronation took place at Powhatan's seat of Werowocomoco, since he refused to go to Jamestown on the (reasonable) ground that this was his country and the English should come to him. Whether by ignorance or design, he likewise resisted kneeling to receive his crown; finally, the English pressed on his shoulders so that his knees gave slightly under the pressure, and Captain Newport popped the crown on his head. Smith completes his description of this travesty with the dry observation that in return for all these valuable items Powhatan gave his old cloak and moccasins to Newport, together with "a heape of wheat [maize] eares, that might contain some 7 or 8 bushels" (1986 [1612]:236–237).[13]

This overture seems to have had little positive effect on Powhatan's disposition toward the English. Smith's attempts to trade with the Indians for corn during the late autumn of 1608 met with little success, and he concluded that Powhatan wished to starve them out. He determined to attack Werowocomoco just at the time —December 1608—that Powhatan invited him there ostensibly to trade but, as events appeared to Smith, in fact to ambush him and his party. Powhatan's ambush failed, as did a number of similar attempts on Smith's life in succeeding months (Smith 1986 [1612]:242–260).

Smith regarded the numerous skirmishes as dangerous because they "would but incourage the Salvages" (1986 [1612]:261). In this he was probably correct, since the fighting sounds much like Virginia Indian engagements—inconclusive but giving prestige to those involved (see Smith 1986 [1612]:167; Spelman 1910 [1613]:cxiii–cxiv). Smith chose instead to terrorize the Indians, killing several, capturing many more, burning the chief's house, and taking their canoes and their fishing weirs. Not surprisingly, there was an embassy for peace soon afterward (Smith 1986 [1612]:260–262).

The subjection of the "savages" received an unexpected boost when Smith seized two Chickahominy brothers as associates of a man who had stolen a pistol from the fort. One brother was sent after the thief and the other put in prison, where Smith provided him with dinner and a charcoal fire. The smoke unfortunately asphyxiated the prisoner, and when his brother returned in the middle of the night with the pistol they found the man apparently dead. Smith told the surviving brother that in exchange for a promise to steal nothing more from them, he would bring the dead man back to life. Somewhat to his own surprise he accomplished this, so dosing the patient with aquavit and vinegar that when he regained consciousness he was also very drunk and appeared to be a lunatic. By morning, however, he was in his right mind, much to his brother's relief; Smith dressed his burns, gave each of them a piece of copper, and sent them away. "This was spread amongst all the Salvages for a miracle, that Captaine Smith could make a man alive that is dead." As a result, all the tribes near Jamestown, and Powhatan himself, sent ambassadors with gifts asking for peace with the English, "and all the countrie became absolutely as free for us, as for themselves" (Smith 1986 [1612]:262).[14]

Following this, the colonists and the Indians enjoyed a serene three months together; when the colonists discovered in the course of reviewing their stores that most of it was rotten or eaten by rats, "for 16 daies continuance, the Countrie brought us (when least) 100 a daie of squirrils, Turkies, Deare, and other wild beastes" (Smith 1986 [1612]:263). The English found this insufficient, though, and so Smith had them try to live off the land, sending small groups to different places down- and upriver to live on oysters, tuckahoe root, sturgeon, berries, and fish; others he sent to live in Indian villages, where they were well treated (in fact, some of them deserted, preferring Indian life to life in the fort).[15] Still, many of the colonists preferred to trade with the Indians for these foods rather than gather them for themselves, with the result that the fort was becoming stripped even of its weapons and the price of food rose considerably (Smith 1986 [1612]:264–265). (It will be remembered that the "Instructions" of the London Council had warned against just such a development.)

In the spring of 1609 the Virginia Company was granted a second charter, under which the colony would have a governor appointed by the London Council rather than a president elected in Virginia. The first acting governor was Sir Thomas Gates, vice Lord de la Warr. Gates sailed with a small fleet—nine ships—in May 1609. The ship carrying himself, Sir George Somers, and William Strachey, among others, was struck by a hurricane on 24 July and became separated from the fleet. It was wrecked off the coast of Bermuda (then known as Somers Isles); many of the passengers survived (Purchas 1906 [1625] 19:6), but in Virginia this was not known. The third supply, arriving in straggling fashion through July and August, offered little actual relief since there was no one in authority. Factiousness and ill-feeling reached a peak. Smith, who was still president, decided to break up his men and sent one group downriver to Nansemond under the leadership of Captain John Martin and another upriver to the falls under the leadership of Master Francis West, brother to Lord de la Warr (see Archer 1910 [1609]:xcvi).

Neither of these colonies survived because both men treated the Indians very badly. Of Martin, for example, the chronicle says, "The people being contributers [paying tribute to Smith] used him [Martin] kindly: yet such was his jealous feare, and cowardize, in the midst of his mirth, hee did surprize the poore naked king, with his monuments [the sepulcher of his predecessors, where images of spirits were kept], houses, and the Ile he inhabited;[16] and there fortified himselfe, but so apparantly distracted with fear, as imboldned the Salvages to assalt him, kill his men, redeeme their king, gather and carrie away more then 1000 bushels of corne, hee not once daring to intercept them" (Smith 1986 [1612]:269–270). Meanwhile West's men were behaving no better at the Falls of the James, where Smith had purchased for them the village of Powhatan from Powhatan in exchange for a promise to defend the area against the neighboring Monacans to the west and an amount of copper.[17] "That disorderlie company so tormented those poore naked soules, by stealing their corne, robbing their gardens, beating them, breaking their houses, and keeping some prisoners; that they dailie complained to Captaine Smith he had brought them for protectors worse enimies then the Monocans themselves; which though till then, (for his love) they had indured: they desired pardon, if hereafter they defended themselves" (Smith 1986 [1612]:271). Assuming these passages to be reasonably close to the truth, they shed much light on

Smith's relations with the Powhatan. He regularly punished them for "insolence," but they nevertheless became his supporters and paid him tribute, quite as if he were indeed a werowance among them. But they met the excesses of his own subordinates with almost instant resistance. The reason for the difference would appear to be, in fact, that Powhatan had proclaimed Smith his son and a werowance, and all Powhatan's subjects treated him as such. For his sake they tolerated West and Martin but only up to a point, when they drove both parties out of their territories in short order.

Sailing down the James to Jamestown, Smith was badly burned when his powder bag exploded. The date of this is not certain, but it seems to have occurred in late August or early September 1609. Since there was no doctor at the fort at that time, it was decided that he should return to England. Doubtless his political opponents saw this as a sensible plan also. George Percy was prevailed upon to become president in Smith's place, and Smith was sent home some time in September or October. His departure signaled the Powhatan to wreak what havoc they could, and it was considerable: "the Salvages no sooner understood of Captaine Smiths losse, but they all revolted, and did murder and spoile all they could incounter. . . . Ratliffe and his men were most slaine by Powhatan. . . . Now for corne, provision, and contribution from the Salvages; wee had nothing but mortall wounds with clubs and arrowes" (Smith 1986 [1612]:275).

What followed is known as the Starving Time, the winter and spring of 1609–1610, during which time the colony lost nearly 90 percent of its population, and some are reported to have resorted to cannibalism (Smith 1986 [1624]:232). In May 1610 the 60 or so survivors were on the verge of abandoning the colony when two ships bearing Sir Thomas Gates and his company appeared. They had been living (fairly well, according to Strachey's account) on Bermuda since the previous summer. They had managed to construct two boats out of timbers salvaged from their own wreck and wood available on the island, and in these they had made their way up the coast to Virginia (Purchas 1906 19:43). Gates quickly realized that the situation in the colony was desperate, however, and that he could do nothing to correct it; he therefore made plans for the entire company to return to England. They were actually sailing out of the James when the ships bringing Lord de la Warr to Virginia appeared with a supply of food, men, and tools (Smith 1986 [1612]:276–277). Jamestown was saved. Other supplies came soon after this one, and the colony was never again in such desperate straits.

During the next several years, the leadership of the colony devolved on different men, mostly because de la Warr was made gravely ill by the climate of Virginia—he returned to England in 1611—and unable to carry out the duties of governor (Craven 1957:25; Smith 1986 [1624]:237–239). Initially Percy, already elected president under the old charter, assumed the governorship; he was succeeded by Sir Thomas Dale, who arrived in May 1611 and set about reestablishing order in the colony with some energy (Smith 1986 [1624]:239). In particular, he instituted a remarkably strict code of laws, the *Lawes Divine, Morall and Martiall.* Although Barbour says that it "was, and is, a controversial code" (1986, 2:240n), Smith defends it on the ground that without it the colony would never have survived (1986 [1624]:240).[18]

Dale was succeeded in 1611 by Sir Thomas Gates, who set about establishing a new fort farther up the river, which he called Henrico. This represents the first successful attempt to move permanently away from Jamestown (which had long been recognized as unhealthy) farther into Virginia and thus to encroach yet further on Indian land and livelihood (see Cronon 1983). Continuing this program of intrusion, Gates attacked the Appomattox on Christmas of that year, supposedly because they had attacked the English but in fact because he coveted their land (Smith 1986 [1624]:242; Hamor 1957 [1615]:31; see Strachey 1953 [1612]:64).

The momentous capture of Pocahontas occurred during Gates's tenure. She had been a frequent visitor at Jamestown until Smith's return to England. At the time of her capture she was visiting a Patawomeck werowance named Iapazaws or Iopassus. Gates had dispatched Captain Samuel Argyll to trade with the Patawomeck Indians, who, while maintaining a tenuous alliance with the Powhatan, were friendly to the English. Thus going that distance to trade was sensible, as the English were more likely to get a better reception than on the James, where they were increasingly unpopular. Apparently Argyll, who knew Iopassus, seized the opportunity to capture Pocahontas by persuading him to betray her for a copper kettle. Argyll's intention was to use her as a bargaining chip in negotiations with her father to recover from him a number of English captives (Smith 1986 [1624]:243-244; Hamor 1957 [1615]:4-6; see de Bry 1618:Pl. 7).

Negotiations were only partly successful, and Pocahontas remained a prisoner in the fort. The outcome of this detention is well known: she became a Christian, was baptized with the name Rebecca, and was married to Sir John Rolfe with her father's approval (Smith 1986 [1624]:245; Hamor 1957 [1615]:11).[19] An immediate consequence of the marriage was, not surprisingly, improved relations between the English and the Indians. The Chickahominy, for instance, offered for the first time to become allies of the English (Smith 1986 [1624]:246; Hamor 1957 [1615]:11-12).

Ethnographic Background

The term "Powhatan" that I have been using throughout is that by which the Indians whom the English found in their new colony have come to be known; their polity is known as the Powhatan Confederacy, although the polity was an empire rather than a confederacy. Since many anthropologists have described Powhatan culture in detail, I give here merely a brief description.[20]

The Powhatan were an Algonkian-speaking group, numbering perhaps 14,000, occupying what is today called Tidewater Virginia from the southern shore of the Potomac River in the north to the southern shore of the James River in the south and from the coast of the Chesapeake (including two tribes on the Eastern Shore) in the east to the edge of the Piedmont in the west, an area of about 8,000 square miles. Their neighbors included the Monacan, a Siouan group, as well as their allies the Saponi, the Tutelo, and the Nahyassan to the west; in the south, the Iroquoian Nottoway and Meherrin and the Algonkian tribes of the Carolina coast; the Algonkian Natchcotank and Tockwogh on the Eastern Shore of the Chesapeake Bay; and to the north the Algonkian Conoy and the Iroquoian Susquehannock and the Massawomecke. The Powhatan were at war with most, if not all, of these people.[21]

The polity was made up of between 27 and 34 small tribes, each with at least one chief, whom the English called "king," all under the paramount chiefship of Powhatan, as he is known today. Since this book is about Powhatan political organization, I say no more on this point here.

The Powhatan were semisedentary, relying on a mixed economy of horticulture (corn, beans, squashes, sunflowers, and tobacco) and foraging (including fishing). The annual cycle found them in Tidewater during the growing season; there they also fished, hunted, and gathered wild plant foods. Once harvest was over, in mid-October, they moved from the Tidewater to the fringes of the Piedmont, where they hunted communally and raided their neighbors to the west, who raided them in return. Warfare was an important part of the culture. In the spring they returned to their Tidewater villages for a new growing season (Williamson 1979). Besides these economic activities, they traded marine and riverine products such as pearls and shell beads inland for products of the Piedmont such as stone, copper, and roots for making an important red dye. On the whole, they seem to have been fairly prosperous and healthy.

What we can say definitely about their social organization is almost nil because of the limitations of the original sources. Succession to chiefship was matrilineal, but, as Speck remarks, "Smith's observation on the maternal descent of Powhatan's dynasty is suggestive but not conclusive" (1924:193). Whether or not they were matrilineal, postmarital residence appears to have been patrilocal (Spelman 1910 [1613]:cvii; Strachey 1953 [1612]:112). The permanent villages were small, most having between 2 and 20 houses; a few were significantly larger. (The hunting camps were temporary and seem to have included both a larger number of people and people from different tribes.) Of what the household consisted is unclear, since the English report both that as many as 20 people might sleep in one house—some on the floor, others on a platform around the walls—and that each household had but one fire. If these structures housed several related families, like those of the Iroquois and Huron to the north (Morgan 1996:315; Tooker 1991:40–41), one would expect at a minimum one fire for every two families. Northern Algonkians tended to have one family and one fire in a dwelling (Russell 1980:51), a residential pattern found also in the deeper Southeast (Hudson 1976:213).

We have more information about Powhatan religion. They recognized at least four major divinities: a creator they called Ahone, one who seems to be the Great Hare of Algonkian mythology, a punisher known as Oke, and the Sun. The English mention sun worship but offer no Powhatan name for this being. Every man was his own priest, to some extent, but there was also a status of religious person whom the English called "priests" and "conjurors"—sacrificers, shamans, and curers. Defining the status of "priest" or "conjuror" and determining its relationship to the chiefs are the substance of this book, so again I defer more detailed discussion until later chapters.

Since the days of Wissler, at least, American Indian cultures have been classified into one or another culture area, and the Powhatan are no exception. The culture area method has obvious drawbacks, but it also has its uses when the information we have about a culture is limited. We can fill in gaps by reference to culturally similar peoples for whom we have more or better information. The question is, of course, which culture area is appropriate in a given circumstance? Anthropologists have differed over the "anthropological position" of the Powhatan. The phrase is Mook's, and he concludes that "culturally they are composite, having possessed a cultural composition consisting of a basic substratum of Algonkian traits [i.e., from the northeast] with an easily recognizable over-deposit of Southeastern influence" (1943:40). Swanton includes the Powhatan in *The Indians of the Southeastern United States* (1987), taking them as the northernmost limit of that cultural province. Kroeber, however, excludes them, saying, "there is little to indicate strong specific influencing by the Southeast, although at the border culture probably shaded over continuously" (1939:94). Hudson (1976) agrees with him; Barker and Pauketat (1992) agree with Swanton.

My interest in identifying the Powhatan as part of a culture area is practical. Where am I most likely to find customs and ideas that shed light on theirs? The Southeast has proven a more fruitful area in this regard than the Northeast, possibly because the Mississippi basin and, ultimately, Mesoamerica are the sources for much that we find in Tidewater Virginia. Many Powhatan customs represent transformations of southeastern ones. For instance, although they did not construct mounds, the Powhatan did build so-called charnel houses, sepulchers for the mummified bodies of their chiefs. Such structures, whether on mounds or not, are well attested throughout the Southeast even into the historical period (e.g., Biedma 1993:230–231; Brown 1975; Rangel 1993:279–289; Emerson 1989:48; Hall 1989:261; Swanton 1931:170, 1911:143, 1987:722);[22] only the mound is lacking in the Powhatan context, and its absence may perhaps be due to the impracticality of building mounds of sandy soil. The bodies were laid on platforms inside these houses. The elevation of the paramount chief, Powhatan, over his people during audiences recalls the elevation of southeastern chiefs also (as well as the platform thrones of the Maya and Olmec). Hall argues persuasively that throughout the Southeast a gift of pearls or other white beads acted as an incorporating device, an equivalent to smoking the calumet elsewhere. On the basis of their use and of their appearance in mythology (e.g., the "Bead-Spitter"; Swanton 1929:2–7, 126–129, 163–164, 172–175, 271), he suggests that pearls were analogous to (white) bodily emissions such as spittle or semen

(Hall 1989:255-256). The English report the same usage of beads and strings of pearls among the Powhatan.

Dual sovereignty was also found throughout the Southeast. A necessarily brief survey of governance among these peoples shows complementary hierarchical statuses, the higher status associated with the village, peace, the elders, and the color white; the lower status with matters outside the village, warfare, juniors, and the color red.[23] The most famous example of this relationship is that between the Great Sun and the Great War Chief among the Natchez (Swanton 1911:100-102, 1987:650; Hudson 1976:234); but the same relationship is reported elsewhere, even if the authority of the supreme chief was not nearly so absolute as it seems to have been among the Natchez. The Timucua recognized divinity in their chief, evidently, as they offered him sacrifices (Swanton 1987:648-649; see Swanton 1998:370; Knight 1990:41). The great chief of the Creeks, the Miko or Mingo, was not so honored, nor were his Choctaw, Chickasaw, and Cherokee counterparts, although Gilbert and Gearing both observe that the Cherokee regarded officials of the white moiety as priests also (Gilbert 1943:325, 339, 346; Gearing 1962). Whether sacred or not, all such "white" chiefs were responsible for the well-being of the people whom they represented (e.g., Swanton 1911:93; Gilbert 1943:358; Gibson 1971:21; Gearing 1962).

A further similarity between the structure of governance among these peoples and that found among the Powhatan is that both peace and war chiefs are reported to have had assistants, whose job was to carry out the decisions of their superiors. An anonymous account of the Choctaw, for instance, says that "in each village, besides the chief, and the war chief, there are two Tascamingoutchy who are like lieutenants of the war chief: a tichoumingo who is like the major, it is he who organises all the ceremonies, feasts, dances, he speaks for the chief, and makes the warriors and strangers smoke" (Anonymous 1931:243-244). The same was true among the Chickasaw (Gibson 1971:21-22), the Timucua of the early contact period (Milanich 2000:7), and the Cherokee (e.g., Gearing 1962).

The evidence of the earlier accounts, though, suggests that even the peace chiefs were subordinate to a religious authority, where they were not its equivalent. That is, dual sovereignty in the Southeast had multiple forms, of which the relationship between peace and war chiefs was one; that between the secular chiefs and the priests or shamans was another, and possibly more inclusive, form. Exploration of this relationship must, in the present circumstances, be limited and inconclusive. Nevertheless, the evidence is suggestive. Bossu, for instance, states that among the Choctaw, shamans had "great authority, and it is to them that they go on every kind of occasion to ask their advice, they consult them like the oracle" (1931 [1768]:260-261). Admittedly, he is unclear to whom "they" refers, but it need not refer only to common people. Gibson implies that, at least in the 18th century, the authority over the whole of the Chickasaw was not a civil chief but a priest (1971:7). Among the Caddo, chiefs had authority over only one community, but a priest was the authority over several (Early 2000:131). The sacerdotal aspect of the Cherokee "white chiefs," whose meetinghouse contained the sacred fire, has been mentioned (Fogelson 1977:190). The Timucua were apparently much the same, regarding their great chief as a great priest if not a divinity (Swanton 1987:648; Milanich 2000:7). The Natchez represent possibly the most extreme case, since the Great Sun was divine and the priest of divinities; he may also have, in Evans-Pritchard's phrase, ruled as well as reigned (Evans-Pritchard 1962; Swanton 1987:649-650, 1911:99-102).

One finds versions of these customs in the Northeast as well, certainly: elevated deposition of the dead, secondary burial, communication by means of beads (wampum), chiefly status, and aggregations of tribes into one polity. The northeastern Indians seem to have been less stratified politically than the southeastern tribes, however, and chiefly status more achieved than ascribed. In particular, we find no suggestion that Iroquoian or Algonkian sachems were sacerdotal or divine, as they were in the deep Southeast. Dual sovereignty among these northeastern peoples took the form of complementarity between the peace chief or judge and the war chief, rather than between the priest and the king, as in the Southeast (Day 1998; McMillan 1988; Morgan 1996; Russell 1980; Simmons 1986; Tooker 1991:42).[24]

I have, consequently, referred more often to the Southeast than the Northeast for help in making this analysis. But as the lack of consensus among anthropologists shows, the Powhatan are neither clearly "southeastern" nor "northeastern." In particular, their language has its affinities in the Northeast and not at all in the Southeast. Thus I have used pertinent examples from the Northeast as well in this reconstruction.

1. The Realm of Powhatan

T he realm of Powhatan, Tsenacommacoh, is conventionally known as the Powhatan Confederacy today. It is supposed to have been a confederation among some number (which is disputed) of small tribes living in the Tidewater area of Virginia. Today most scholars recognize that this was not a confederacy (e.g., Lurie 1959:40; Potter 1993:164; Rountree 1989:117; contra, e.g., Feest 1966; Axtell 1988), although consensus on how to classify it is lacking. This polity can reasonably be called a paramount chiefdom (Rountree 1989:117), but it might as properly be called an empire or a kingdom. More useful than any such labeling, though, is the understanding of the constitution of the polity. The English descriptions say consistently that this was an association of small, semiautonomous political groups, each with its chief and his immediate subordinate chiefs, all more or less united under the leadership of one man, known as Powhatan, the mamanatowick.[1] According to what Powhatan informants told the colonists, he had inherited the leadership of some of these groups, and the rest he had conquered.

What the colonists have to say on this subject needs no particular knowledge of Renaissance culture for its understanding. Therefore, I take what they say at face value here and try to relate it to modern anthropological terms.

Powhatan "Tribes"

Smith refers to the constituent groups of this polity as "nations," and Strachey uses the term "shires." Most modern writers about the Powhatan follow Jefferson (1832:96) in calling the constituent parts of this polity "tribes" (Mooney 1907; Speck 1924; Mook 1944; Swanton 1987; Feest 1978; Rountree 1989; Gleach 1997; Turner [1985] says "groups"). None of them defines what is meant by "tribe." Their reluctance is understandable, since the difficulties in defining this word are well known (Helm 1968). For purposes of this analysis, we may set aside the arguments over whether the tribe is a necessary stage in political or social evolution, but even so we confront a considerable list of possible characteristics of the tribe, most if not all of which are contested: a common culture; a common language; a common, bounded territory; a common name; political integration and political autonomy; self-definition; mutual obligations of an economic, political, or military nature (Dole 1968:87). What sort of mechanisms there might to be for mobilizing joint activities or making decisions is also a matter of debate.

These discussions arise from a wish to have a definition that will allow valid cross-cultural comparison. The problems associated with such comparison are themselves well known: either the cases that suit all the criteria are too few to make a valid argument, or one expands the definition to include all "reasonable" cases—or cases that conform to a majority but not all the criteria—and vitiates the analytical value of the category (Dole 1968:87; Fried 1968:7; see Fried 1967:170). Since this analysis anticipates the comparison of structures rather than of supposedly discrete parts of a culture, the terms used for parts of the structure are less important than the relationships among these parts. In this circumstance, retaining the term "tribe" for these constituent groups should be acceptable.

In addition, what we know of these groups from the English colonists shows them to have conformed in many regards to the anthropological criteria for a tribe. Each tribe enjoyed a degree of political autonomy, and each had "a common and distinct name," "a common and distinct territory," and apparently "a moral obligation to unite in war" (Evans-Pritchard 1940:122). Only in one regard do these groups differ markedly from the conventional idea of "tribe": they were ranked societies, not egalitarian, each tribe having a principal chief and one or more subordinate chiefs as well as a council composed of outstanding persons in the tribe. Even so, since modern scholarship calls them "tribes," I prefer to do so as well, if only to avoid the possibility that introducing a different term might distract from the main issue.

Smith, listing the names of the different tribes, also confirms that though they were not independent of Powhatan himself, none had sovereignty over any of the others. "The most of these rivers are inhabited by severall nations, or rather families, of the name of the rivers" (Smith 1986 [1612]:146). He gives an estimate of the number of "fighting men" for each tribe he identifies and says that each of them has a "severall commander, which they call Werowance" (Smith 1986 [1612]:146; Strachey 1953 [1612]:43). Smith's map shows many more villages than "king's houses." Some "king's houses," like Kecoughtan, seem isolated from other settlements and may indeed have been the only village of that tribe. Smith says, in fact, that the Kecoughtan were a small tribe with "not past 20. fighting men" (1986 [1612]:146). Others, like Kupkipcock or Menapucunt on the Pamunkey River, are surrounded by several ordinary villages, and Smith reports that the Pamunkey tribe was large. Strachey identifies several villages for some tribes, for example, the Appomattox, Weanock, Nansemond, and Pamunkey.

Such variation in size appears to have been both widespread and long-lasting. Harriot, writing in 1590 about the Carolina Algonkians, reports a similar situation in those tribes: "In some places of the countrey one onley towne belongeth to the gouernment of a *Wiroans* or chiefe Lorde; in other some two or three, in some sixe, eight, & more; the greatest *Wiroans* that yet we had dealing with had but eighteene townes in his gouernment, and able to make not aboue seuen or eight hundred fighting men at the most" (1972 [1590]:25). Over a century later (1705), Beverley writes: "The method of the *Indian* Settlements is altogether by Cohabitation, in Townships, from fifty to five hundred Families in a Town, and each of these Towns is commonly a Kingdom. Sometimes one King has the command of several of these Towns, when they happen to be united in his Hands, by Descent or Conquest" (1947 [1705]:174).[2] These reports imply a varying relationship between the name of the tribe and that of the "king's house" at its center. Some, probably the smallest and least dispersed, seem to have shared the name; others, larger and occupying more territory, had a name distinct from that of their major settlement. In any case, it seems clear that each of these tribes had a distinct name.

Regarding land tenure Smith writes: "They all knowe their severall landes, and habitations, and limits, to fish, fowle, or hunt in, but they hold all of their great Werowance Powhatan" (1986 [1612]:174, 1986 [1624]:127; Strachey 1953 [1612]:87). According to Strachey, Powhatan himself divided up the territory into "shires" and placed a werowance in charge of each. These divisions "all . . . haue their precincts, and bowndes, proper, and Commodiously appointed out, that no one intrude vpon the other, of severall forces" (Strachey 1953 [1612]:63). Both writers state that all territories were held directly from Powhatan, and Strachey reports a small piece of history in support of this contention. According to him, "Vpon the death of an old Weroance of this place [Kecoughtan] some 15. or 16. yeares synce (being too powerfull neighbours to syde the great Powhatan) yt is said Powhatan taking the advantage subtilly stepped in, and conquered the People killing the Chief and most of them, and the reserved he transported over the Riuer, craftely chaunging their seat, and quartering them amongest his owne people, vntill now at length the remayne of those lyving haue with much sute obteyned of him *Payankatank,* which he not long since . . . dispeopled" (Strachey 1953 [1612]:68).[3] In an earlier section, Strachey describes the "dispeopling" of Piankatank: "in the yeare 1608. Powhatan surprised the naturall Inhabitantes of *Payankatank* his neighbours, and subiectes, the occasion was to vs vnknowne; . . . Twenty fower men they kil'd, (the rest escaping by fortune, and their swift footemanshipp) and the long hayre of the one syde of their heades, with the skyn cased off with shells, or reeds, they brought away to Powhatan: they surprised also the women, and Children, and the Weroance, all whome they presented to Powhatan" (1953 [1612]:44; also Smith 1986 [1612]:175). He remarks in his description of the territory that it was inhabited by the survivors of the Piankatank and of the Kecoughtan, whom Powhatan had moved there in 1608. Given this sort of activity, Strachey's statement that Powhatan had himself divided the whole country into smaller territories is understandable.

But he may not have been correct, even so. His own account suggests that the areas were already tribal, that is, associated with named, politically distinct groups of people. A statement to the effect that "the Kecoughtans" were moved to "Piankatank" supposes that both the tribal name and the territory were permanent and semi-independent, that is, that the name of the people was not necessarily a function of the name of the territory nor vice versa.

Some less direct evidence supports the conclusion that each of these groups had its own territory. The singular, enduring hostility that the Paspahegh showed the English (which was reciprocated; Smith calls them a "churlish and trecherous nation" [1986 (1608):39]) almost from the beginning was due to the English having settled (albeit unwittingly) in their territory (Percy 1910 [1607]:lxvi–lxvii; Smith 1986 [1608]:39, 91, 93; Strachey 1953 [1612]:107). Following Smith's capture, the paramount chief, Powhatan, "proclaimed me [Smith] a werowanes of Powhatan, and [declared] that all his subjects should so esteeme us, and no man account us strangers nor *Paspaheghans*, but Powhatans" (Smith 1986 [1608]:67; emphasis added). Although the Paspahegh did not want them there, Powhatan and the rest had apparently come to think of the English as "Paspahegh" because they were living in their territory. We have also a purported statement from the werowance of the Powhatan tribe (who was a son of the paramount, Powhatan) to his people, which Percy quotes in his "Observations." Although Captain Newport greatly pleased this werowance with the gift of a hatchet, "But yet the Sauages murmured at our planting in the Countrie, whereupon this *Werowance* made answere againe very wisely of a Sauage, Why should you bee offended with them, as long as they hurt you not, nor take any thing away by force. They take but a little waste ground, which doth you nor any of vs any good" (Percy 1910 [1607]:lxix). The "savages' murmuring" apparently arose from a sense of trespass that they would not allow among themselves. (Why the werowance would tolerate it is another question; see Hantman 1990 for an answer.)

The terms in which Strachey describes the attacks on the Piankatank and Kecoughtan suggest that each tribe had an obligation to unite in war. Other evidence supports this as well. Smith and Strachey give estimates of the number of fighting men in each of the tribes. Smith, for example, writing in 1612 (1986:146), says: "The first and next the rivers mouth are the Kecoughtans, who besides their women and children, have not past 20. fighting men. The Paspaheghes . . . have not past 40. The river called Chickahamania neere 200. The Weanocks 100. The Arrowhatocks 30. The place called Powhatan, some 40." And so on. Smith's including these numbers may reflect English colonial, not native, interests, of course. From Strachey, who is more explicit about what "fighting men" means, we learn that the number of warriors was probably of interest to both sides, as one chapter heading includes the promise to identify "what forces for the present they ar hable to furnish Powhatan in his Warrs" (1953 [1612]:63).

According to Strachey, not only Powhatan but the subordinate werowances could conscript men for a raid. The chief would send "an officer" to run from village to village, striking the requested men over the back with a "bastynado" and announcing the time and place of meeting. A man so summoned "dare not at the tyme appointed be absent" (Strachey 1953 [1612]:104). Strachey is the only writer who mentions this forcible draft, though. Clayton seems to imply less conscription and more willingness when he writes that "every one that in any nature can serve his Prince, is ready to do it, & to do it gratis" (1965 [1687]:22). According to Beverley (1947 [1705]:192), when a chief wished to stage a raid he summoned a council, called *matchacomoco*, to which young men came decorated in a frightening manner as for war and carrying their weapons.[4] Once in the meetinghouse they performed a "Grotesque Dance" and afterward planned their raid. Beverley's account does not mention conscription but rather conveys that a chief had but to announce a projected raid to have all the eligible men volunteer, which sounds more like what one finds among the peoples of the deep Southeast (Hudson 1976:242). The question is significant because "a moral obligation to unite" is not at all the same as a draft, as modern Americans know very well. The weight of the evidence favors the former in this case. Strachey is the only writer to mention something like a draft, and even he seems to contradict this when he describes Powhatan and other werowances giving copper gifts to their allies in return for military support (1953 [1612]:68–69, 107). The others do not, admittedly, say that chiefs did not press warriors, but their accounts give the impression that all participants in warfare were volunteers, and eager at that. Motivation for joining a raiding party is not far to seek. Spelman writes, "And they that kill most of ther enimies are heald the cheafest men amonge them" (1910 [1613]:cxiv).

All these passages suggest that the English took each group to be a self-governing entity because the Powhatan themselves did. They suggest, moreover, that the Powhatan conceived of social relations in terms of tribes and not of individual persons. A consequence of this must have been that hostilities were a tribal, not a personal, matter; we may conclude that they had "a moral obligation to unite in war."

What about the polity as a whole? Was it morally obliged to unite for a concerted effort against the Monacans, the enemies of the Powhatan; to assist Powhatan himself to attack one of the Tidewater tribes supposedly subject to him; or both? The answer appears to be no. Both the explorers of the Outer Banks and the Jamestown settlers report that werowances offered gifts to their neighbor chiefs to enlist their aid in an attack and that the paramount chief (including Powhatan) sent gifts to supposedly subordinate chiefs for the same reason. The gift could be accepted or rejected as the recipient pleased, without prejudice (Hakluyt 1907 [1589], 6:146, 155, 157; Smith 1986 [1612]:227, [1624]:308; Strachey 1953 [1612]:107).

Composition of the Polity

Despite the variety of interpretations of this material, one fact seems plain regarding the Powhatan: it was a congeries of culturally similar small tribes who had probably once been independent of each other politically, if not economically, but were now allied or subject to one man, Powhatan. Smith provides the earliest statement to this effect: "The forme of their Common wealth is a monarchicall governement, one as Emperour ruleth over many kings or governours. Their chiefe ruler is called Powhatan" (1986 [1612]:173).

The reports do not agree on the number of tribes or of werowances. Smith's map shows 30 "king's houses" that definitely belong to werowances allied or subject to Powhatan; the remainder belonged to the Conoy, the Monacan, the Mannahoac, and Algonkian tribes living on the Eastern Shore of Maryland. Smith marks on his map some "king's houses" that he does not identify in the text as "nations, or . . . families" (1986 [1612]:146). For example, he identifies Orapaks, at the head of the Chickahominy River, in this way, although it was not the capital of a tribe of that name. Powhatan moved there from Werowocomoco to put some distance between himself and the English (Smith 1986 [1612]:147; Strachey 1953 [1612]:57; see Smith 1986 [1612]:139). Smith also identifies Uttamussac, on the north bank of the Youghtanund River, as a "king's house," but from the text we know that this was the main "temple" of the polity (Smith 1986 [1612]:169). In his text, Smith identifies 28 "nations" altogether, including two groups on the Eastern Shore of Virginia (1986 [1612]:146-148).

Strachey agrees with this for the most part, but he offers some additional material. In one passage, which he copied largely from Smith, he lists but 23 tribes, which he calls "shires." He omits the Weanock, the Pamunkey, the Chickahominy, and the two Eastern Shore tribes (Strachey 1953 [1612]:43-46). But subsequently, in a general statement about the "greatnes and Bowndes of [Powhatan's] Empire," he says, "he seemes to comaund South and North from the *Mangoags*, and *Chawanookes*, bordering vpon *Roanoak* or South-Virginia, to *Tockwogh*, . . . : South-west to *Anoeg*[5] (not expressed in the Mappe) . . . 10. dayes iournye distant from vs, from whence those inhabiting Weroances sent vnto him of their Commodityes . . .

and west-ward, he Commaundes to *Monahassanugh*,[6] which standes at the foot of the mountaynes, from *Chesapeak* or the mouth of our Bay 200. myles: Nor-west, to the bordures of *Massawomeck*, and *Bocootawwonough:* Nor-east and by east to *Accohanock, Accowmack*, and some other petty Nations, lying on the East syde of our Bay" (Strachey 1953 [1612]:56–57). He provides a list of 32 werowances, which includes Weanock and which identifies what Smith calls "Pamunkey" as "Opechancanough," the name of Powhatan's brother and successor (Strachey 1953 [1612]:63–69).

Strachey mentions the Chickahominy Indians in this catalog as well, describing them as "a warlick and free people, albeyt they pay certayne dutyes to Powhatan, and for Copper wilbe waged to serve and helpe him in his Warrs, yet they will not admitt of any Weroance from him to governe over them, but suffer themselves to be regulated, and guyded by their Priests, with the Assistaunce of their Elders whome they call *Cawcawwassoughs*" (1953 [1612]:68–69). This is partly copied from Smith, who had written that the "Chickhamanians . . . are governed by the Priestes and their Assistants or their Elders called *Cawcawwassoughes*" (1986 [1612]:146). Strachey's is the clearer statement, though, and thus more useful in sorting out the somewhat obscure relationship between werowances and *cockarouse*s, as well as that between the chiefs themselves and the priests. He makes it plain that the term *cawcawwassough*, "later anglicized as 'cockarouse'" (Barbour 1986, 1:146n), refers to the elders of the Chickahominy and not to a religious status; he states that, at least among the Chickahominy, the "priests" took precedence over the elders in the matter of government. Ralph Hamor, rejoicing over the separate peace the English had concluded with the Chickahominy following the marriage of Pocahontas to John Rolfe, confirms Smith's and Strachey's assessment of the semi-independent political status of the Chickahominy. He identifies them as "our next neighbours" who "haue long time liued free from *Powhatans* subiection, hauing lawes and gouernors within themselues" but have no "principall commander or *Weroance*" (Hamor 1615:11). In accepting this treaty, which was drawn up at their request, the Chickahominy agreed to accept King James as their sole werowance (thus breaking with tradition, one reason for Hamor's delight at this turn of events), with the governor, Sir Thomas Dale, as his deputy. But since Dale could not live among them they requested "to be gouerned as formerly by eight of the elders and principall men amongst them, as his substitutes and councellers" (Hamor 1615:12).

Strachey includes several "shires" not found in Smith. What Strachey calls the "shire" of Cantaunkack, whose werowance he names Ottahotin, Smith also includes on his map but not as a "king's house." Other names in Strachey's list have but a distant similarity to names in Smith and may not in fact refer to the same places. Yet others are not found in Smith at all. A comparison of Smith's list of "king's houses" and "nations" with Strachey's "shires" and werowances reveals that the English were in pretty close agreement about the tribes closest to themselves, which were also those at the heart of Powhatan's empire, and that they were comparatively vague about tribes successively farther away from themselves. We can, however, resolve some of the discrepancies, especially the references to Pamunkey. Smith identifies Pamunkey as the land embraced by the confluence of the present Pamunkey and Mattaponi Rivers to form the York and says that it has "neere 300 able men" (1986 [1612]:147). This is the area Strachey calls "Opechancanough." The difference in their reports is probably due to the fact that a werowance and the territory went by the same name, although which comes first is uncertain.

Archer says of the werowance of Arrohattoc, "his name is *Arahatec:* the Country *Araheticoh*" (1910 [1607]:xliii). Archer identifies Powhatan as a person (1910 [1607]:xliii), but both Smith and Strachey identify it as a place also (Smith 1986 [1612]:146; Strachey 1953 [1612]:43). On this first exploration up the James River, the English met a chief they thought was the "great Emperor" Powhatan of the Virginians (Smith 1986 [1608]:29), but they later discovered that this was a "lesser" Powhatan, called Tanxpowhatan or

Tantspowhatan, a son of the "great" Powhatan; he was in fact the werowance of the place called Powhatan at that time (Strachey 1953 [1612]:63–64). Smith states that the paramount chief, Powhatan, was called after this place, which was his "principall place of dwelling. . . . But his proper name is Wahunsonacock" (1986 [1612]:173, [1608]:29). Why Smith identifies the place Powhatan in this way is puzzling, since elsewhere he presents Werowocomoco as Powhatan's seat and the center of the polity. Strachey says that Powhatan was called that as a young man because he was born there, "taking his denomynacion from the Country Powhatan," and that the people of that region—including the "frontier neighbour princes"—still called him that even though he then lived elsewhere for the most part. But Strachey also says that the people called Powhatan a variety of names, some of which referred to "his divers places." Powhatan's "owne people," for example, might call him Ottaniack, Mamanatowick (which Strachey translates as "great king"), and Wahunsenacawh, the last of which is his "proper right name which they salute him with (himself in presence)" (Strachey 1953 [1612]:56).

Although we cannot today reconstruct the subtleties of Powhatan linguistic usage, these remarks suggest that a werowance assumed a title, if not a personal name, from his tribal territory on his accession. Possibly the reciprocal occurred also, the territory coming to be called after the personal name of the werowance, as when Strachey calls Pamunkey "Opechancanough." This is the sole example of such a thing, however, and a more reasonable inference is that Strachey assumed a reciprocal usage not typical of the Powhatan.

Smith lists no "king's house" for Pamunkey as such, but he does identify the village of Cinquoteck as a residence of two of Powhatan's brothers, who were werowances of this tribe (1986 [1608]:77). Strachey lists three werowances for the tribe. These were "all three Powhatans brethren, and are the Trium-viri as yt were, or 3. kings of a Country called *Opechancheno* vpon the Head of Pamunky [York] river" (Strachey 1953 [1612]:69). In his earliest account of Virginia, however, Smith identifies Menapacute (a variant of Menapucunt) as the residence of Opechancanough (1986 [1608]:51). Uttamussak was "their principall Temple or place of superstition . . . , neare unto which is a house Temple or place of Powhatans" (Smith 1986 [1612]:169). Neither Smith nor Strachey positively associates Kupkipcock with any particular werowance or tribe; but Smith places it in Pamunkey territory, for which Strachey lists three werowances. Presumably it was the residence of at least one of them, as Menapucunt is reported to have been for Opechancanough.

Strachey lists the werowances of nine villages whose relationship to those listed by Smith is in most cases obscure. The one exception is Cantaunkack, which both writers mention, although Smith does not call it a "king's house." Strachey says (1953 [1612]:69) that it had a werowance and was able to provide 100 men for warfare. Another village, Pataunck, for which he lists one werowance (Strachey 1953 [1612]:69), may be Smith's village of Potauncac (south bank of the Pamunkey), but Smith does not say it has a "king's house." Likewise, Strachey's Ochahannauke may be Smith's Oquornock village (north bank of the Rappahannock River), but again Smith does not call it a "king's house." Strachey gives the name of the werowance of Cassapecock as Keyghaughton (1953 [1612]:69), which seems to be a variant spelling of Kecoughtan. He gives no indication where the village of Cassapecock is, and Smith has no village with a name like this, nor does he show or describe villages in the vicinity of Kecoughtan. Of the remaining villages, none can be found on Smith's map. Smith himself indicates two "king's houses" on the Rappahannock River—Pissaseck and Oposcopank—that he does not list as "nations," and Strachey mentions them not at all. Each is shown fairly obviously separated from other tribes on that river, and the impression is that they are true "nations," which for some reason Smith omitted from his list.

Depending on how one takes these data, there may have been, at a minimum, 27 Powhatan tribes; at a maximum, 43. The smaller number is probably more realistic, and certainly no modern scholars have accepted anything like the larger one. Jefferson, Mook, Swanton, and Rountree say there were 30 (Jefferson 1832:97; Mook 1944; Swanton 1952; Rountree 1989); Feest identifies 27 (1978:257). My preference is to regard Orapaks, Kupkipcock, Uttamussack, and Manpucunt as Pamunkey villages; to treat the Opiscopank and Pissasec as independent tribes; and to treat all of Strachey's unidentifiable villages as part of one of the other tribes. This results in 30 tribes.

Internal Relations

According to the colonists, who say they are reporting what the Indians told them, Powhatan himself established this "common wealth" primarily by means of conquest. Smith and Strachey report that he had inherited 6 (or possibly 7 or 8) of these 30 tribes (Smith 1986 [1612]:173, [1624]:126; Strachey 1953 [1612]:44, 57). These were the Arrohattock, Appomattox, Pamunkey, Youghtanund, Mattaponi, and Powhatan, and possibly the Werowocomoco and Chiskiak (Smith 1986 [1612]:104, 147). Archer reports of the werowance of Arrohattock: "This we found to be a kynge subiect to *Powatah* the Cheife of all the kyngdomes" (1910 [1607]:xliii). He also describes a meeting with the "little" Powhatan, during which the English learned that some number of tribes—Archer is not more specific—were "all one with him or vnder him" (1910 [1607]:xliii). Later in the account, Archer says of the "queen" of Appomattox, "she is subiect to *Powatah* as the rest are" (1910 [1607]:l). Smith reports further that in each of these territories Powhatan had a longhouse kept ready for his entertainment (1986 [1612]:51; see Strachey 1953 [1612]:61), and at Werowocomoco he had four or five such houses.

The fact that the distinction between inherited and conquered tribes was evidently important to the Powhatan themselves prompts several hypotheses about relations among the tribes and between the individual tribe and the mamanatowick, Powhatan. One would imagine that the relationship between Powhatan and his conquests must be different from that between himself and his inheritance.

What was true of the inheritance may not have been true of the conquest and vice versa. The conquered tribes may well have seen themselves as "subiect to *Powatah*" as a person rather than to a status or to an idea of empire. The inherited ones may also have done so, or they may have formed a more solidary unit within the polity as a whole. If that were so, they may have regarded Powhatan as the embodiment of their union rather than as someone who had imposed himself on each of them separately. There may have been differences in how each group saw itself temporally, too—the inheritance as a union outlasting any individual reign, the conquests as such only for their conqueror's lifetime (if that long). And each group may have seen the other group as different from itself.

Because the English were not interested in such distinctions, they do not provide clear answers to these questions. Their political concern was simple: whom did they treat with? They wanted to add Virginia to the dominions of James I. To whom did they go for submission? If the chiefs they met claimed to be a subject of a more powerful ruler, as it seemed to them that they did, they would seek that ruler and treat with him. They did not wonder about the subtleties—possible or actual—of being "subject." This is clear in the statements that appear in accounts for the next 15 or 20 years that Powhatan alone is responsible for the hostility or amity of tribes toward the English. "Subject" to the English meant that the ruler could and did exact certain kinds of action from his people; he could and did prohibit them from other actions equally effectively.

The English were mistaken to think that "subject" meant in Virginia quite what it meant in Europe. A first step in rectifying their mistake is to try to address the hypotheses posed above. I take the English evidence—not all of it about relations between leader and supporters—to mean that the inheritance was qualitatively different from the conquest in the ways I have mentioned. Geographically and politically it was the core of the polity, without doubt. If we cannot know, now, that these six or seven tribes helped Powhatan establish his polity, we can make a case that they helped him maintain it.

But the Powhatan defined a space in terms of its center rather than its periphery or boundary. Thus the inheritance seems to have been emerging, if not established, as a conceptual core as well.[7]

Archer's report that "the kyng of *Paspaeiouh* and this king [the werowance of Weanok] is at odds, as the *Paspeians* tould me, and Demonstrated by their hurtes" shows that relations between tribes were not necessarily peaceful (1910 [1607]:xli). They were not necessarily uneasy, either. Smith notes than when the Pamunkey took him prisoner in December 1607, they were hunting together with people from the Paspahegh, Youghtanund, Mattaponi, Chiskiac, and Chickahominy—a combination of inherited, conquered, and semi-independent tribes. He mentions in the same passage that the Chickahominy and the Paspahegh were in league to "surprise us at worke, to have had our tools" (Smith 1986 [1608]:91). A werowance established an alliance with other werowances by means of gifts. Strachey states that "the before remembred Weroance of *Paspahegh*, did once wage 14. or 15. Weroances to assist him in the attempt vpon the Fort of Iames Towne for one Copper-plate promised to each Weroance" (1953 [1612]:107; "wage" in this passage means "give wages to," not "lead into battle," although the result is the same in this case). In this regard, Powhatan seems to have been no different, since Strachey says he also offered gifts to win potential allies (1953 [1612]:107). The English who attempted to settle on the Outer Banks met with similarly organized resistance: "First that Okisko king of Weopomeoik with the Mandoages should bee mooved, and with great quantitie of copper intertained to the number of 7. or 8. hundreth bowes, to enterprise the matter thus to be ordered" (Hakluyt 1907 [1589], 6:155). If tribal relations in Tidewater Virginia were like those in other parts of the world (which we know rather better ethnographically), they almost certainly oscillated between alliance and enmity, and the current status always admitted the possibility of establishing its opposite.

But we may discern a consistent separation between inherited tribes and conquered tribes, with the former exerting some control over the latter. The relationship of inherited to conquered seems also to have been the relationship of Powhatan to the conquered, in that Powhatan relied on his inheritance to accomplish his conquest. Thus these need to be discussed together.

Archer's report that in mid-June two "salvages" came to the fort to offer the English help in dealing with hostile tribes provides a good starting point. The visit occurred very soon after the English arrived, and so it gives us a picture of political relations as close to aboriginal as we are likely to get. These men—one of them an Arrohattock whom they had met on their exploration up the James —"certifyed vs who were our frendes, and who foes, saying that king *Pamaunke* [Pamunkey] kyng *Arahatec*, the kyng of *Youghtamong* [Youghtanund], and the king of *Matapoll* [Mattaponi] would each assist vs or make vs peace with *Paspeiouk* [Paspahegh], *Tapahanouk* [Quiyoughcohannock], *Wynauk* [Weanock], *Apamatecoh* and *Chesciak*, our Contracted Enemyes" (Archer 1910 [1607]:lv). Archer's "frendly" tribes were all part of Powhatan's inheritance; the "Enemyes" were part of the conquest, with one exception: Smith, Strachey, and Archer himself identify the Appomattox as one of the inherited tribes. The phrasing of the intelligence implies that the four friendly tribes could control the others. Wingfield (the first president) reports a later event with similar implications: "June the 25th, an Indian came to vs from the great *Poughwaton* with the worde of peace; that he desired greatly our freindshipp; that the wyrounnces, *Paspaheigh* and *Tapahanagh* should be our freindes; that wee should sowe and reape in peace, or els he would make warrs vpon them with vs. This message fell out true; for both those wyraounces haue ever since remayned in peace and trade with vs" (1910 [1607]:lxxv–lxxvi). Wingfield's report is so like Archer's that one concludes that Powhatan was behind both embassies. Powhatan and Opechancanough both took much friendly interest in the English at this time, although only Opechancanough had met them. Wingfield writes that besides this visit he received in early July two gifts of deer, one from Powhatan and one from the Pamunkey (1910

[1607]:lxxvi); and Smith writes that Opechancanough sent a peaceful embassy to James Fort on 21 June.[8]

Smith, at least, singles out the Weanock and the Paspahegh as particularly inimical (1986 [1608]:31, 39, 49, cf. 91–93, [1612]:261, [1624]:192, 236), and Wingfield (1910 [1607]:lxxvi) mentions that the werowance of Tappahannock (Quiyoughcohannock) had been "in the feild against vs" some time before July 1607, although Percy (1910 [1607]:lxv) describes a very friendly meeting with him in early May, and none of the sources mentions a battle with this tribe. The reported inclusion of the Appomattox among the inimical tribes is somewhat puzzling. Percy says that on their first visit, on 8 May, the English met great hostility, but they persuaded the people that they meant no harm and were allowed to "land in quietnesse" (1910 [1607]:lxvi). Archer met the "quene" of this country (Percy's party had apparently met the werowance, her brother) nearly three weeks later and found her distant but hospitable (Archer 1910 [1607]:l; Smith 1986 [1608]:31). Possibly the werowance retained a lively animosity to the strangers despite his letting them come ashore; the ambassadors from Powhatan would know more about that than the English. Likewise, Archer's reference to the Chiskiak is also puzzling since the English do not report having met them at this point. Their lands were just behind Jamestown, however, and possibly they and the English had encountered each other without the English realizing it. The English report fairly constant harassment at their fort during that summer but say the perpetrators are "salvages" without specifying the tribe. Possibly the Chiskiak were among them.

Evidently, Powhatan, Opechancanough, and the inherited tribes generally were confident they could control the conquered tribes of the polity. Wingfield's comment that "this fell out true" proves that their confidence was not misplaced, and his account of subsequent incidents confirms it. First, "The 7th of Iuly, *Tapahanah* [Quiyoughcohannock], a wyroaunce, dweller on *Salisbery* side [i.e., the south side of the James], hayled vs with the word of peace."

Wingfield diplomatically ignored the fact that they had last met on the field of battle, answered his questions about the movement of the English ships, and received a promise that when the harvest began the people of Quiyoughcohannock would bring food to the fort, "which promise he truly performed." From this reconciliation came another. In September "*Paspaheighe, by Tapahanne's* mediation, was taken into friendshipp with vs." The werowance of Paspahegh had already sent them a runaway boy, suggesting that he was disposed to cease hostilities even before the intervention of Quiyoughcohannock (Wingfield 1910 [1607]:lxxvi–lxxxii). The activities which, from the English point of view, were behind the scenes are not hard to reconstruct.

Whether Powhatan attempted to suppress fighting among his subject tribes is not clear, but several reports suggest that he did not. He seems to have ignored the fight between the Paspahegh and the Weanock and likewise a war between the Tappahannock and the Moraughtacund on the Rappahannock River in the summer of 1608 (Smith 1986 [1624]:173–174). Possibly he left them to it so long as they also did what he wanted.

But he did attack them from time to time. Smith and Strachey both describe attacks that he made on the Kecoughtan, the Piankatank, and the Chesapeake. These seem to confirm not only the report that the polity was formed primarily by conquest but also the modern view that Powhatan kept it together by force.[9] But other evidence suggests that Powhatan was pursuing a policy of incorporation by affinity and kinship as well. A reasonable inference is that his intention was to establish so many ties of this kind in his domains that force—always expensive—would no longer be necessary.

Strachey, who seems to have been more interested than any of his comrades in Powhatan and the nature of political relations in Powhatan's domain—according to his own account, he made systematic inquiries into the matter almost in the manner of a modern anthropologist—provides most of the relevant information here, but there are a few comments by other colonists that support this argument.[10] In his catalog of werowances, Strachey identifies as Powhatan's sons the werowance of the Powhatan tribe, called Tanxpowhatan or "little" Powhatan; that of the Kecoughtan; and that of the Quiyoughcohannock (1953 [1612]:63, 67, 65; see Spelman 1910 [1613]:cii). Strachey says that Powhatan himself had established the Quiyoughcohannock werowance in his status, replacing a man called Pipsco, whom he deposed for seducing a wife of Opechancanough's. At the time Strachey was writing, the werowance was still too young to take over the entire tribe; his regent was his mother, one of Powhatan's wives. The son was "for the most parte in the governement of *Chopoke* at *Chawopo* one of Pipscoes brothers" (Strachey 1953 [1612]:64–65). The so-called quene, or *werowanqua*, of the Appomattox, whom Strachey identifies as subordinate to her brother, the werowance of the entire tribe (Strachey 1953 [1612]:64), was another of Powhatan's wives, according to Smith (1986 [1608]:65). This should mean that in due course the son or sons born to both would become werowances of the Appomattox.

The Appomattox and the Powhatan were "inherited" tribes, but the Kecoughtan and the Quiyoughcohannock were not, and the Kecoughtan is one of those tribes the mamanatowick, Powhatan, attacked early in the colonial period. On the other hand, Strachey identifies no other werowances of "inherited" tribes as relatives of Powhatan with the exception of those of the Pamunkey, who were his brothers. Strachey's comments, though brief, suggest no correspondence between "inherited" tribes and those with one of Powhatan's sons in charge.

The curious events surrounding John Smith's further acquaintance with the natives of Virginia may be seen as an example of Powhatan's strategy.[11] To summarize: a group of Powhatan under the leadership of Opechancanough surprised and captured Smith as he was exploring the upper reaches of the Chickahominy River in the winter of 1607. Some weeks later, still a captive, he met Powhatan himself, who adopted him as his son, having (according to one of Smith's versions) first threatened his death by bludgeoning, a fate from which Powhatan's daughter Pocahontas rescued him. The speeches that Smith reports Powhatan making on this occasion are worth quoting. The first version, published in 1608, says: "This [the English promise of assistance against the Monocans and Pocoughtronack] so contented him, as immediatly with attentive silence, with a lowd oration he proclaimed me a werowanes of Powhatan, and that all his subjects should so esteeme us, and no man account us strangers nor Paspaheghans, but Powhatans, and that the Corne, weomen and Country, should be to us as to his owne people" (Smith 1986 [1608]:67). In 1624 Smith described the event thus:

> Two dayes after [the rescue; 7 January 1608], Powhatan having disguised himselfe in the most fearefullest manner he could, caused Captaine Smith to be brought forth to a great house in the woods, and there upon a mat by the fire to be left alone. Not long after from behinde a mat that divided the house, was made the most dolefullest noyse he ever heard; then Powhatan more like a devill then a man with some two hundred more as blacke as himselfe,[12] came unto him and told him now they were friends, and presently he should goe to James towne, to send him two great gunnes, and a gryndstone, for which he would giue him the Country of Capahowosick,[13] and for ever esteeme him as his sonne Nantaquod (Smith 1986 [1624]:151).

Smith says in his earlier account also that Powhatan wished him to move to Capahowosick: "He desired mee to forsake *Paspahegh*, and to live with him upon his River, a countrie called Capahowasicke" (Smith 1986 [1608]:57).

Considerable internal evidence, both direct and indirect, points to the Powhatan, and Powhatan himself, having taken Smith to be the werowance of the English colony. When he was captured, Smith's Indian guide told Opechancanough that Smith was a werowance: "He [i.e., the guide] discovered me to be [i.e., revealed that I was] the Captaine" (1986 [1608]:47; see Barbour 1986, 1:102n). Smith's English companions were killed either on the spot or somewhat later (1986 [1608]:47, [1624]:146–147), but he was spared. Since

Powhatan custom was to spare only the werowance among the men they captured in raids, their leaving Smith alive suggests that they regarded him in this light. Smith's guide may simply have lied about Smith's status in an effort to save Smith's life—Smith's account implies this sort of loyalty in the man—but it is more likely that the Powhatan had already marked Smith as a werowance; if the man's comment was not redundant, it was intended to inform Smith himself of the Powhatan point of view. In his trading activities throughout the lower Tidewater area, Smith acted like a werowance, being the only person to engage in exchange with the Powhatan; within the fort he was obviously the leader, organizing and motivating men to work. The Powhatan may have decided to capture Smith because, as they saw it, he was a werowance. Powhatan could then adopt him and place him in a country of his own, Capahowosick. This was near Werowocomoco, where Powhatan could keep him under control and out of Paspahegh, where his presence was disruptive.

Although the accounts of the colonists give us minimal information about Powhatan kinship, they do state clearly that the status of mamanatowick passed "not to his sonnes nor children, but first to his brethren, . . . and after their decease to his sisters. First to the eldest sister then to the rest and after them to the heires male and female of the eldest sister, but never to the heires of the males" (Smith 1986 [1612]:17, [1624]:127; also Strachey 1953 [1612]:77). In this circumstance, Powhatan could ensure that his sons became his subordinate werowances by marrying the sisters of incumbents. According to both Smith and Strachey, Powhatan—like all werowances—had many wives, Powhatan more than others. Strachey's comments, although they follow Smith's fairly closely, are the more entertaining:

> According to the order and custome of sensuall Hethenisme in the Allowaunce of Poligamy, he [Powhatan] may haue as many women as he will, and hath (as is supposed) many more then one hundred. . . .
>
> Of his women there are said to be about some dozen at this present, in whose Company he takes more delight then in the

matrilineal

polyggamy

rest, being for the most parte very young women, and these Commonly remoue with him from howse to howse . . they observe certayne degrees of greatnes, according to the neerenes they stand in their Princes love, and amourous entertaynment. (1953 [1612]:61; see Smith 1986 [1612]:174)

The list of wives that Strachey provides does not identify any of them as a werowance's sister nor yet as a *werowanqua,* but this may mean no more than that those august wives were by now too old to be still attractive.

As Figure 1 shows, Powhatan's marriages with such women could have several political consequences. He made these same werowances his brothers-in-law. We have no information about the expected or actual relations between men so connected, but it is not unreasonable to assume that they were allies and that the association benefited both. A son of such a marriage would succeed his mother's brother, becoming at the same time politically as well as jurally subordinate to his own father and later to his father's brother(s). In the next generation, too, the sons of Powhatan's daughters by these same women would be the heirs to his own sons in those tribes. By that time, Powhatan would himself be dead and very likely his brothers, too. The next heir would then be Powhatan's eldest sister's eldest son. (Although the sources state that sisters succeed brothers, there are so few instances of werowanquas in Powhatan that the statement is dubious [but see McCartney 1989]. In any case, the English never mention any of Powhatan's sisters specifically.) If the scheme outlined here were indeed part of Powhatan's political planning, his sister's son would find at least some of his subordinate werowances his own MBSS and MBDSS, that is, matrilateral kin.[14] If we project Powhatan's dynastic activities into subsequent generations, we can see that after only two or three generations all the werowances of the polity would have been kin to one another.

This reconstruction is largely hypothetical, if only because with the advent of the English any such planning went by the board. Nor

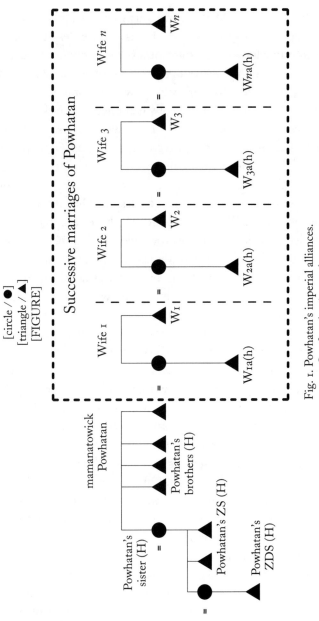

[circle / ●]
[triangle / ▲]
[FIGURE]

Fig. 1. Powhatan's imperial alliances.
● = female; ▲ = male

W = werowance; (H) = heir to mamanatowick; (h) = heir to werowance
ZS = sister's son; ZDS = sister's daughter's son

have we evidence that Powhatan consciously had such plans in mind or that such planning was any part of this culture despite Smith's characterizing Powhatan and "some others" as "provident" regarding their own food supply (1986 [1612]:163). The evidence we do have is spotty. For instance, although we know that some werowances were his sons and that at least two of his numerous wives were sisters to werowances, neither Strachey nor anyone else says who the mothers of Tanxpowhatan and the werowance of Kecoughtan were.

In favor of this reconstruction, however, is the fact that we seem to find something like it on a smaller scale in each of the constituent tribes, which is good reason to assume that it was a custom established before Powhatan's polity. We have acceptable, if not always consistent, evidence that werowance was an inherited status like mamanatowick and that werowances within a tribe were kin to each other. The earliest report from this region, that of the Spanish Jesuits, states that "Don Luis," their captive, was a *cacique* himself, the brother of "a principal chief of that region," and nephew to another—presumably zs, but the sources are not specific (Lewis and Loomie 1953:15, 23, 44). Smith does not say explicitly that the rule of succession that he reports for Powhatan's status applied to werowances (Beverly [1947 (1705):193] says that it was), but Strachey says that the deposed werowance of Quiyoughcohannock, called Pipsco, had that status by right of birth. He says also that there were a werowanqua and three werowances at Quiyoughcohannock and that they were all kin: the "quene," who was married to Powhatan; her two brothers; and her son by Powhatan. Only one of the men, though, was the tribal werowance; the others were chiefs of subordinate villages. Likewise, the werowances of the Pamunkey were brothers, as were the werowances of the Potomac and of the Accomack; and the chiefs of the Appomattox were siblings. We can conclude that within each separate tribe there was a chiefly family ranked internally by some means, almost certainly by age, and that the highest-ranking was the tribal chief, while the others were chiefs of subordinate villages.

In short, at the time the English began settling in Virginia, there seems to have been a chiefly family in each tribe—perhaps not unlike the Natchez Sun clan—some of whose members functioned as chiefs in the constituent villages of the tribe. What I suggest about Powhatan's attempts to solidify the entire polity is an application of the same principle on a much larger scale, just as he seems to have increased the scope of the status of werowance.

The one tribe with whom such relations were impossible was the Chickahominy, since they had no werowances but were governed instead by their priests (who never married) and a group of eight elders whose title the English wrote as *caw-cawwassoughes*. (Hamor [1615:14] says that one of these was preeminent among them, but the other sources do not mention this.) Thus Powhatan could neither put one of his own followers in as werowance nor marry the incumbent's sister in the expectation that a son would succeed him. The geographical and political position of the Chickahominy seems to have been unique.[15]

If the area nearest Powhatan's base, Werowocomoco, was pretty firmly under his control, what about the tribes farther out? The English came to know these areas only gradually, by which time political relations between them and Powhatan may have deteriorated somewhat. The few reports we have suggest that while Powhatan was nearly as capable of exacting compliance on the Eastern Shore, the Rappahannock River, and possibly even the Potomac as on the James, Pamunkey, Mattaponi, and York, his control was less assured in these regions. Strachey's statement that Powhatan offered gifts to his werowances to help him in military undertakings may explain the different kinds of reception the English got on their explorations of Chesapeake Bay in 1608. The Accomac and Accohannock, on the Eastern Shore, were friendly. Powhatan told Smith that he received tribute of these tribes, for the collection of which he sent canoes across the bay. The tribes of the Potomac River attacked the English when they first explored it (the summer of 1608), while the tribes of other polities made them welcome. The attackers quickly gave up, apparently disliking the noise of gunfire; they explained that Powhatan, urged by malcontents at the fort, had ordered them to attack the English (Smith 1986 [1612]:227). The tribes of the Rappahannock River, on the other hand, greeted the English hospitably (Smith 1986 [1624]:173). Possibly a chief with whom Powhatan sought to form an alliance could refuse such an overture, at least on that occasion. In 1624 Smith wrote that Opechancanough, Powhatan's brother, had sent "two baskets of beads" to the Potomac chief just after the massacre of 1622, asking him to kill a couple of Englishmen who were there. The recipient debated for a couple of days before sending the beads back, telling the Pamunkey to stay out of his country. He offered as explanations that the Emperor Opitchapam (Powhatan's successor) was his brother and that he himself was a friend of the English (Smith 1986 [1624]:308).

However it came into being, in 1607 Powhatan's realm consisted of about 30 tribes more or less under his command: those closer to the center more, those at the periphery less. His command depended partly on military strength, which seems to have been considerable even though he was himself beyond the age of fighting. But it also depended on the categorical conceptions that the people of this polity as a whole had of their leaders, the werowances; the shamans, or *quiyoughcosoughs;* and the mamanatowick himself. How they defined these different statuses and related them to one another is the subject of the remainder of this book.

2. "Civilizing" the Powhatan

Arriving at an understanding of the ideal working of Powhatan's polity requires a close examination of the colonial documents on several levels in order to identify their genuine anthropological content. Most generally, we may ask why the English chose to include what they did in their accounts of Virginia. A modern anthropologist living in a chiefdom automatically inquires how one becomes chief; but there is no reason to assume that an early-17th-century explorer-colonist would automatically do so or would have the same reasons for asking. What the Jamestown colonists included reflects not only the colonial interests in increasing James I's dominions, enriching his kingdom, and saving the souls of the "salvages," but also the contemporary concerns over the nature of kingship and over the relationship between sovereign and subject, especially as these ideas were being worked out in England. An effect of their choices (whether consciously aimed at or not) is to "civilize" the Powhatan; that is, to make them seem "civil" to Englishmen and women still in England.[1]

Sources

Sources for Virginia Algonkians at the time of contact are limited in the sense that, while we have accounts from a number of men, most include information about the Powhatan only as it bears upon the likelihood of the colony succeeding. Besides working with patchy information, the modern anthropologist must also translate the Renaissance English translation of the Powhatan into modern anthropological terms. As a necessary first step in this process, I discuss the most important of the colonial sources for the study of the Powhatan.

The works of Captain John Smith must take precedence. The controversies over Smith's veracity are well known and need not be rehearsed here.[2] As far as his accounts of Indian life are concerned,

noble savage

he is as reliable as any of his colleagues. Like them, he considered the Powhatan inferior beings for the most part but worthy of admiration in some regards.

Smith left three principal works regarding Virginia: the *True Relation* (1608), the *Map of Virginia* (1612), and the *Generall Historie* (1624). This last work includes the text of the 1612 publication, with some minor alterations, and brings it up to date.[3] In these accounts, Smith is concerned to show that Virginia, as a colony, has a future. (He is also, in the 1624 work, concerned to show that that future should include him; but his superiors thought otherwise.) Thus he addresses everything in the territory that could be of importance in establishing the colony, including the climate, the fertility of the soil, useful native plants and animals both wild and domestic, the possibility of producing European commodities there, and the disposition of the natives to help or hinder these projects. Partly because of the importance of this last matter, he includes descriptions of such aspects of native life as seem relevant to it: their economy, since the English were there to trade; their political organization, since the English wished to annex the territory to the nascent British empire; their religion, since it was hoped that they would become Protestants. The result is not in any modern sense ethnography; but in conjunction with other descriptions of Virginia, it allows us to produce something akin to modern ethnography.

Others among the first settlers at Jamestown wrote accounts of their first weeks or months there. The earliest is Captain Gabriel Archer's "relatyon," probably written in June 1607, describing the colonists' first ascent of the James River (Archer 1910 [1607]). An important goal of the expedition was to discover the degree of civility among the natives and their inclination to welcome strangers, the two being, of course, closely related. Thus he describes not only something of the geography of the river but also as much of Indian custom as he could observe.

Master George Percy, who became president of the colony following Smith's accident with the gunpowder, wrote his "Discourse" in 1607 as well (1910 [1607]). Percy was a younger brother of the "wizard earl" of Northumberland, who was an intimate of Harriot, Raleigh, and their circle. His presence at Jamestown provides some continuity with that earlier expedition to North Carolina, sponsored by Raleigh, of which Harriot was a member. Percy describes Virginia as so beautiful "as I was almost rauished at the first sight thereof" (1910 [1607]:lxi). He, too, mentions the exploration of the James, as well as of tributary rivers to the north and south, but he provides us with more detail than Archer does about Indian life. From him we learn what the Powhatan looked like, how they entertained visitors, what sorts of things they ate, a tantalizingly small bit about their religion, and something about their music and dances.

At the end of the "Discourse," Percy mentions yet other customs discovered by one William White, who had lived among the Powhatan, but he provides us with few details. We know from other sources, Smith's *Map of Virginia* among them, that White observed a *huskanaw,* or male initiation, and either wrote an account of it or gave it orally to Percy and possibly to other colonists.

Percy wrote another account of Virginia in about 1612 entitled "A Trewe Relacyon of the Procedeinges and Ocurrentes of Momente wch have hapned in Virginia" (Percy 1922 [1612]), a depressing document recounting the misfortunes of the colony after Smith's departure. These included a nasty fight with the Nansemond, the massacre of Ratcliffe and his men, and the sacrifice of two messengers the English had sent to treat with the Nansemond.

In addition to Smith's *Map of Virginia,* we have another substantial source, *The Historie of Travell into Virginia Britania,* written by William Strachey probably in 1612 but not published until 1849 (Wright and Freund 1953:xviii). Strachey came to Virginia with Sir Thomas Gates and lived there until August 1611, becoming secretary of the colony (Culliford 1965:122). Strachey had obviously read Smith's work; indeed, he copies from it without acknowledgment in a way that would be actionable today. But although much of what he says seems not to be independent corroboration, to dismiss it would be overhasty, since we may assume that Strachey would not have taken so much from Smith had he not, of his own experience, concluded that Smith's account was accurate. Strachey's is not simply a reiteration of Smith's work, though. He includes information that Smith did not or could not include—he arrived after Smith had left the colony—and he includes his own opinions, too. Strachey may have admired Smith, but he evidently thought himself a cut or two above the captain, as he lards his history with Latin tags and references to classical authors, many of which his modern editors cannot identify. One must be made aware of his Cambridge education.

The second wave, as it were, of publications about Virginia includes several smaller works, each valuable in its own way if not as comprehensive as those of Smith and Strachey. I have already mentioned Percy's "Trewe Relacyon" of 1612. Captain Gabriel Archer also wrote a second, brief, letter at the end of August 1609 announcing that the third supply had arrived and describing the situation in Jamestown (1910 [1609]). A more substantial work is *Good Newes from Virginia* (1613) by Rev. Alexander Whitaker, "the son of a Cambridge University professor, . . . a moderate Puritan who went to Virginia as a minister," where he drowned while still young (Kupperman 1980:27). As a minister, he took great interest in the Indians' religion and in the possibilities of their conversion. Kupperman characterizes Whitaker's attitude to the Powhatan as "harsh and censorious" and regrets that he "wrote about them in curt generalizations and seemed little interested in the details of Indian culture" (1980:27). His communication is certainly brief, but it is not uninformative; he reserves his harshness for Powhatan shamans, whom naturally he detested quite as fervently as did Strachey. He describes the Powhatan otherwise as "a very vnderstanding generation, quicke of apprehension, suddaine in their dispatches, subtile in their dealings, exquisite in their inuentions, and industrious in their labour" (1613:25).

From about the same year we have a valuable "Relation of Virginea" by Henry Spelman (1910 [1613]), whose writing is surprisingly awkward considering that his family were gentry. He appears to have been a tiresome boy, as his family disinherited him; possibly in consequence of this, but certainly "in trouble at home," he emigrated to Virginia (Barbour 1986, 1:xlix). As he himself explains, he came to Virginia in October 1609 when he was young, possibly in his early teens (Spelman 1910 [1613]:ci, cx). Shortly after his arrival, Smith gave him to the "little" Powhatan in part in exchange, so Spelman thought, for the village of Powhatan, in which Smith intended to settle Captain Francis West and his men.[4] Returning to Jamestown after only four or five days, Spelman found himself ordered by Smith to go to the great Powhatan with Thomas Savage, whom Captain Newport had given to Powhatan at their first meeting in 1608 (Smith 1986 [1612]:216). While living with Powhatan, Spelman witnessed the massacre of Captain Ratcliffe and his men. This and other things persuaded Spelman that Powhatan meant to kill him also, so after perhaps six months he attached himself to a visiting werowance of Potomac and followed him home. He lived with this chief at the village of Pasptanzie until rescued by Captain Samuel Argyll in 1610 (Spelman 1910 [1613]:ci–civ).

Although Spelman's account is generally informative, it is infuriatingly imprecise as well as badly written. He lived with three different chiefs; the political status of the last, the werowance of Potomac, vis-à-vis the Powhatan is unclear. Most probably he was at this time a chief independent of, but uneasily allied to, Powhatan (see Rountree 1989; Potter 1993; chapter 3). Spelman calls all these people "king" pretty much indiscriminately, and it is not always possible to tell from the context to which of them he refers. We should expect a difference between Powhatan and his son the werowance, but whether there was any difference between Powhatan and Potomac werowances—and if so, of what kind—is obscure. The Potomac seem to have been culturally and linguistically somewhat different from the Powhatan (Potter 1993; Dent 1995; Rountree 1989); moreover, since that werowance seems not to have been Powhatan's subordinate, he may have maintained a state very similar to that of

Powhatan. Spelman's account is particularly frustrating because he alone mentions some important Indian customs, but determining to whom the information pertains can be difficult and is sometimes impossible. But for the same reason he cannot be ignored. Thus, despite its shortcomings, this is an essential source for reconstructing Powhatan culture.

Another work from about this time is a short "True Discourse" by Ralph Hamor, whom Barbour (1986, 1:xxxvii) describes as "a staunch supporter of the colony." He was among those shipwrecked on Bermuda in 1609; he arrived in the colony in 1610, where he stayed until 1614. During this time, he became clerk of the council. In 1614 he returned to England, and he published his "Discourse" a year later to counter unpleasant rumors circulating in England about the difficulties in Virginia, particularly with the Indians (Rowse 1957:xii–xiii). He does not set out to describe Powhatan culture specifically, but because he wishes the English to support the colonial project, he includes information about the Powhatan as part of the basis for his optimism. He had some firsthand experiences with the Indians, too, as one of the ambassadors sent to Powhatan after the capture of Pocahontas to negotiate for the return of English prisoners and English arms. Later, after the marriage of Pocahontas, Governor Sir Thomas Dale sent Hamor back to Powhatan to ask him for another of his daughters, this time to be Dale's wife (see de Bry 1618:Pl. 10).[5]

Many of these accounts found their way into the compendium of Samuel Purchas, *Purchas his Pilgrimage,* the first edition of which appeared in 1612. With the approval and help of the younger Richard Hakluyt, Purchas undertook to continue Hakluyt's collection of English voyages, but with a difference: "The weakness of Hakluyt was that he never attempted any synthesis of the vast material at his disposal: Purchas, on the other hand, drew all his reading together in order to develop a single theme, a survey of the world from the point of view of its peoples and their religious practices" (Taylor 1934:54). The result is nevertheless harder to read than Hakluyt:

more ornate and, to a modern reader, distractingly inclined to see the hand of God in every reported event (see Taylor 1934:55). But he does give us information not found elsewhere. He was greatly interested in the Virginia enterprise, and he had a number of friends in the company, including Smith, who provided his manuscript of the *Map of Virginia* for inclusion in the first edition. In the third edition, of 1617, Purchas adds the report from Whitaker and some (refutatory) comments by John Rolfe; but the most interesting addition is information he had acquired from a Powhatan man of importance, Tomocomo, who had accompanied Pocahontas on her visit to England. He apparently acted as an informant for Purchas and told him things about the religion, in particular, that are found nowhere else (Purchas 1617:954). The different editions also include versions of the huskanaw collected from William White.

In the first book of his *Generall Historie* (1986 [1624]), Smith includes the already-published accounts of the Carolina Algonkians written by the expeditions of the middle 1580s. He does this for two reasons: to show that England has a legitimate claim to Virginia and because the Carolina Indians' "Clothing, Townes, Houses, Warres, Arts, Tooles, handy crafts, and educations, are much like them in that part of Virginia we now [1607-1624] inhabite" (1986 [1624]:78). Just as Smith regarded the earlier accounts as a proper supplement to what his contemporaries knew about Virginia Indians, so today modern students of Powhatan culture rely on Harriot, Philip Barlowe, and Ralph Lane as well as on the Jamestown colonists to reconstruct the culture.

Of these, Harriot's is the most important: it was written expressly for publication, and it is illustrated with engravings made from the watercolors of John White, a member of the expedition. His paintings include pictures of flora, fauna, and "naturals" (Hulton 1984). Harriot has been introduced earlier. His work, *A Briefe and True Report of the New Found Land of Virginia* (1972 [1590]), was the first in a series of works, the *Great Voyages*, about the discovery of the New World begun by Theodor de Bry and continued after his death in

1598 by his son, Johann Theodor de Bry (Yates 1972:71), and published between 1590 and 1634 (Bucher 1981:xiii).

Theodor de Bry was a Protestant native of Liège exiled with his family to Frankfort for his religion. An engraver as well as a publisher, de Bry realized early the value of copperplate engraving for publishing pictures of foreign lands, and especially the New World (Bucher 1981:6–7). He intended his series not simply to bring discoveries and conditions in the New World to the attention of Europe but specifically to make public the Catholic (i.e., Spanish) atrocities there and to show, by contrast, the Protestants' humane treatment of the indigenes and their land (Bucher 1981:10; Yates 1972:71). To make it accessible not only to the nobility but to middle-class literate persons (potential investors in such explorations), de Bry published Harriot's work in Latin, English, High German, and French (Bucher 1981:11).

From White's watercolor paintings, de Bry and his collaborator, Gysbert van Veen, produced a series of 23 plates depicting Carolina Algonkian men and women of different ages and social statuses; various activities such as making a dugout, cooking, and dancing; two villages, one with palisade and one without; their "idol"; and the so-called charnel house where the mummies of chiefs were kept. (De Bry produced one original engraving for this publication, for the title page: a wonderful amalgam of images from the other engravings displayed about a Palladian facade that includes garlands, a broken pediment, and two Doric columns of empire.) For getting a sense, even at four hundred years' remove, of what the Carolina Algonkians looked like, White's original watercolors are at least as informative—in some cases even more informative—than de Bry's engravings (Kupperman 1980:33, 2000:41; Oberg 1999:9). But de Bry's publication has the merit of commentary by Harriot, who wrote not only the full text but also an explanation of each of the pictures.

Even with these additions, Harriot's *Report* contains on balance more about the economic possibilities of the region than about its

native inhabitants, an emphasis in keeping with the recommendations of the Hakluyts themselves. He begins his work with a discussion "Of Marchantable Commodities," goes on to discuss what
there is to eat using the Indian diet as the example, and then describes a miscellaneous collection of items that colonists should
know, including available building materials and medicinal plants.
He ends with an account "Of the nature and manners of the people."
Here he describes their appearance, habitations, government, economy, warfare, and religion. Harriot also notes something of how the
Indians interpreted the English. He concluded "that they in respect
of troubling our inhabiting and planting, are not to be feared; but
that they shall haue cause both to feare and loue vs, that shall inhabite with them" (Harriot 1972 [1590]:24). Since "feare and loue,"
as I discuss below, were appropriate sentiments for a subject to feel
for the monarch, Harriot's conception of the relation between the
English and the Carolina Algonkians is obvious.

Besides Harriot's *Report,* there are accounts by two other important colonists, Ralph Lane and Philip Barlowe, that describe Carolina Algonkian culture and intimate something of political relations
among the various chiefdoms there (Hakluyt 1907 [1589], 6:121–
162). Together these supply information with which we can, with
caution, supplement the reports of Smith, Strachey, and others on
the Virginia Algonkians.

With equal caution I have made use of a few sources from nearly a
century after the establishment of Jamestown, most notably Robert
Beverley's *History and Present State of Virginia* (1947 [1705]), which
includes a substantial section on the Powhatan. Beverley relies on
Smith's work but not slavishly: he offers differences of opinion or
criticisms where he finds them appropriate. It is a testament to
Smith's reporting that Beverley does not often dissent. Beverley was
a sympathetic and interested observer of Indians, whom he seems to
have preferred to some of his Anglo neighbors; these neighbors, in
turn, probably viewed his approbation of the savages with disfavor.
He adds not only historical material to what we have from James-

Fig. 2. Title page of Harriot's *Briefe and True Report*.
Courtesy of the Library of Virginia.

town but also some, very limited, ethnographic observation. As a result, we can identify changes and continuities in Powhatan culture during the first century of intense contact with England. The status of chief seems to have changed, for instance, while Powhatan religion seems to have persisted: the attempts to convert the Powhatan to Christianity had not been successful at that time. Some of Beverley's most interesting ethnographic comments result from his investigation—in fact, a violation—of a Powhatan "temple," which confirm the earlier descriptions of such structures by Harriot and Strachey.

Two other later documents, both brief, include a few references to Virginia Algonkian culture: one anonymous (Anonymous 1959 [1689]) and one written by Rev. John Clayton, a minister in Virginia in the late 17th century (1965 [1687]). Like Beverley's book, these provide evidence of cultural changes since 1607, confirming the persistence of the native religion and suggesting that the status of chief has altered.

A discussion of documents relating to Virginia Algonkians would not be complete without reference to the accounts from the short-lived Spanish mission to the Chesapeake in 1570, mentioned in the previous chapter. This endeavor was at least partly a consequence of an earlier Spanish reconnaissance of the bay between 1560 and 1565, during which a Powhatan Indian chief was persuaded to go with the explorers (or, alternatively, proposed himself; the circumstances are obscure). He was baptized Don Luis de Velasco, after his Spanish sponsor. At his urging, a Jesuit mission went with him to Virginia in 1570 and settled in an area not clearly identified today but probably in the region of the Chiskiak, on the York River. Initially, Don Luis helped the missionaries, but then he returned to his people and, much to the dismay of the Jesuits, seemed to abandon Spanish culture and religion altogether. Facing a winter without food and concerned for the state of Luis's soul, the leader of the mission sent several messages of reproof and entreaty to him. The last of these provoked an attack that killed all the party except a boy, Alonso, who was taken away by one of the attacking party and kept safe until his rescue by a Spanish relief ship the following spring (Lewis and Loomie 1953).[6]

The reports surviving from this mission allow us to see through a glass darkly one small part of the realm of Powhatan in 1570. Contacts between the Spanish and the Indians were few and limited. Only one letter from the missionaries survives, the rest being accounts by those sent to relieve the colony; the primary concern in these documents is to know, first, how easily the Indians may be converted and, second, what happened to the mission and what could be done about it. Almost as an aside, the Spanish convey some information about the status of chief among the Powhatan at that time, something about relations among chiefs, and something about the nature and importance of exchange within and among tribes. By themselves these data would be inadequate as a basis for any analysis of the culture, but when put together with the later accounts, they confirm and even extend slightly what these accounts say about Powhatan political organization.

Interpretation

The English literature promoting expansion, epitomized in the writings of the two Hakluyts, stressed commerce, conversion, and assimilation. The reciprocating works from the resulting colonies concentrate on these aspects of the enterprise, and they do so in terms they and their readers took for granted. A result of this is that the Powhatan government so described emerges as a slightly distorted version of the English government: something approaching the civilized, if not so industrious. They saw in the Powhatan their own Anglo-Saxon ancestors at the time the Romans arrived, a resemblance that gave them hope for mutual cooperation and assimilation (Kupperman 2000:16).

This conclusion is debatable, of course. It agrees with Kupperman's argument that "neither savagery nor race was the important category for Englishmen looking at Indians. That is, English colonists assumed that Indians were racially similar to themselves and that savagery was a temporary condition which the Indians would quickly lose. The really important category was status" (1980:2). In her opinion, Europe, and England, would have made little headway in North America had it not been for the devastation of European diseases (Kupperman 1980:186; see Cronon 1983:85–90; Crosby 1986). In other words, European domination at this period was accidental and not a result of a systematic extirpation of an inferior race. Gleach's more recent assessment of the value of these documents for anthropology (1997:3–4) is not dissimilar, though when he points out that the English attempted to civilize the Indians he means in a direct, proselytizing sort of way rather than rhetorically. Indeed, he accuses the English accounts of presenting a "Europeanized caricature" of Powhatan culture (1997:3). This, I think, misrepresents the colonists' motivations: a caricature suggests an intent to ridicule, whereas the Jamestown writers generally appear to take the Indians seriously, even when they criticize.

A radically opposed position is that of Sheehan (1980), who argues that the English persisted in seeing Indians as "savage" rather than "civil," despite all sorts of evidence to the contrary. This interpretation led to their representing the Indians in the literature first as noble savages in a state of prelapsarian innocence, then as ignoble savages in thrall to the Devil and motivated by blood lust and other antisocial qualities, and finally as beasts of the field (Sheehan 1980:5; see Bucher 1981; Oberg 1999). At each turn, he argues, they got the Indians wrong; he says of the paradisaic interpretation, for example, that it "could not work in its fullness. The real world was bound to intrude" (Sheehan 1980:23, 34). The evils that today we associate with colonization resulted from what he characterizes as a refusal to respect "the integrity of native life" (Sheehan 1980:42).

There is no question that Europeans did consider Indians "savages" and more particularly that the English refer to the Powhatan as "salvages" (but they also call them "naturals" and "Virginians"), that they describe Virginia in somewhat Edenic terms, and that they condemn certain customs of the Indians, their religion above all. Still, Sheehan's conclusions are too general. They reflect nothing of the ambivalence of Europeans toward what they found in the New World. Even Captain John Smith, that skeptical critic of Virginian life, admits that the Powhatan showed signs of civility, and his shifting characterization finds parallels in virtually all the other colonial accounts.

Sheehan's reiteration that the English never did, because they never could, understand Indian culture raises a separate, and critical, question: whether we really can discern the "true Powhatan culture" in these documents (see Galloway 1989:255). Even if we can identify and discount political concerns and cultural biases in individual statements, and thus recover some specific facts about the Powhatan (e.g., shamans lived apart from society, succession to chiefship was matrilineal), can we ever recover the *whole* culture—its underlying premises, by which the Powhatan related such disparate facts—from documents whose own underlying premise is how best to translate Powhatan religious and political forms into English in order more easily to assimilate the Powhatan into the realm of James I and the kingdom of God? The answer has implications far beyond the present study, of course. If it is no, then much if not all anthropological analysis based on colonial documents is invalid. That this book exists is evidence that I think the answer is yes.

A first step in addressing this question is to pose another: by whose reckoning did the English get the culture wrong? By modern anthropological standards, perhaps; but the colonists were not anthropologists, nor were they trying to be. To expect modern fieldwork of them is anachronistic. According to their own lights, we must assume, they did understand a good deal of what the Powhatan were doing; they agree with each other on the cultural forms they observed, and moreover both sides—English and Powhatan—were able to treat with each other for decades. Condemning a cultural practice does not mean failing to understand it.

Sheehan's assessment of the success of colonial understanding, and thus of the value of sources, finds an echo in Greenblatt's comment that

> the authors of the anecdotes with which this book concerns itself were liars—few of them *steady* liars, as it were, like Mandeville, but frequent and cunning liars none the less, whose position virtually required the strategic manipulation and distortion and outright suppression of the truth. But though they were liars, European voyagers to the New World were not systematic, so that we cannot have the hermeneutic

satisfaction of stripping away their false representations to arrive at a secure sense of reality. Instead we find ourselves groping uneasily among the mass of textual traces, instances of brazen bad faith jostling homely (and often equally misleading) attempts to tell the truth. (1991:7)

The authors to whom he refers are earlier than those considered in this book; they were still under the influence of medieval cosmography, which expected, and found, monsters and unnatural beings beyond the limits of civilization (Hodgen 1964). By the time Harriot arrived at Roanoke, such fancies were no more than that. He and his companions expected, and found, human beings with a society, language, and customs the sense of which they could understand and emulate. But perhaps we should brand them liars as well. Their writings are frankly promotional, even propagandist (see Jones 1946; Sheehan 1980:10). They overrate the friendliness and tractability of the Indians, which might be called "brazen bad faith," and they represent them as having English-like institutions, which we could say is a "misleading attempt to tell the truth."

Just as one may ask in whose judgment the English got Virginia Indian culture wrong, one may ask whether it is not overly critical to call these rhetorical forms lies, and more, whether doing so serves any purpose. Today, who can say in what frame of mind anyone in Virginia in 1607 wrote of the Indians? A positive report may indeed be a deliberate concealment of a dire situation; but it could just as easily be the sober truth as the writer saw it, or it could be wishful thinking. The writer himself might not have been able to say. (There is no reason, either, to assume that only positive reports must be dubious.) More important than these considerations is the fact that one finds these motivations in modern ethnography as well. It is well known that two different anthropologists—Mead and Fortune perhaps come most readily to mind—may study the same people at the same time and arrive at quite different conclusions about them, but neither considers herself or himself a liar, nor does anyone else. Moreover, it is ethically proper to conceal the names of informants and even the locus of fieldwork if revealing these would compromise those whom one studies. Our assumption is that the structure of the culture will emerge just the same, and be quite as informative, as if the whole truth were made public. The same is true of these early colonial sources.

Hallpike suggests that "social anthropology might be defined as the study of the lies that natives tell to anthropologists"; he writes as one who has had to work with a people among whom, he claims, "truthfulness for its own sake is not a virtue" (1977:33; but see Needham 1985:75). Still, he argues, it is possible to arrive at an anthropological truth about the culture despite the misrepresentations of one's informants, whether those are deliberate or inadvertent, and with that conclusion I agree. In the present case, my informants are not so much the Powhatan—although in a tenuous way they are—but rather the writers of the accounts of colonial Virginia. I do not consider that they lie, but rather I recognize that their way of representing the Indians is far removed from my own, which is to say, from that of modern anthropology. But one extends the same courtesy to informants in Africa or Oceania, and, moreover, one respects their authority over one's own.

One reason to resist calling these informants liars is that they use terms that, while they probably do not represent the Powhatan "truth" in Powhatan terms, are nevertheless those the English knew for discussing social institutions, including political status and process. Thus we find terms such as "king," "magistrate," and "tyrant"; stress on "commanding" and "obedience"; and phrases such as "only the law whereby he [Powhatan] ruleth is custome," "his will is lawe," and "power of life and death over their people." Even their negative statements present what to contemporary readers was a familiar, if undesirable, situation.

In using such rhetoric, the Jamestown colonists represent the Indians in Virginia as politically similar to the English and thus assimilable in the nascent British empire. That is, they translate the culture as well as "civilize" it (Elliott 1970:18) rather than misrepresenting it past hope of reconstruction. We cannot expect the colonists to use a terminology or a set of ideas other than those with which they are familiar. There are other reasons, anyhow, to treat the accounts as veracious. One is that there is considerable concurrence among the various sources. Strachey, an astute and traveled man capable of independent observation, agrees with Smith's opinion of the status of werowances in Virginia. Beverley, writing a century later, likewise confirms the great authority of the werowance (1947 [1705]:225–226). Indirectly, their statements are corroborated by much that we know of southeastern chiefs generally. Moreover, the Jamestown colonists' accounts are circumstantial. In justifying what may appear a somewhat pat characterization of Powhatan political status, they cite evidence and contexts in greater detail than a sustained lie could be expected to support.

In consequence, contra Greenblatt's conclusion, I think we can "arrive at a secure sense of reality" about the people represented. It is possible to distinguish in the Jamestown documents two sorts of statements: one is a fairly literal record of what the writer saw or was told, and the other is his interpretation of his experience (Galloway 1995:77). Admittedly, there is no observation unaffected by one's cultural background. Nevertheless, there is an important difference between, for example, Smith's statement that "Powhatan hath three brethren, and two sisters, each of his brethren succeeded [each] other. For the Crowne, their heyres inherit not, but the first heyres of the Sisters, and so successively the weomens heires" (1986 [1608]:59–61), and Rev. Alexander Whitaker's statement that Powhatan shamans lived "much like the popish hermits of our age" (1613:26). In the first case, Smith must be reporting what he was told. He was not able to see an act of succession; if he had, he would still have needed an Indian explanation of it. In the second case, Whitaker offers an interpretation of a Powhatan custom by showing its similarity to a European custom. While not necessarily invalid, the second sort of statement requires a consideration for its acceptance that the first sort of statement does not.

The first, which I call a report, is as close as we can get today to a "native voice" (Waselkov 1989b:129; Galloway 1995:77; Kupperman 2000:32), and in my analysis I have relied on such reports more than on interpretations like Whitaker's. One need not, nor ought one, simply to dismiss interpretations, however; in their way they offer us information also. In this chapter, I illustrate this by referring the rhetoric of the colonists' statements regarding Powhatan chiefs to contemporary political concerns and ideas about sovereignty and thus render their cultural bias more nearly neutral. The result is a collection of facts about Powhatan chiefs and chiefship that is closer than the original statements to data that a modern cultural anthropologist would acquire in the field, if not their equal in quantity or quality.

Whitaker's comment about Powhatan "priests" is a case in point. It occurs in the midst of his wholesale condemnation of these religious persons: it is one of the ways he tries to convey to his Protestant readers just how abhorrent the shamans are, and how much in need of stamping out.[7] But whatever one's opinion of hermits, the fact remains that they live completely apart from human society and engage in subsistence activities minimally if at all. Thus in expressing his moral outrage, Whitaker inadvertently says something useful to anthropology about Powhatan shamans. The other interpretations the colonists offer us, subjected to the same kind of treatment, yield similarly useful information.

What follows in this chapter are statements from the early colonial sources regarding the rights and obligations of werowances, their habits, and their appearance, matched against relevant contemporary cultural ideas. I concentrate first on this aspect of both Renaissance and Powhatan culture because this book is primarily about Powhatan governance. Since the approach of this analysis is holistic, though, I address other aspects of Powhatan culture—and thus also of English culture—as relevant in subsequent chapters.

At this point, my intention is only to identify the contemporary English ideas embedded in these descriptions. The idea of kingly or chiefly power would appear to be the most important of these, if only because it has most seriously affected how modern scholarship has looked at Powhatan politics. Moreover, the power of the monarch interested Renaissance Europe, as is well known. But the physical appearance and actions of the Renaissance monarch constituted a great part of his or her definition, and we find these concerns expressed in the Jamestown documents as well. All these matters, though, were expressions of a more general concern about civility and civil life. Thus I take up that problem first in order to provide a ground for a discussion of the term "power" in these documents.

A word of caution is necessary first. In this chapter, I call all the chiefs whom the English encountered werowances, despite the fact that Powhatan's title was not werowance but mamanatowick, which Strachey says means "great king" (1953 [1612]:56). The linguistic difference between the two terms suggests that the mamanatowick was more than an exaggerated version of the werowance. But for analytical purposes in this chapter, referring to all persons of authority as werowances is justified on the ground that the English saw the difference between Powhatan, whom they called an emperor, and the others, whom they called kings, as one of degree and not kind. Thus they not only describe them in similar terms but explicitly draw parallels between them.

Civility and the Savage

The question of civility obviously occupied the Jamestown colonists as they tried to understand what the "salvages" of Virginia were about. Two things may claim our attention in trying to get a grasp of "civility": how the colonists answered their own overriding question, were the Indians civil or not; and how they understood the term themselves, which is of course a logically prior question. Their accounts reflect a widespread ambivalence in Europe regarding the moral status of inhabitants of the Americas (see Kupperman 2000:20), which in turn was due to some question about what "civil" meant at all. I offer only the merest outline here to give some sense of the meanings and importance of the concept in England in the early 17th century.

The modern senses of "civil"—pertaining to the community, as in "civil defense," or pertaining to manner, as in "a civil response"—differ little from those in use in the late 16th and early 17th centuries. The *Oxford English Dictionary* (OED) provides the following definitions from the period of Elizabethan and early Stuart expansion: "of or belonging to citizens; consisting of citizens, or men dwelling together in a community"; "of or pertaining to the whole body or community of citizens; pertaining to the organization and internal affairs of the body politic, or state"; "having proper public or social order; well-ordered, orderly, well-governed"; "in that social condition which accompanies and is involved in citizenship or life in communities; not barbarous, civilized, advanced in the arts of life"; "educated"; "humane, gentle, kind"; "polite or courteous in behaviour to others" (*OED, s.v.* "civil"). Orderly, social life was then, as it is now, the more important thing; being humane or educated is a means to that end.

For Europeans encountering the inhabitants of the New World, the issue of civility was not simply a matter of classification: it had practical consequences as well, perhaps more obviously important for the Indians than for the Europeans, though not without consequences for the latter also (Hodgen 1964; Elliott 1970). These explorers accepted the Aristotelian argument that any people incapable of forming and submitting to a government of their own therefore needed to be governed by others and were naturally the slaves of those governors (Elliot 1970:44; Pagden 1995:21). Thus enslaving or even killing savages was acceptable and even obligatory, just as one might put a horse to work or exterminate vermin from one's barn. On the contrary, a group recognized as civil—that is, living in an orderly society properly governed—deserved civil treatment: exchange, marriage, political treaties, the gift of Christianity.

The meanings of "civil," "barbarous," and "savage" changed as a result of contacts with the peoples of the New World (Elliott

1970:44). Of savages, there were two possible kinds: noble and ignoble. The noble were like Adam and Eve before the apple: innocent, happy, virtuous but also unimaginative and passive, since they had no difficulties to contend with and experienced no changes (Elliott 1970:42; Sheehan 1980:21-25). The ignoble were not only irrational but acted solely according to "passion"; their "only grip upon the world seemed to be the undifferentiated rage that they released upon anyone foolish enough to come within reach" (Sheehan 1980:37). Such abstractions had constantly to be tempered by events. Even other people's rages become comprehensible with familiarity and may prove to be as obligatory as anything else, so the classification of Indians as savage was under attack from the early days of Spanish colonizing. Even in the first half of the 16th century some argued in favor of the Indians being somewhat civilized, since they had monumental architecture, hierarchical polities, marriage, and so on—in other words, they recognized law and abided by laws. "Rationality, measured by the capacity for living in society, was the criterion of civility; and if this civility was not crowned, as it should have been, with Christianity, this tended to be a misfortune rather than a crime" (Elliott 1970:45; see Pagden 1995:20). Of course, the basis for judging the orderliness was most usually European society, but even so a certain cultural relativism was developing. By 1570 people began to argue that the Indians might as easily call the Spanish barbarians, as the Spanish did them, since it was known that the men of ancient times had used the word to refer to anyone outside the society of the speaker. Montaigne's comments to this effect, "we call barbarous anything that is contrary to our own habits" (1958:108), is echoed in the passage in 1 Corinthians: "There are, it may be, so many kinds of voices in the world, and none of them is without signification. Therefore if I know not the meaning of the voice, I shall be unto him that speaketh a barbarian; and he that speaketh shall be a barbarian unto me" (14:10-11; cited in Elliott 1970:47). By the period relevant to this analysis, then, people were increasingly willing to entertain the idea that alien societies were called barbarian merely because of their differences but that they were nonetheless societies with their own merits and prerogatives (Elliott 1970:46–47).

This latitude was in turn related to the conviction that savagism or barbarity was a temporary rather than a permanent state (so, for that matter, was civilization). Thus Europeans might hope with time and care to bring any savages, whether American or other, to their own level (Sheehan 1980:5, 110–111; Elliott 1970:49; Oberg 1999:8). Indeed, some explorers argued that the Indians were already civil for the most part—that is, they thought of them as human (Hodgen 1964:379–380; Kupperman 2000:2–4).

The Jamestown documents call the Powhatan "salvages" and constantly compare them either explicitly or implicitly to "civil" society, sometimes concluding that they are civil, sometimes that they are not. In that they had a language, that they lived in villages and gardened, that they ordered society hierarchically and expressed due deference to superiors, and that among these superiors were both an emperor and kings, they were civil; in that they were transhumant, that they seemed passionate and "inconstant," that they were pagan and not Christian, and that they could or would not recognize the obvious superiority of the English, they were savage (see Pagden 1995:19; Kupperman 2000:78). In short, the colonists provide us with no clear, unequivocal assessment of the moral status of the Indians. This is partly because the terms themselves tended to ambiguity and partly because the opinions of the writers themselves shifted as the rapport or hostility between indigenes and intruders waxed and waned. Of the two, "civil" is the less ambiguous: it was a term of approbation and hope, and its use signals the recognition of rationality and sociality in the Indians. Calling them "salvages" may convey that the writer thinks them utterly beneath consideration, but it may as easily mean that the Indians are unspoiled innocents. In any case, the tone of the context conveys which sense the writer had in mind.

Kingly Authority and Power in Virginia

In the Introduction, I mentioned the troublesome matter of the supposed absolute power that Powhatan chiefs had over their subjects, so much at odds with what we know about American Indian chiefs generally (see Clastres 1977, 1994; Lowie 1967) or in the Southeast particularly (e.g., Anonymous 1931:243; Bossu 1931:258; Gearing 1962:4, 6, 38; Gibson 1971:22; Gilbert 1943:358; Hudson 1976:223), and the fact that modern anthropological opinion has ranged from unquestioning acceptance (e.g., Feest 1966:73) through ambivalence (e.g., Rountree 1989) to mild skepticism (e.g., Gleach 1997:29). As a first step in resolving the issue, I present the relevant texts, which are found only in Smith (1986 [1612]) and Strachey (1953 [1612]), although other writers offer indirect corroboration.

Smith, no great admirer of the Powhatan, nevertheless praises their government: "Although the countrie people be very barbarous, yet have they amongst them such governement, as that their Magistrats for good commanding, and their people for du subjection, and obeying, excell many places that would be counted very civill" (1986 [1612]:173; see Whitaker 1613:26). His further comments provide the earliest statement about the powers of the chiefs, including Powhatan:

> [Neither Powhatan] nor any of his people understand any letters wherby to write or read, the only lawes whereby he ruleth is custome. Yet when he listeth his will is a law and must bee obeyed: not only as a king but as halfe a God they esteeme him. His inferiour kings whom they cal werowances are tyed to rule by customes, and have power of life and death at their command in that nature. . . . What he commandeth they dare not disobey in the least thing. It is strange to see with what great feare and adoration all these people doe obay this Powhatan. For at his feet they present whatsoever hee commandeth, and at the least frowne of his browe, their greatest spirits will tremble with feare: and no marvell, for he is very terrible and tyrannous in punishing such as offend him. (Smith 1986 [1612]:174)

Strachey's description of chiefly power is almost identical. Like Smith, he calls this a "monarchall gouernement," and he mentions the "great feare and adoration" with which "all these people doe obey this Powhatan" (Strachey 1953 [1612]:59). And, like Smith, he says the Powhatan have no "posetiue lawes, only the law whereby he [Powhatan] ruleth is custome; yet when he pleaseth his will is lawe, and must be obeyed. . . . His inferiour kings are tyed likewise to rule by like Customes, and haue permitted them power of life and death over their people as their Comaund in that nature" (Strachey [1612] 1953:77). Strachey implies the absolute status of Powhatan in his own polity in a passage, original to him, in which he compares Powhatan's "owne Weroances" with "his neighbours . . . all the great and absolute Weroances about him" (1953 [1612]:57–58); unfortunately, he does not say who these chiefs were. Another original comment on Powhatan's state is yet more significant. Strachey calls it wonderful

> how such a barbarous and vncivill Prynce, should take into him (adorned and set forth with no greater outward ornament and munificence) a forme and ostentacion of such Maiestie as he expresseth, which oftentimes strykes awe and sufficient wonder into our people, . . . but such is (I believe) the Impression of the divine nature, and howsoever these . . . heathens forsaken by the true light, haue not that portion of the knowing blessed Christian-spirit, yet I am perswaded there is an infused kynd of divinenes, and extraordinary (appointed that it shalbe so by [the] king of kings) to such who are his ymediate Instruments on earth (how wretched soever otherwise vnder the Course of misbelief and Infidelity). (1953 [1612]:60–61)

Strachey's digression is all the more remarkable because he is even less favorably disposed toward the manamatowick, Powhatan, than is Smith. He says that Powhatan has been both "cruell" and "quarrellous," and, like Smith, he refers to Powhatan's "tyranny" (Strachey 1953 [1612]:57, 92). He cites as evidence the passage in Smith describing the torture and execution of "Malefactors"

(Strachey 1953 [1612]:60; this passage is quoted and discussed below); but he makes other, more specific charges as well. His descriptions of Powhatan's attacks on the Piankatank, Kecoughtan, and Chesapeake tribes convey his opinion that Powhatan acted more capriciously than judiciously, with scant regard for the well-being of those for whom he was responsible; he also states that the people of the Lost Colony at Roanoke "were by practize and Commaundement of Powhatan . . . miserably slaughtered without any offence given him" (Strachey 1953 [1612]:44, 68, 104–105, 91; regarding Piankatank, see Smith 1986 [1612]:175). He suggests (Strachey 1953 [1612]:91–94) that in order to bring the Powhatan to recognize Christ and King James (in that order) as their lords, the English point out to the lesser werowances that Powhatan is a worse master than either or both these alternatives. That this is so must be immediately apparent to them, because "Powhatan doth at his pleasure, dispoyle them both of their lyves and goodes, without yeilding them any reason, or alleadging or proving any iust cause against them" (Strachey 1953 [1612]:91–92]). Strachey charges also that these lesser chiefs cannot "enioy freely the fruictes of their owne Territoryes" because the best they have to offer is "forbidden them and reserved and preserved to Powhatan," and that he "robbes them as you haue heard of all they haue" (1953 [1612]:92). By "robbing," Strachey means what he calls the tribute that the lesser werowances offered annually to Powhatan, which, according to Strachey amounted to 80 percent of his people's products.[8] Strachey disapproved of this arrangement. Apparently, he saw it simply as an expression of greed, if not parasitism, for he says in the same paragraph, "so he robbes the poore in effect of all they haue even to the deares Skyn wherewith they cover them from Could" (Strachey 1953 [1612]:87). In short, so far as Strachey and Smith were concerned, neither the bodies nor the possessions of Powhatan's subjects were immune to his cruelty and rapacity.

Taking them at face value today, these accounts conjure a grim picture indeed: poor, naked Indians toiling away in all weathers to provide their overlord with luxuries, only to be capriciously done to death if and when it pleased him to do so. But of course the one thing we cannot do is take the descriptions at face value. What, then, was their contemporary sense? The terms "emperor," "king," and "monarchicall" require elucidation first of all.

The reiterated description of the remarkable obedience of the Powhatan to their chiefs, especially to Powhatan, and of the "good commanding" of the "Magistrates," a synonym for "king" or "prince" in the works of King James I (McIlwain 1918:xvi; James I 1918 [1598]:64), reflects a salient Stuart political concern (e.g., James I 1918 [1598]:56, 59, 64–69; see Stone 1965:21; Elton 1965:xxi; Willson 1956:131; Pocock 1967:16). The matter of commandment and obedience emerged from debates over the most important political issue in the kingdom of James I — as in Europe at that time — namely, the sources of kingly authority. There were three possibilities: that it came from above, that is, from God; that it was accorded from below, that is, from the people; or both. In England, at least before the accession of James I, kingly status was recognized as having a dual source: God and the governed, the latter represented by Parliament (Elton 1965:xxxii).

Governed and governors together made the commonweal, a hierarchical organization in which — ideally at any rate — superiors and subordinates met the complementary obligations of just rule and due obedience for their mutual benefit and the maintenance of social harmony (e.g., Bacon 1985 [1625]; see Laslett 1971:183; Wrightson 1982:37, 57–59; Amussen 1988:137; Sharpe 1989:14; contra, Stone 1979:109–110). This was a reflection of the cosmic harmony ordained by God and was to be found also in the relations between husband and wife, parent and child, lord and vassal, as well as between mind and body. (The parallel to dual sovereignty in other cultures will be apparent.) The king, although he was the head of the social hierarchy, was nevertheless but a subordinate to God, whom he was as obliged to obey as his subjects were to obey him. As God's representative to his people, the king was obliged to be the principal source of harmony and balance, in part by ensuring the distribution of justice (Sharpe 1989:9; see Wrightson 1982:15–19; Underdown 1985:9–11). He was thus a Hocartian king, at least in theory: a governor in the literal sense, one who by his power regulated the workings of the society with which he was entrusted and who was obliged to do so. His motivation, it must be noted, was love (in which he tried to emulate his own authority, God), not fear (Sharpe 1989:25–26). Or, rather, the only fear a subject should have was the loss of the prince's love (Bacon n.d.:250).

Besides obedience, subjects owed a monarch counsel as well (Amussen 1988:3, 38; Sharpe 1989:16). Bacon, citing both classical and scriptural authority, urged the monarch's acceptance of counsel with the reassurance that it in no way diminished the majesty or power of the Crown (Bacon 1985 [1625]:63). The appropriate counsel for a monarch was the nobility (Sharpe 1989:83). Bacon's opinion was that "a *Monarchy*, where there is no *Nobility* at all, is ever a pure, and absolute *Tyranny*; . . . For *Nobility* attempers *Soveraignty*" (1985 [1625]:41). Lesser persons offered a sort of counsel in the form of petitions, to which the king was as obliged to attend as he was to listen to the advice of those of the higher estate (Sharpe 1989:16).

This was an ideal that informed and allowed judgment of actual events which, of course, not infrequently failed to measure up (Sharpe 1989:20). James I, moreover, agreed with only a part of it. His espousal of the old doctrine of the divine right of kings is well known, but he had his own interpretation of what that meant.[9] McIlwain (1918:xxxiii–xxxv) summarizes his argument: divine right meant that the king represented God on earth; therefore he was responsible for everything in his kingdom, but only to God, not to the people; and his "powers were commensurate. They included nothing less than the complete disposal of his subjects' persons and property." If the established laws of the kingdom constituted a hindrance to the exercise of this power, then, James argued, "the [royal] prerogative was *above* the ordinary course of that law" and could be suspended at the king's will, when necessary. James, then, found the locus of authority only in the power superior to himself, that is, in God.

One of King James's political works is entitled, ironically, *The Trew Law of Free Monarchies: or The Reciprock and Mutuall Dutie Betwixt a Free King and his naturall Subjects:* ironical because it denies that reciprocal duties of a king and his subjects are necessary or even possible, since in his opinion the monarch was beyond the sphere of ordinary life (McIlwain 1918:xlii). In this treatise, James states that "*Monarchie* is the trew paterne of Diuinitie" (James I 1918 [1598]:54); in his speech to Parliament following the abortive Gunpowder Plot, he asserted that "kings were gods, adorned and furnished with some sparkles of divinity" (James I 1918 [1605]:281; see Bacon n.d.:249–250). Just as a man obeys God without question, the subject must render unquestioning obedience to his king, however despotic. A king is like a father to his people; he is "ordained for them, and they not for him" (James I 1918 [1598]:55): ordained by God, and God only, as the context makes clear. In the *Trew Law,* the king cites three authorities for his conclusions: Scripture (King David calls kings gods), the laws of nature, and the laws of Scotland ("positive" law; Kantorowicz 1957:135).

The fact the laws of Scotland were in large measure Roman law (Willson 1956:257) is of considerable importance to this discussion. "Roman law . . . laid stress upon the concepts of will, command and the legislator, and tended therefore to encourage the already existing idea that each institution had originated at a particular time in the will of a particular individual who had established it in substantially its present form" (Pocock 1967:18). It is not surprising, then, that James maintained that kings make laws, not the reverse, and that therefore "the King is aboue the law, as both the author and giuer of strength thereto" (James I 1918 [1598]:63). Since this is so, the king owns everything in his kingdom: "And as yᵉ see it manifest, that the King is ouer-Lord of the whole land: so is he Master ouer euery person that inhabiteth the same, hauing power ouer the life and death of euery one of them: For although a iust Prince will not take the life of any of his subiects without a cleare law; yet the same lawes whereby he taketh them, are made by himselfe, or his predecessours; and so the power flowes alwaies from him selfe" (James I 1918 [1598]:63). In other words, James denies the argument put forward by supporters of the common law that the authority of a prince comes from below as well as from above. Thus his use of the phrase "free monarch": "By a free monarch he meant one free from all control" (Davies 1938:30). The only possible judge for a king is God.

If the king were really above the law, what might be the limits to his authority? This question naturally exercised his subjects not a little. "The sixteenth and seventeenth centuries were throughout western Europe a time of collision between the authority of kings and local or national privileges, liberties and constitutions" (Pocock 1967:16; see Hill 1980:37; Figgis 1965:93; McIlwain 1918:xl). According to James I, ideally the will of the king should impel him to follow the laws he (and his predecessors) had created, if only to set a good example to his own people. But more important, a king who willfully ignores the established laws imperils his soul (and his punishment will be unusually severe because of his exalted position); he also endangers his kingdom, whose well-being should be his first care. Should he prove despotic, however, "tyrannizing ouer mens persons, sonnes, daughters and seruants; redacting noble houses, and men, and women of noble blood, to slauish and seruile offices; and extortion, and spoile of their lands and good to [his] owne priuate vse and commoditie, and of his courteours, and seruants" (James I 1918 [1598]:59), he has a greater right to do so than have his subjects to rebel against him. This is so partly because, as we have seen, he owns the entire kingdom in the first place and partly because "a wicked king is sent by God for a curse to his people, and a plague for their sinnes" (James I 1918 [1598]:67).

In the *Basilikon Doron, or His Maiesties Instrvctions to his Dearest Sonne, Henry the Prince* (James I 1918 [1599]), the king distinguishes the tyrant from the good king in terms of their motivations. A good king wishes only the good of his kingdom and the welfare of his people, and to this end he makes and executes appropriate laws. He must not think of himself but of them. The tyrant is just the opposite: secure only when his people are divided among themselves and making laws that benefit himself at the expense of those he governs, "inuerting all good Lawes to serve onely for his vnrulie priuate affections" (James I 1918 [1599]:19). Bacon's summary of tyranny likewise emphasizes the private, as distinct from the public, origin of regal decisions: "it sometimes happens, that, being depraved by long wielding of the sceptre, and growing tyrannical, they would engross all to themselves; and slighting the counsel of their senators and nobles, conceive by themselves; that is, govern according to their own arbitrary will and pleasure" (n.d.:505).

It was all very well for James I to insist that people should trust him or take royal mismanagement and abuses as a punishment justly due to a sinful people. Many were unwilling to extend such trust, nor did they care to accept their king as the scourge of God. But more fundamental in this debate was the perennial question about the source and nature of the law, the answer to which entailed a certain attitude to the source of kingly authority. (This is, however, a question that cannot be resolved because of the liminality of a monarch.) The characteristics of Roman law, which so appealed to James I, are countered by those of the common law. Roman law was temporal. It had a known beginning, a known creator; it was written and therefore seemingly permanent; but because it was devised at a particular time, it was appropriate only to the circumstances of that time and would inevitably become outdated as history unfolded. Therefore it must also have an end, if only because it must be altered to suit new circumstances, among which might be its inconvenience to the monarch (Pocock 1967:18). Roman law reflects a notion of unilinear, nonrecurring time. In the ideas about the nature of common, or customary, law we find, on the contrary, an idea of time not so much cyclical as endlessly regenerating. Customary law was not written down or codified, and therefore it "could never become obsolete." "Custom was . . . always immemorial and always perfectly up-to-date." That is, it was constantly subtly modified by the collective will as the times themselves called for such modification. Law so conceived was "a thing ancient, immanent and unmade, proof against invasion by human wills because no will had made it." In particular, the king had not made it, and thus he could not bypass or unmake it. This was the basis of the challenge to claims of royal sovereignty. As James I insisted on his royal prerogative both to create and to set aside the law, English lawyers countered by developing and extolling the idea of custom, or common law (Pocock 1967:30).

This background allows us to make an informed reading of the early Jamestown descriptions of Powhatan. In Smith's 1612 statement, which Strachey echoes, we learn that "only the law whereby he ruleth is custom." This is puzzling in part because of an archaic ordering of words, which might better be, as Arber and Bradley's edition puts it, "the only lawes whereby he ruleth is custome" (Smith 1910 [1612]:81). In this connection, note that when Strachey amplifies his assessment of Powhatan's power, he says, "His [Powhatan's] inferiour kings are tyed likewise to rule by like Customes" (1953:77). This and the context—the Powhatan have no writing—suggest that the sense of the statement is that the chief's authority is limited by common law. Indeed, one of the beauties of common law, so its supporters argued, was that it was not written or codified; therefore it was endlessly pertinent and useful. Powhatan and his lesser chiefs are thus presented as subjects of their own law and laudable on that ground.

But the subsequent phrase, "when he pleaseth his will is lawe," which has been taken as the strongest evidence of Powhatan despotism, represents an entirely opposite point of view. This is a fundamental point in Roman law, whose jurists argued that the king's "will" had the power of law insofar as he was a public, and not a private, person; he willed, as a public person, on behalf of his state. This being so, what he willed must be equivalent to, and have the power of, the law (Kantorowicz 1957:95–96). As a tenet of Roman law, this phrase is not reliable evidence about Powhatan political ideas. The Powhatan may have agreed with their European contemporaries, but that must be proven rather than assumed; and, in fact, they did not.

The statement that Powhatan's will is law is one of two statements that have led to the modern assumption that the Powhatan enjoyed but a despotic rule. The other is that the chiefs had the power of life and death over their subjects. But it will not have escaped notice that King James uses precisely the same phrase in stating what he thought were the rights and prerogatives of a king: "the King is ouer-Lord of the whole land: so he is Master Ouer euery person that inhabiteth the same, *hauing power ouer the life and death of euery one of them*" (James I 1918 [1598]:63; emphasis added).

What follows Smith's statement that chiefs had such power is also instructive in this regard: a report of land tenure among the Powhatan. According to Smith and to Strachey, each werowance held his territory from Powhatan, who owned the whole area; they imply that the tribute he received constituted a form of return for these appointments, much as a tenant pays rent to a landlord or a vassal to a lord. "They all knowe their severall landes, and habitations, and limits, to fish, fowle, or hunt in, but they hold all of their great Werowance Powhatan, unto whome they pay tribute of skinnes, beades, copper, pearle, deare, turkies, wild beasts, and corne" (Smith 1986 [1612]:174; Strachey 1953 [1612]:63). This juxtaposition of Stuart political ideas is another example of "civilizing" the Powhatan. In Smith's mind, as in his king's, there is a connection—a holdover, no doubt, of the old feudal law (Pocock 1967:65)—between the ownership of land and rights over those who live there.

Smith and Strachey, then, present Powhatan and his subordinate werowances in such terms as must make them acceptable—civilized—to everyone who read their accounts, whether they supported a common law or a Roman view of monarchy. Saying so much implies that the ambiguity was calculated, and it may have been. But since both Smith and Strachey express considerable ambiguity about

the Powhatan generally, it seems more likely that Powhatan chiefship presented them with a paradox: a monarch who was obliged by
custom to appear to be willful and autocratic.

Smith and Strachey write of the rights of the werowances in
terms of "power," a word King James uses as well. Its uncertain
definition in anthropology I have discussed already. Pinning down
its meaning in 1607 is even more difficult. The word is used ambiguously and infrequently, but there is a strong presumption that it
meant efficacy and not coercion—at least coercion was not its primary meaning. God is called "powerful" because God is the creator
of the universe and its order and because God can damn the un-
repentant (Amussen 1988:36; Sharpe 1989:14); the king, as God's
agent and image, is also powerful in the same way. The just king
used his power to maintain harmony and did so not by coercion but
by persuasion or love—ideally, anyhow.[10] Cosmic order was understood to include both God and the king and therefore to constrain
their actions. Parliament was said to be the greatest power in the
land, though the king was absolute (Sharpe 1989:14–15).

Bacon's use of the word "power" is informative. In his essay
"Great Place" (1985 [1625]:33–36), he states, perhaps enigmatically
to the modern reader, "It is a strange desire, to seeke Power, and to
lose Libertie; Or to seeke Power over others, and to loose Power over
a Mans Selfe." He writes this while pondering the mystery of why
men aspire to great place, since their success makes them "Servants
of the Soveraigne or State; Servants of Fame; and Servants of Busi-
nesse. So as they have no Freedome; neither in their Persons; nor in
their Actions; nor in their Times" (Bacon 1985 [1625]:33). In answering his question, he gives some notion of how he and his contemporaries thought of power: "But Power to doe good, is the true and
lawfull End of Aspiring. For good Thoughts (though God accept
them,) yet towards men, are little better than good Dreames; Except
they be put in Act; And that cannot be without Power, and Place;
As the Vantage, and Commanding Ground" (Bacon 1985 [1625]:34).
In this passage, Bacon makes power the means by which the poten-

tial may be made actual. He considers it a good thing, but only—and this is a significant limitation—if the power of a great man be put not to the service of his own private ends but be used for the benefit of others, whose servant he is. In his essay "Of Empire" (1985 [1625]:58–63), Bacon distinguishes "power" from "authority" in a way that suggests that "power" means efficacy: "And certaine it is, that Nothing destroieth Authority so much, as the unequall and untimely Enterchange of Power *Pressed* too farre, and *Relaxed* too much." The essay concludes, "*Princes* are like to *Heavenly Bodies,* which cause good or evill times;[11] And which have much *Veneration,* but no *Rest.* All precepts concerning *Kings,* are in effect comprehended in those two Remembrances: *Memento quod es homo;* And *Memento quod es Deus,* or *Vice Dei:* The one bridleth their Power, and the other their Will" (Bacon 1985 [1625]:188–189).

The weight of this evidence suggests that "power" in the Jamestown documents had less in common with its modern popular meaning and more in common with its use to represent certain American Indian ideas about efficacy. For this reason, too, I suggest that the alleged despotism of Powhatan has been misunderstood in modern analyses.

The personal use of power in a public person, king or counselor, constituted tyranny. As we have seen, both Strachey and Smith refer to Powhatan as a tyrant, incontinent and rapacious, attacking his own people without provocation, and demanding inordinate quantities of tribute from them. To these two writers, at least, Powhatan's actions exceeded what was acceptable in a monarch because self-gratification, rather than the general welfare, motivated them. It is noteworthy, though, that they attribute no such evil intentions to his "lesser werowances." The reason is that Powhatan resisted any sort of friendly commerce—read subordination or alliance—with the English, but several of his subordinates agreed to it. And, as Hocart argues, we need to be cautious in accepting these statements at face value, since accounts such as those on which the present study is based concentrate on what appears to be chiefly or kingly license and not on the restrictions of the office (1970a:152).

Despite all this, Strachey concludes his account of the paramount with the observation that though he was "uncivill" he was nevertheless a "Prynce" with "a forme and ostentacion of . . . Maiestie" that "strykes awe and sufficient wonder into our people" (1953 [1612]:60). Strachey attributes the incongruously savage majesty to the "impression of the divine nature," which will make its appearance even among those who do not know what it is (1953 [1612]:60). He claims to see divinity in Powhatan because God always contributes some portion of himself to "such who are his ymediate Instruments on earth" (Strachey 1953 [1612]:61). Such language clearly echoes that of James I, who argues that a king is in some sense a god himself: "*Monarchie* is the trew paterne of Diuinitie. . . . Kings are called Gods by the prophetically King *Dauid,* because they sit vpon GOD his Throne in the earth" (James I 1918 [1598]:54). Bacon makes a similar statement: "A king is a mortal god on earth, unto whom the living God hath lent his own name as a great honour: but withal told him, he should die like a man, lest he should be proud and flatter himself, that God hath with his name imparted unto him his nature also" (n.d.:250).

Strachey's statement that even the savage prince Powhatan reflects the divine nature and Smith's to the effect that the Powhatan esteem their paramount chief as "halfe a god," would seem to reflect Stuart ideas of kingship more than those of the Powhatan.[12] Strachey was nevertheless correct. Powhatan, the mamanatowick, was a true monarch: priest and shaman, judge and warrior, in one person. As the primary intermediary between the spirits and his people, Powhatan was structurally the Virginian equivalent of James I, head of the Church of England and God's vicar there. Powhatan may have been considered semidivine as well.

Besides telling their compatriots about the authority and power of the Virginian chiefs, Smith and Strachey include careful statements about succession among them, the first of which I have quoted earlier in the discussion of method: "Powhatan hath three brethren, and two sisters, each of his brethren succeeded [each] other. For the Crowne, their heyres inherite not, but the first heyres of the Sisters, and so successively the weomens heires" (Smith 1986 [1608]:59–61). In 1612 Smith wrote more fully: "His kingdome descendeth not to his sonnes nor children, but first to his brethren, whereof he hath 3. namely Opitchapan, Opechancanough, and Catataugh, and after their decease to his sisters. First to the eldest sister then to the rest and after them to the heires male and female of the eldest sister, but never to the heires of the males" (1986 [1612]:174). It is not at once clear why Smith thought this information so important or why he includes it in the context of his discussion of laws, customs, and the monarch's will. Modern anthropologists are accustomed to thinking and writing about kinship and descent, so no one has wondered why these two writers mentioned this particular fact, instead seizing on it as evidence for the mode of descent among the Powhatan. At least as significant as what Smith and Strachey say, though, is that they say it at all. The importance of succession and the association with laws were alike related to the central issue of the source of monarchical power and authority.

For some centuries in England, monarchy was, as we might say today, partly an achieved status: whoever was king was king by right regardless of how he became king. According to this doctrine, kings were elected by the people (represented by the Parliament), who made their choice under the inspiration of God (Kantorowicz 1957:296). King James, however, rejected the notion of election. He insisted that divine right was hereditary (this was itself a Scottish doctrine), "inalienable and indefeasible," rather than adventitious (McIlwain 1918:xxxvii). At the time of his accession, political concern was less with the continuity of the political body (the kingdom) than with the continuity of the dynasty. In 1609 Coke stated that the English king succeeds "by descent from the blood royal, 'without any essential ceremony or act to be done *ex post facto.*'" The ceremony of coronation ratified, but it was not necessary to, the title;

although the king was still consecrated by the priests, the importance of this act, in constitutional terms, "had been decreasing for many centuries" by the time of James I. It was now assumed that the automatic heir, and the proper heir, was the monarch's oldest son, that there was no election, and that the king and his son "were considered one person" in law. God's will was still manifest, however, because God created the heir. In this sense the heir is already anointed and chosen by God. "The royal blood now appeared as a somewhat mysterious fluid" (Kantorowicz 1957:317–331).

The fact that the Powhatan had a law of succession, then, was another indication that their society had some claim to be called civil. Smith and Strachey probably had a practical political reason for including these facts, but that was not their only motivation. The issue of inheritance versus election was a touchy one in England at that time, the legitimacy of Elizabeth I's reign, and therefore of James I's, being questionable; moreover, Smith and Strachey inform us of this law in connection with their discussion of monarchical rights and duties in Virginia. That association is not random; on the contrary, to the Stuart mind these ideas were inextricably bound up together.

Kingly State or the King as the State

Besides reporting the political status of Powhatan chiefs, the colonists also describe their physical appearance and presence (see Kupperman 2000:41). This reflects an allied concern of Renaissance England: the monarch as embodiment of the kingdom. As Kevin Sharpe says, "the monarchy itself we might study as a text—not least because the comparison came easily to contemporaries" (1989:34). James I's political admonitions to his heir, Prince Henry, express this well. In a section of the *Basilikon* entitled "Of a kings behaviovr in indifferent things," the king writes: "The whole indifferent actions of a man, I deuide in two sorts: in his behauiour in things necessary, as food, sleeping, raiment, speaking, writing, and gesture; and in things not necessary, though conuenient and lawfull, as pastimes or exercises, and vsing of company for recreation" (James I 1918

[1599]:43). These are important, he argues, because a king is always on display (see Smuts 1987:28); in terms of what he does, and how, his people will determine and judge his inner state and disposition. The king accorded the greatest importance to eating: "one of the publickest indifferent actions of a King, and that maniest, especially strangers, will narrowly take heed to; is his maner of refection at his Table, and his behauiour thereat" (James I 1918 [1599]:43). This by itself makes it necessary for the king to eat in public, but there are other reasons, too. Any sign that the king does not care for company is an indication that he is a tyrant, and eating in private gives rise to the conviction that he is a glutton. His people will want to see what he eats as well as how and with whom. A king should eat only to sustain his body, not for pleasure. Likewise, he should avoid drunkenness above all else (another irony in King James's life). James also urges moderation in dress, neither too fancy nor too slovenly or mean. The king must convey in his dress that he is both a judge and a warrior. He deplores the use of the codpiece since it contravenes the law of God, which is to wear clothing for modesty's sake (James I 1918 [1599]:43–45).

In short, the king must exemplify the idea of kingship, and he must embody his state and its condition. In adjuring the prince to adopt a style of dress combining the attributes of the warrior with those of the judge, signifying his status as both the defender of the faith and the judge of his people, James I was expressing a contemporary attitude: he knew that his subjects considered the king a kind of text in his own right, a symbol or assemblage of symbols of England and thus its embodiment.[13]

Such ideas about the meaning of the monarch inform the attention of the Jamestown colonists to the appearance, state, liberality, and lodging of Virginia werowances. They wrote of them using the same rhetoric that English ambassadors and merchants had used of such princes as the shah of Persia, the Grand Turk, and Ivan the Terrible in the middle of the previous century. In those texts, as in the Jamestown documents, we can identify four immediate concerns:

the appearance of the king, the manifestations of his authority, what he ate or provided for others to eat, and the organization of space around him. The implicit comparison between the werowances and Eurasian princes emphasizes similarities at the expense of disparities, so that these descriptions of events tend to "civilize" the Powhatan quite as much as the structural inferences about monarchical authority.[14]

From the first, the Jamestown colonists expressed admiration of the physical appearance of the chiefs they encountered. Only Spelman says that in appearance "the King is not know by any differenc[e] from other of y^e [*better*] chefe sort in ye cuntry" (1910 [1613]:cxiii; editors' interpolations and emphasis). All of the other sources describe chiefs as distinctive in actions and in appearance. One of the earliest, and fullest, descriptions of a werowance comes from Percy, himself the son and brother of peers. In May 1607 the werowance of Quiyoughcohannock, which in this passage Percy erroneously calls Rapahanna, sent word to the English that he would welcome a visit from them. Percy writes of the meeting:

> When wee landed, the Werowance of Rapahanna came downe to the water side with all his traine, as goodly men as any I haue seene *of Sauages or Christians:* the Werowance comming before them playing on a Flute made of a Reed, with a Crown of Deares haire colloured red, in fashion of a Rose fastened about his knot of haire, and a great Plate of Copper on the other side of his head; with two long Feathers in fashion of a paire of Hornes placed in the midst of his Crowne. His body was painted all with Crimson, with a Chaine of Beades about his necke; his face painted blew besprinkled with siluer Ore as wee thought; his eares all behung with Braslets of Pearle; and in either eare a Birds Claw though it, beset with fine Copper or Gold.
>
> He entertained vs in so modest a proud fashion, *as though he had beene a Prince of ciuill gouerment;* holding his countenance without laughter or any such ill behauiour. (1910 [1607]:lxv; emphasis added)

If the werowance is as dignified, physically imposing, well-off, and well-attended as a "ciuill" prince, how did Percy's compatriots describe such princes? We can compare Percy's encomium with this description of Ivan the Terrible, written from Moscow in 1553:

> [the English visitors] being entred within the gates of the Court, there sate a very honorable companie of Courtiers, to the number of one hundred, all apparelled in cloth of golde, downe to their ankles: and therehence being conducted into the chamber of presence, our men beganne to wonder at the Majestie of the Emperour: his seate was aloft, in a very royall throne, having on his head a Diademe, or Crowne of golde, apparelled with a robe all of Goldsmiths worke, and in his hand hee held a Scepter garnished, and beset with precious stones: and besides all over notes and apparances of honour, there was a Majestie in his countenance proportionable with the excellence of his estate: on the one side of him stood his chiefe Secretarie, on the other side, the great Commander of silence, both of them arayed also in cloth of gold: and then there sate the Counsel of one hundred and fiftie in number, all in like sort arayed, and of great state. (Hakluyt 1907 [1589], 1:280)

Like that of Quiyoughcohannock, this description of a "civil" prince mentions his court, his majesty and dignity, his clothing and face, and the evidence of wealth in the kingdom. Apart from the differences of material—gold and gemstones against copper and feathers—the two monarchs are made to be equivalent. The literature of Tudor exploration furnishes many such examples (e.g., Hakluyt 1907 [1589], 1:423, 2:14; Taylor 1934:40).

The Jamestown colonists, too, provide additional examples. Archer gives us a rare glimpse of a werowanqua: Opossunoquonuske, the sister of Coquonasum, werowance of Appomattox; she ruled one village in the territory (Strachey 1953 [1612]:64). Archer reports a meeting less than cordial, possibly because the "quene" had a low opinion of the English. But we see the same themes reiterated:[15]

assending a pretty Hill, we sawe the Queene of this Country comminge in selfe same fashion of state as *Pawatah* or
Arahatec; yea rather with more maiesty: she had an vsher before her who brought her to the matt prepared vnder a faire
mulbery tree, where she satt her Downe by her selfe with a
stayed Countenance. . . . she is a fatt lustie manly woman: she
had much Copper about her neck, a Crownet of Copper upon
her hed: she had long black haire, which hanged loose downe
her back to her myddle, which only part was Covered with a
Deares skyn, and ells all naked. She had her woemen attending on her adorned much like her selfe (save they wanted y^e
Copper). [She] requested him [Captain Newport] to shoote
o[f] a peece, whereat (we noted) she shewed not neere the like
feare as *Arahatec* though he be a goodly man. (Archer 1910
[1607]:xlix-l; editors' interpolations)

In contrast to these chiefs, Powhatan's brother, Opechancanough,
the werowance of Pamunkey, failed to impress Archer and his companions, despite the richness of his land and his personal ornament:
"This kyng (sitting in maner of the rest) so set his Countenance
stryving to be stately, as to our seeming he became foole" (Archer
1910 [1607]:l).

Strachey's lyrical description of the wife of a former werowance of
Quiyoughcohannock, Pipsco, deserves inclusion here even though
she seems not to have been a "quene" in her own right. Strachey
gives no name for this woman, so anonymous she must remain. I am
inclined to think she was a werowance's sister, sister's daughter, or
both, partly because of her demeanor and partly because our (admittedly meager) evidence about chiefly marriage suggests a tendency
to endogamy among them. Again, copper was worn only by men or
by chiefly women. But it is equally possible that she was the Powhatan equivalent of a tradesman's daughter married to an earl and
gave herself airs. Whether she was of chiefly stock or merely wished
to give that impression is irrelevant for this discussion, though, because—as he says in his final comment—Strachey took her as an
example of the civility of the "better sort" among the Powhatan.

nor is so handsome a savadge woman, as I haue seene amongest them, yet with a kynd of pride can take vpon her a shew of
greatnes: . . . I was once earely at her howse (yt being Sommer
tyme) when she was layd without dores vnder the shadow of a
broad leav'd tree, vpon a Pallett of Osiers spredd over with 4.
or 5. fyne grey matts, her self Covered with a faire white drest
deare-skyn or towe [two], and when she rose, she had a Mayde
who fetch't her a frontall of white Corall, and pendants of great
(but imperfect coulored, and worse drilled) pearles, which she
putt into her eares, and a Chayne with long lynckes of Copper, which they call *Tapaantaminais* and which came twice or
thrice double about her neck, and they accompt a iolly Ornament, and sure, thus attyred with some variety of feathers, and
flowers stuck in their hayres, *they seeme as debonayre, quaynt,
and well pleased, as (I wis) a daughter of the howse of Austria
behoung with all her Iewells,* Likewise her Mayd fetch't her a
Mantell, which they call Puttawus, which is like a side cloak,
made of blew feathers, so arteficially and thick sowed togither,
that yt showes like a deepe purple Satten, and is very smooth
and sleek, and after she [the "Mayd"] brought her water for
her handes, and then a bunch or towe of fresh greene ashen
leaues, as for a towell to wipe them; *I offend in this digression the willinger, synce these were Ceremonies which I did little
looke for carrying so much presentment of Civility.* (Strachey 1953
[1612]:65; emphases added)[16]

Contributing to the state of a monarch—and thus a primary means
of determining it—was the size of his or her train. The description
of Ivan IV of Russia, quoted earlier, is typical in enumerating and
identifying the czar's courtiers, followers, and the like. Likewise, the
Jamestown explorers made a note of the size of each chief's company. Even in the extremity of his capture, Smith took the trouble to
note the orderly military progress of his captor, Opechancanough.
"The King well guarded with 20 bowmen 5 flanck and rear, and each
flanck before him a sword and a peece, and after him the like, then a
bowman, then I on each hand a boweman, the rest in file in the reare,

which reare led foorth amongst the trees in a bishion, eache his bowe and a handfull of arrowes, a quiver at his back grimly painted: on eache flanck a sargeant, the one running alwaies towards the front the other towards the reare, each a true pace and in exceeding good order" (Smith 1986 [1608]:47).[17]

Smith's is an informed approval, since he had fought successfully in diverse wars under different commanders (Smith 1986 [1630]). In mentioning the order of soldiers, their weaponry, their clothing (or in this case their body decorations), and their recognition of authority, his description reads, moreover, like that of a Russian military review in December 1557: "the Emperors Majestie and all his nobility came into the field on horsebacke, in most goodly order, having very fine Jennets & Turkie horses garnished with gold & siver abundantly. . . . his noble men . . . did ride before him in good order by 3. & by 3. and before them there went 5000 harquebusiers, which went by 5 and 5 in a ranke in very good order, every of them carying his gun upon his left shoulder, and his match in his right hand, and in this order they marched into the field where as the foresayd ordinance was planted" (Hakluyt 1907 [1589], 1:423).

However marvelous the appearance of chiefs and their wives, the splendor of Powhatan eclipsed them all. Given the contemporary attitude to rank, the colonists no doubt expected him to outshine any of his subordinates. Smith, the first of the colonists actually to meet Powhatan, describes him in 1608

> proudly lying uppon a Bedstead a foote high upon tenne or twelve Mattes, richly hung with manie Chaynes of great Pearles about his necke, and covered with a great Covering of *Rahaughcums* [raccoon skins]: At his heade sat a woman, at his feete another, on each side sitting uppon a Matte upon the ground were raunged his chiefe men on each side the fire, tenne in a ranke, and behinde them as many yong women, each a great Chaine of white Beades over their shoulders, their heades painted in redde: and [he] with such a graue and Majesticall

countenance, as drave me into admiration to see such state in a naked Salvage, [. . .] hee kindly welcomed me with good wordes, and great Platters of sundrie Victuals, assuring mee his friendship, and my libertie within foure days [Smith was his prisoner at this time]; hee much delighted in Opechanca-noughs relation of what I had described to him, and oft examined me upon the same. (Smith 1986 [1608]:53; editor's ellipsis; [1624]:150–151)

In his second account, the *Map of Virginia*, published in 1612, Smith described Powhatan and his state:

He is of parsonage a tall well proportioned man, with a sower looke, his head somwhat gray, his beard so thinne that it seemeth none at al, his age neare 60; of a very able and hardy body to endure any labour. About his person ordinarily attendeth a guard of 40 or 50 of the tallest men his Country doth afford. Every night upon the 4 quarters of his house are 4 Sentinels each standing from other a flight shoot, and at every halfe houre one from the Corps du guard doth hollowe, unto whom every Sentinell doth answer round from his stand; if any faile, they presently send forth an officer that beateth him extreamely. . . .

He hath as many women as he will, whereof when hee lieth on his bed, one sitteth at his head, and another at his feet, but when he sitteth, one sitteth on his right hand and another on his left. . . . When he dineth or suppeth, one of his women before and after meat, bringeth him water in a woden platter to wash his hands. Another waiteth with a bunch of feathers to wipe them instead of a Towell, and the feathers when he hath wiped are dryed againe. (1986 [1612]:173–174)

In the earlier passage, Smith tells us the same kinds of things about Powhatan that the English ambassadors to Christian and Moslem princes tell us about them. We learn that the paramount chief is majestical, awe-inspiring, commander of many people, and willing to be approached. In his later account, Smith describes something of the state in which the "savage" chief lives, and again an implicit parallel is drawn with the state of European kings.

These themes are reiterated in Smith's two descriptions of Powhatan's meeting with Captain Newport. Shortly after the event, which occurred early in 1608, he wrote,

> Before his [i.e., Powhatan's] house stood fortie or fiftie great Platters of fine bread; being entred the house, with loude tunes they all made signes of great joy. This proude salvage, having his finest women, and the principall of his chiefe men assembled, sate in rankes as before is expressed, himself as upon a Throne at the upper ende of the house, with *such a Majestie as I cannot expresse, nor yet have often seene, either in Pagan or Christian;* with a kinde countenance hee bad mee welcome, and caused a place to bee made by himselfe to sit. I presented him a sute of red cloath, a white Greyhound, and a Hatte; as Jewels he esteemed them, and with a great Oration made by three of his Nobles, if there be any amongst Salvages, kindly accepted them, with a publike confirmation of a perpetuall league and friendship. (Smith 1986 [1608]:65; emphasis added)

Like the ambassadors to Moscow, Turkey, and elsewhere, Smith puts this sovereign on a throne, endows him with majesty, and surrounds him with courtiers; and he places himself as a favorite in the midst thereof.

He conveys the magnificence of the monarch not only directly, in words, but also indirectly by describing the gifts he offers him, since a gift must be "fitting to the character of the recipient" (Needham 1979:34). The hat is of especial interest. In England at this period it was a fine marker of rank, worn by everyone for the purpose either of doffing it to a superior or keeping in on in the presence of an inferior. (Quarrels could result, of course.) Children bared their heads to their fathers, commoners to lords, everyone to the king (Stone 1965:34–35; but see also Wrightson 1982:115). Portraits of James I show him always with his hat on his head. Interestingly enough, the portrait of Pocahontas shows her with her hat on also, indicating her royal rank in English eyes. Giving a hat to Powhatan did not simply provide him with another article of civilized dress: it acknowledged his right to wear one in any company. If he did not understand the message, nevertheless we may be sure he agreed with it.

In his next account, Smith elaborates somewhat on this meeting, with what to us must be interesting results:

> Powhatan strained himselfe to the uttermost of his greatnes to entertain us, with great shouts of Joy, orations of protestations, and the most plenty of victuall hee could provide to feast us. Sitting upon his bed of mats, his pillow of leather imbroydred (after their rude manner) with pearle and white beades, his attire a faire Robe of skins as large as an Irish mantle, at his head and feet a handsome young woman; on each side his house sate 20. of his concubines, their heads and shoulders painted red, with a great chaine of white beads about their necks. Before those sate his chiefest men in like order in his arbor-like house. . . . 3. or 4. daies were spent in feasting dancing and trading, wherin Powhatan carried himselfe so prowdly, yet discreetly (in his Salvage manner) as made us all admire his natural gifts considering his education. (1986 [1612]:216–217)

Except that the specific items are different, these might be, in their various ways, the description of Czar Ivan IV: he, too, stuns beholders by his majestical countenance; he sits above the others on a throne, where Powhatan rests on a "bedstead"; the czar wears cloth of gold, Powhatan a fur cloak; Powhatan is supported by a woman on either side, Ivan IV by his chief secretary and his commander of silence (also in cloth of gold); and Ivan has his council of 150 where Powhatan has 20. The tenor of these comments suggests that such differences are to be expected, but they are of little importance compared to the generally great similarities between the styles of these two rulers.

In these descriptions, the wealth and liberality of the monarch are foci of interest. In early Stuart society, status was so closely related to expenditure and display that it is difficult at times to know which

POWHATAN

*Held this state & fashion when Capt. Smith
was deliuered to him prisoner
1607*

Fig. 3. Powhatan in state. Courtesy of the Library of Virginia.

was a function of which. Certainly contemporaries expected "noble" or "gentle" status to be allied to suitable income (Stone 1965:27)— "suitable" referring not just to its size but also to its source, since anyone who was not required to do physical labor for a living was a "gentleman" (Laslett 1971:33; see Rabb 1967:12).[18] Even in early Stuart times aristocratic families still held, despite half a century of inflation (Hill 1980:11), to the medieval tenet that "the prime test of rank was liberality, the pagan virtue of open-handedness," maintaining feudal hospitality in their large houses, supporting many servants and dependents, dressing opulently, and being buried with ostentation (Stone 1965:42, 187, 547).

These convictions find expression in the minute descriptions of the dress, ornament, and attendants of a sovereign, as we have seen, and of their liberality, especially with food. In his descriptions of Powhatan's reception of Newport, Smith takes care to mention the kinds of food offered, in what quantities, and over what period of time. Again, we can compare what he says with the description of how Ivan IV received the emissaries of the Moscovy Company:

> Within one houre after [the ambassador's audience with the czar] in comes to my lodging a duke richly apparelled, accompanied with fiftie persons, ech of them carying a silver dish with meat, and covered with silver. The duke first delivered twenty loaves of bread of the Emperors owne eating, having tasted the same, and delivered every dish into my hands, and tasted of every kind of drinke that he brought.
>
> This being done, the duke and his company sate downe with me, and tooke part of the Emperors meat, and filled themselves well of all sorts, and went not away from me unrewarded. (Hakluyt 1907 [1589], 2:84–85)

The embassy of 1583 lists a "new and much larger allowance of diet for the ambassador," staggering the recipient, who asked (unsuccessfully) to have it reduced. The provisions included, per day, two live geese, twenty hens, seven sheep, a third of an ox, a side of pork, ten pounds of butter, 70 loaves of white bread, ten pounds of salt, half a pound of pepper and smaller amounts of other spices, and what the English considered an overwhelming—in every sense— amount of drink including burnt wine, six sorts of mead, and two sorts of beer. The czar also allowed three bushels of provender a day for the horses (Hakluyt 1907 [1589], 2:257–258).

The king's generosity, the size of his court, and the richness of their dress were expressions, on their part, of the wealth and well-being of the kingdom as a whole and were so taken by visitors. The logic of this assumption lies in the understanding of the king as "text," or as the emblem of his kingdom. The men of this period, it must be remembered, regarded super- and subordinate as allied, not at odds. Therefore a rich court was not interpreted as a sign of a poor subject population—poor because exploited—but rather the reverse. The reports that Tudor ambassadors wrote about their missions to Hyrcania, Russia, and so on are ostensibly just that: statements about the success of the mission and whether it is worthwhile to pursue it. But their approach differs notably from that of a modern group attempting to answer similar questions. They spend very little time describing the economic potential of the land and its people and concentrate instead on the splendors of the monarch and his or her court.

Hocart observes that a monarch's opulence represents the wealth of the realm, but that he or she is also the source of that wealth, a veritable cornucopia (1970a:202; see Feeley-Harnik 1985:288). In judging kings by their gifts, our explorers again show themselves products of their age. Stone finds fault with Elizabeth I for not supporting her nobility adequately, as a monarch was supposed to do. If she erred in being too parsimonious, James I went to the other extreme, being profligate beyond what all but the most rapacious could tolerate (Stone 1965). Despite their extremes, they show us that the English looked to their monarch for both direct and indirect economic support in the form of court appointments, pensions, grants of land, and monopolies. The Moscow visitors were delighted with a gift of bread from Czar Ivan's own table not just because it came from the *king*, but because it *came from* the king. Such liberality was reassuring not just because it showed the king to be generous but also more generally because it was a gage of the royal will and ability to promote prosperity and life for the kingdom.

The same points can be made with regard to what the colonists tell us about chiefly liberality. Their interest in this was due in part, without doubt, to the fact that they themselves had very little to eat much of the time. But they received gifts other than food—for instance, they classify a "frendly wellcome" as a gift — and they used all such gifts as an index of the Indians' civility, noting who gave how much of what even in the very earliest encounters, before their provisions ran short. Archer, again our earliest source, describes their first meeting with a James River werowance, the chief of Arrohattock. "We found here a *Wiroans* (for so they call their kynges) who satt upon a matt of Reedes, with his people about him: He caused one to be layd for Captaine *Newport*, gave vs a Deare roasted; which according to their Custome they seethed againe: His people gave vs mullberyes, sodd wheate and beanes, and he caused his weomen to make Cakes for vs. He gave our Captaine [Newport] his Crowne which was of Deares hayre, Dyed redd" (Archer 1910 [1607]:xlii–xliii). Later the exploring party met the neighboring werowance of Powhatan, who "caused his weomen to bring vs vittailes, mulberyes, strawberryes &c. but our best entertaynment was frendly wellcome" (Archer 1910 [1607]:xliv). The English had many similar receptions on their passage along the James. As they returned from the falls, the werowance of Arrohattock "caused heere to be prepared for us *pegatewk-Apyan* which is bread of their wheat made in Rolles and Cakes; this the weomen make, and are very clenly about it; we had parched meale, excellent good; sodd beanes, which eate as sweete as filbert kernells in a maner, strawberryes and mulberyes new shaken of the tree dropping on our heads as we satt: He made ready a land turtle which we eate, and shewed that he was hartely reioyced in our Company" (Archer 1910 [1607]:xlviii–xlix).[19] Archer reports, too, that at Appomattox they had their "accustomed Cates, Tobacco and wellcome" from the *wiroanqua*, despite her unfriendly demeanor.[20] At Weanock, by contrast, the Indians provided "neither victualls nor Tobacco" (Archer 1910 [1607]:l, li).

Although, according to Archer, the Indians "seemed not to craue any thing in requitall," Captain Newport nevertheless gave them gifts including a hatchet, a gift to "little" Powhatan; and his red waistcoat, which he bestowed on the werowance of Arrohattock (1910 [1607]:xliii, xlvii, xlix, l). Wingfield mentions two occasions on which the colonists received a deer as a gift: the first time from Opechancanough, the second from "great" Powhatan himself; in return he gave them "trifles," including a hatchet (1910 [1608]:lxxvi).

Some part of Powhatan's generosity in entertaining Newport has been described. In addition, on that occasion, he caused the "Queene of Appomattoc . . . to give me [Smith] water, a Turkie-cocke, and breade to eate," and later provided yet more bread and a "quarter of Venizon"—all for Smith alone. Having met Newport, and unable to persuade him to stay for the evening meal, Powhatan "sent bread after us . . . and venizon, sufficient for fiftie or sixtie persons" (Smith 1986 [1608]:65, 67, 71). As the logic of chiefship would lead us—and led the colonists—to expect, his liberality surpassed that of his werowances; but they were not niggardly. Even as their prisoner, Smith received such vast quantities of food, not only from them but from other chiefs whom they took him to visit, that it "made him thinke they would fat him to eat him" (Smith 1986 [1624]:148, 1986 [1608]:51). His first night as a captive saw him provided with "a quarter of Venison and some ten pound of bread . . . , what I left was reserved for me: each morning 3. women presented me three great platters of fine bread, more venison then ten men could devour I had" (Smith 1986 [1608]:49). After his release and return to Jamestown, he continued to receive substantial gifts of food from Powhatan and other werowances (Smith 1986 [1608]:61, [1612] 215).

The early interest of the Jamestown colonists in what their hosts gave them to eat, and how much, and with what freedom, all echo the concerns of the English half a century earlier in Russia, Persia, and elsewhere in Asia. Even though the Virginians' fare was neither so rich (they ate little oil) nor so varied as that found in the courts of Europe and the Middle East, nor was the setting for their meals in any way similar, nevertheless the colonists describe their friendly welcome in the same gratified terms with which Anthony Jenkinson and his colleagues write from Moscow and Turkey. This was the language of successful contact with civility, understood by the

Jamestown colonists and by their readers in England. In their liberality, as in their command over their subjects, Powhatan werowances
were equivalent to civilized princes.

The colonists' attention to chiefly state in Virginia took account
of spatial symbolism as well: the separation from, or proximity to, a
chief and the dimensions and layout (though not the orientation) of
their houses. We have already seen Smith situating himself, literally,
in Powhatan's inner circle. Archer's account of the colonists' first
meeting with the lesser Powhatan includes this observation: "Heere
we were conducted vp the Hill to the kyng ["little" Powhatan], with
whome we found our kinde king *Arahatec:* Thes. 2. satt by themselves
apart from all the rest (saue one who satt by *Powatah,* and what he
was I could not gesse but they told me he was no *Wiroans*): Many
of his company satt on either side: and the mattes for vs were layde
right over against the kynges" (1910 [1607]:xliii–xliv). Archer lets his
readers know in what favor they stood with these "kings:" their own
people kept their distance, but the visitors were invited to sit at his
side. A day or two later the English were able to return the favor, and
"king *Powatah* [the "little" Powhatan] with some of his people satt
with vs, brought of his dyet, and *we fedd familiarly,* without sitting in
his state as before" (Archer 1910 [1607]:xlv; emphasis added). Here
they are, hobnobbing with a king, says Archer: perfectly civilized
and friendly. They received a similar welcome the first time they
landed at Kecoughtan, although it is not clear whether the English
sat "right against" the "chiefest of them" or just some of the Indians gathered there (Percy 1910 [1607]:lxiii). The "quene" of Appomattox stands out in this catalog of friendly attentions: "she would
permitt none to stand or sitt neere her" (Archer 1910 [1607]:l).

These encounters took place out of doors, indeed out of villages
in the neutral territory between settlement and wilderness. Such was
the Powhatan rule for greeting any visiting person of importance.
Once invited into the village, visitors had a house placed at their disposal by the werowance (Smith 1986 [1612]:167–168; Beverley 1947
[1705]:189). Compared to the great houses of Europe, Indian houses

must have seemed hardly worth the name. Nevertheless, the colonists describe them and say something of their mode of construction: "Their houses are built like our Arbors of small young springs
bowed and tyed, and so close covered with mats, or the barkes of
trees very handsomely, that notwithstanding either winde, raine or
weather, they are as warme as stooves, but very smoaky" (Smith 1986
[1612]:161). Strachey says that the bark covering indicates a "principall howse" (1953 [1612]:78), and other Jamestown colonists mention a distinctive werowance's house. Smith's map identifies "Kings
howses" and "Ordinary howses." Percy calls the house of the werowance of Quiyoughcohannock a "palace," but he offers no description (1910 [1607]:lxv). Spelman also mentions a "king's house" in
several contexts, saying that "the Kinges houses are both broader
and longer then ye rest hauing many darke windinges and turnings
before any cum wher the Kinge is" (1910 [1613]:cvi).

The colonists considered not just the size but also the number
of houses a chief owned. Powhatan is reported to have had several
large houses, at least one in each of his inherited territories (Spelman
1910 [1613]:cv; Smith 1986 [1608]:17–18, 1986 [1612]:79). According to Strachey, each house had a cohort of his wives living there
(1953 [1612]:61). A report dated 1618 mentions that "Powhatan goes
from place to place visiting his Country taking his pleasure in good
friendship w^{t}h us" (Kingsbury 1935:92). In making such progresses,
he was seen to be acting like a European monarch: more particularly,
like Elizabeth I, who, unlike James I, regularly moved through at
least the Home Counties of her kingdom. If at the time her subjects
dreaded the expense of her presence, in the reign of James I they
came to value the king's visits as the epitome of regal condescension
(Smuts 1987:16–18).

In general, the Jamestown colonists' discussion of space and architecture in Virginia present the Powhatan as civilized. An important aspect of a civil society is sedentism, which implies structures
of some substance. Rhetorically, too, the colonists echo here as in
other ways their predecessors' accounts from Europe and Asia of

palaces and the spatial disposition of persons about the monarch. The first embassy to Moscow reported that the czar's "chiefe Secretarie" stood on one side of the czar and the "great Commander of silence" on the other; a contrary case was the shah of Persia, of whom an embassy reported in 1574 that "sometimes in a moneth or six weekes none of his nobilitie or counsaille can see him, yet goe they daily to the court, and tary there a certaine time untill they have known his pleasure" (Hakluyt 1907 [1589], 2:130). One may imagine with what gratification Arthur Edwards reported to the Moscovy Company that he had met with the shah "(as I thinke) two houres. He willed me twise to come neerer him, demanding what were my requests: and having heard them, he promised me his gracious letters. Afterwards he called me twise againe to come neerer him" (Hakluyt 1907 [1589], 2:42). Abdullah Khan favored Anthony Jenkinson on his first trip through Hyrcania in a similar manner: "I was sent for to come to the king. . . . I came before his presence, who gently interteined me, and having kissed his hands, he bad me to dinner, and commanded me to sit down not farre from him" (Hakluyt 1907 [1589], 2:14).

There is no surprise in finding spatial relations a symbol for social relations, but we may not be aware of their singular importance in the Renaissance. There are two reasons, at least, for these writers' interest in who was where and with whom. One is the overriding concern with rank.[21] Social relations were primarily hierarchical relations: on this basic point everyone agreed. But in early Stuart commentaries on social life "rank and status emerge as having been far from autonomous conditions" (Wrightson 1982:22). Usually one was being defined by someone else; in the case of the ambassadors and merchants that was certainly so, since they were foreigners. Spatial arrangement was an obvious, public, immediate way to determine rank, whether one's own or other people's. Girouard writes of "the constant series of retreats that make up the history of palace planning," so that by the time of Elizabeth I an appropriate lodging for an important guest would include a great chamber for large numbers of miscellaneous people and beyond it a "withdrawing chamber, a bedchamber and an inner chamber," all en suite (1978:57, 108). Each of these rooms represents increasing separation from the world in general and corresponding difficulty of access.[22]

If space were equivalent to social order, these ambassadors would naturally observe the disposition of persons in space to understand the order and their own place in it. And with such royal behavior at home, we may understand why they rejoiced to have a king admit them to his presence, feed them from his table, urge them to come closer: these were signs not just of enormous favor but of incorporation into the local hierarchy. In Virginia, the same considerations ruled: the chiefs showed themselves, and were shown in print to be, civil in that they recognized not only the worth of their visitors but the concept of worth itself.

Evaluation

This minute examination of the Jamestown texts is necessary to allow us to identify their contemporary meanings and intention. Because the language of political debate in early modern England uses terms and refers to relationships still in existence today, it is easy to assume that the meanings have remained the same as well. But the English Renaissance conception of polity was significantly different from modern political notions of the same, and indeed it closely resembled what we have come to expect of American Indian political ideas. It was a different culture, like the Bemba or the Bororo, and we must treat it as such. By this means we discover that the Jamestown documents have different, and greater, meaning than had been supposed. Admittedly, since translation is always imperfect, the fact that we must translate our source documents into modern terms before we can understand their translation of Powhatan political forms might be held to vitiate the undertaking. This is excessive pessimism, however. Without a sense of the contemporary meanings in these documents, any attempt to reconstruct Powhatan culture must be futile. More important, the colonists' cultural bias predisposed them to understand the relationship between superior and subordinate in the same way as the Indians and probably better than a modern observer brought up to mistrust hierarchy. Their accounts taken in modern terms are of no value and can be misleading, but taken on their own terms they provide us with more than enough information on which to base a study of Powhatan culture.

3. Kings and Councilors in Tidewater Virginia

The Jamestown explorers identify several ranks of person among the Virginia Algonkians. They call these "king" and "queen," "priest" and "conjuror," and "the chief sort" or "the better sort." They also offer a limited native vocabulary: mamanatowick, werowance, cockarouse, quiyoughcosough. In the manner of an anthropological analysis based on ethnographic field-work, I have tried to define each of these in native terms and to show its relationship to the others. This chapter concentrates on the more secular half of the sovereignty of the Powhatan, namely, the werowance and the cockarouse; the following chapter examines the more spiritual or mystical half, the "priests" and "conjurors." The relationship between the spiritual and mundane is examined in chapter 5.

Since the colonial accounts make the Powhatan seem more English and less "savage," it is reasonable to ask whether their comments about "kings" and "the better sort" may be more of the same. The colonists came from a hierarchical society, and they were keenly sensitive to evidence of gradation in rank. We can suppose two possible consequences of this: either they wished the coastal Algonkians to be ranked—that would make them "civil"—and so they saw evidence where there was none, or they were exceptionally well prepared to recognize and understand it in even an unfamiliar social setting. There is no doubt, though, that these societies were ranked—the English did not make it up. If anything, their conviction that hierarchy was the only possible way to organize a society made them good observers of the system.

But when we have said this we are still confronted with difficulties of interpretation. What the colonists say about chiefs and their councils is neither so comprehensive nor so consistent as one could wish; in fact, their accounts seem to contradict one another to some degree. The challenge is how to treat the contradictions. If they represent English ignorance, we cannot use them as evidence about the Powhatan. This seems extreme. The English may have regarded the Powhatan with something like tunnel vision, but they did see them (see Kupperman 2000:2). Another possibility is to gloss over the discrepancies, as recent anthropological analyses of Powhatan political structure do (e.g., Rountree 1989; Gleach 1997). A result of this is that the same text can be made to support different, equally plausible, interpretations, but none of them can be conclusive. We need not dismiss, nor should we ignore, these contradictions, however. Anyone who has done ethnographic fieldwork knows that even "the natives" can disagree about the meanings and proper uses even of important terms and, moreover, that the differences in usage can be significant in themselves. I assume that although the Jamestown accounts are not strictly speaking the "native voice," nevertheless these discrepancies do reflect native cultural forms and therefore have something useful to tell us about the relations between chief and councilor (see Darnton 1984:262).

The fact that Smith and Strachey, at least (cf. Whitaker 1613), took the attitude that Powhatan acted only and always in his own selfish interests, and that his werowances did so as much as they could, presents us with limitations also. The colonial writers and their modern adherents may be right. Powhatan may have been a monster of selfishness. Such a conclusion is based, though, on the faulty premise that the king is an individual rather than "a more or less autonomous point of emergence of a particular collective humanity, of a *society*" (Dumont 1972:39). Strachey, like his contemporaries, saw a distinction between the individual will and the collective custom or law and called a tyrant any king who appeared to put the promptings of his own private will above his obedience to the law. That monarchs do act, or appear to act, willfully is undeniable. Any incumbent of an office brings to it something per-

Fig. 4. A werowance. Courtesy of the Library of Virginia.

sonal, too. No chief is exactly like any other, even if their titles be the same. The extent to which a chief stamps his office with his own style makes him "more or less autonomous," like anyone else. At the same time, trying to determine whether a monarch's actions are due to cultural constraints or to individual motivations is exceedingly tricky. Even if it were a fruitful endeavor in a living society, we cannot now legitimately make such a distinction in Powhatan's case. Thus it is preferable to consider kingly actions as expressions of cultural ideas about kingship rather than as expressions of an individual psychology. This is true even if they really are expressions of an individual psychology, because the legitimacy of such expressions in kingly action is itself a cultural fact.

This line of thought follows Hocart's argument in *Kings and Councillors*. Kingship is a social, not a psychological, phenomenon (e.g., Hocart 1970a:97–98); therefore Hocart views with skepticism accounts like those from the Jamestown colony when they concentrate on what appears to be chiefly or kingly license and not on the restrictions of the office (1970b:152). He insists that a king's life is limited rather than licentious because his ultimate duty is to be "the life of the group" (Hocart 1970a:99; see Dumézil 1988:44), "to promote life, fertility, prosperity by transferring life from objects abounding in it to objects deficient in it" (Hocart 1970a:3).[1] As Needham observes, Hocart's use of "life" is vague; nevertheless, Hocart does provide "a useful enough indication of what he has in mind" (Needham 1970:xxxii–xxxiii): "fertility, prosperity, vitality . . . something which [distinguishes] the animate from the inanimate . . . life" (Hocart 1970a:32). This sacerdotal function subsumes every particular thing the king does. No action of his can be without social and even cosmic significance and consequence; therefore none can be unregulated.

Elsewhere in native North America, we find that the primary duty of the chief is to look after others' welfare and the welfare of the group—the two are not the same—even if it means giving up his own comfort and possessions (e.g., Clastres 1977; Lowie 1967; Lévi-Strauss 1967). As a result, the widow and orphan are cherished, and the criminal discovered and dealt with. Perhaps more important is that the group realizes (i.e., grasps the reality of) the resources it has. Among the tribes of the deep Southeast, where rank and seeming privilege are common, we can discern this pattern: the expectation that what a chief does is for the benefit of the whole group, not for his own (e.g., Swanton 1911:93; Gilbert 1943:358; Gibson 1971:21; Gearing 1962). Given this nearly universal pattern, its lack among the Powhatan would be remarkable indeed.

Werowance and Cockarouse Distinguished

The colonial documents use the terms "werowance" and "cockarouse" to refer to the secular or civil leaders of Powhatan society. What exactly each of these terms meant and how they were related to each other are not obvious. The simplest interpretation of the colonial sources is, as others have proposed, that the Powhatan did recognize two distinct ranked statuses, which we can gloss as "chief" and "councilor." The relationship between the two was more complex than this, though. It was a dialectical relationship between ranks and functions, and it constituted one of the forms of dual sovereignty in Powhatan society.[2]

The English discovered werowances in 1585 during their attempt to establish a colony in the Outer Banks. A report of his men's activities written to Sir Walter Raleigh says that the Carolina Algonkians "called all our principall officers" by this term, and also that "there be [on the Chesapeake] sundry Kings, whom they call Weroances" (Hakluyt 1907 [1589], 6:155, 142).[3] Harriot translates the term as "chief Lord" (1972 [1590]:25, Pls. 3, 7), and he calls them "princes" and "governors," a term he also uses for the "priests" (1972 [1590]: Pl. 3, 25–26). Werowance was still in use more than a century later. Beverley writes that the titles of respect among the Virginia Algonkians were "King," "Queen," "cockarouse," and "werowance," the last of which he identifies as "a Military Officer, who of course takes upon him the command of all Parties, either of Hunting, Travelling, Warring, or the like, and the word signfies a War Captain." The cockarouse he calls both a councilor and "a brave fellow" (1947 [1705]:226, 149). The "king" was "at once Governour, Judge, [and] Chancellour" within his kingdom; he was also a warrior (Beverley 1947 [1705]:174).

There is a significant difference between Harriot's "governor" or "prince" and Beverley's "war captain," and if we are to elucidate sovereignty among the Powhatan we have to know which is closer to the aboriginal mark. Since customs and meanings undoubtedly changed between 1585 and 1705, we could simply accept Harriot's translation as the closest we are likely to get to the 16th- and early-17th-century sense of the word were it not that Smith and, after him, Strachey define werowance in terms more like Beverley's than Harriot's. They raise the question whether werowance was a title not of chiefs alone but bestowed on any man with outstanding (military) accomplishments—perhaps an alternative to cockarouse, as "monarch" and "sovereign" may be interchangeable—or whether it was appropriate to a social class, like the Natchez Sun (see Swanton 1911:93, 100–107).

Each of the constituent tribes of the polity had "some Governour, as their king, which they call *Werowances*," or "a severall commander, which they call Werowance" (Smith 1986 [1612]:146). In this passage, Smith also introduces the term "cockarouse," which he spells "caw-cawwassoughes" (plural) and seems to translate "elders" (1986 [1612]:146, [1624]:103). Still later he amplifies his definition of werowance: "But this word Werowance which we call and conster for a king, is a common worde whereby they call all commanders: for they have but fewe words in their language, and but few occasions to use anie officers more then one commander, which commonly they call werowances" (Smith 1986 [1612]:174; see Strachey 1953 [1612]:59). He repeated this in the *Generall Historie* with an amplification: "but few occasions to use any officers more then one commander, which commonly they call Werowance, or *Caucorouse*, which is Captaine" (Smith 1986 [1624]:127). In describing preparations for Powhatan warfare, Smith writes that "every Werowance, or some lustie fellow, they appoint Captaine over every nation" (1986 [1612]:165, see 167), and in recounting the circumstances of his capture he says that his Indian guide (who was Smith's captive at that point) "discovered me to be the Captaine" (1986 [1608]:47), or werowance.

In the earlier work, Smith equates werowance, commander, and captain; at the same time he seems to disparage translating werowance as "king," although he so translates it in describing the disposition of Powhatan tribes along the rivers and in his word list (1986 [1612]:146, 139). In the later work, he adds cockarouse to this collection of terms. Strachey repeats many of Smith's earlier statements, including the apparent disparagement; but he, too, translates *wiroance* as "a king or great Lord" in his word list (1953 [1612]:190, 89, see also 204, where he has "*Veroance*—a king or a great man"). Harriot, writing about the Algonkians of Carolina and the lower Chesapeake, calls the chiefs "governors." Hamor glosses werowance as both "king" and "principall commander" (1615:9, 12).

What appears to be confusion in these statements is not due to any change in the meanings of the terms during the past 400 years. Although "captain" and "commander" identify different ranks in the Royal Navy today, during the period in question they were virtually synonymous. According to the *Oxford English Dictionary*, "captain" could refer to "a chief or headman," "one who stands at the head of others and leads them, or exercises authority over them," "a military leader; a commander of a body of troops, of a fortress, castle, etc.," or "a subordinate officer holding command under a sovereign, a general, or the like." "Commander" referred most broadly to "one who commands or orders anything" or "one who has the control or disposal of anything"; more specifically, to "one who exercises authority, a ruler or leader" or "the officer in command of a military force." "Governor" meant "one who governs, or exercises authoritative control over, subjects or inferiors; a ruler" and "the commander of a company, esp. an armed force, naval or military." Only this last definition is now obsolete. In short, in 1607 all the terms, with the possible exception of "governor," referred to a military leader, sometimes but not always in a subordinate status. Thus we cannot assign, for instance, "captain" to the werowance and "commander" to the cockarouse, making them into anticipatory equivalents of British naval officers. The persistent synonymy in Smith's statements implies that the Powhatan made no distinction between the werowance and the cockarouse either.

If the werowance was a war captain, a "commander" in that sense, was he nothing more? If so, it suggests that leadership among the Powhatan was based on military achievement, not inheritance; it suggests also the corollary that Powhatan society was not ranked but egalitarian, at least in terms of opportunity. We seem to get confirmation of this interpretation in Spelman's saying that nothing distinguished the "king" (presumably he means Powhatan, but the text is unclear) from other persons of high rank except that people gave him unusually lavish gifts when he visited their houses (1910 [1613]:cxiii–cxiv). This otherwise reasonable hypothesis does not, however, take into account all the facts we have about the wero-wance.

In Tidewater Virginia, several persons in one tribe could be called werowance. All the evidence argues not just that they were kin but that they had chiefly status for that reason. They were ranked at least to the extent that one of them was paramount. This was the oldest man. Smith reports Powhatan's statement that his siblings would succeed him in order of sex and age, brothers to sisters and oldest to youngest (1986 [1612]:174, [1624]:196). Although we should not automatically assume that what applied to the mamanatowick also applied to his werowances, in this case it did. Lewis and Loomie report that Don Luis, the Spaniards' captive chief, was the elder brother of the incumbent in his territory, who offered on the don's return to Virginia to relinquish his status in favor of his brother (1953:44). Strachey's detailed discussion of werowances further con-firms the rule, and we have no examples of werowanquas who out-rank their brothers or who rule on their own.

Although in the *Generall Historie* Smith seems to say that the term "cockarouse" means war captain and that it is interchange-able with werowance, other statements represent the cockarouse as foremost a councilor rather than a warrior and as distinct from the werowance (cf. Gleach 1997:34–35). Smith himself implies as much when he says the Chickahominy "are governed by the Priestes and their Assistants or their Elders called *Caw-cawwassoughes*." This is ambiguous: does "Caw-cawwassoughes" refer to the elders or to the "priests," the word for which the English usually write quiyough-cosoughs (Smith 1986 [1612]:172; Whitaker 1613:26)? But Strachey clarifies it in his statement that the Chickahominy are "guyded by their Priests, with the Assistaunce of their Elders whome they call Cawcawwassoughs"; he says explicitly that the Chickahominy do not recognize the status of werowance among themselves (1953 [1612]:69; see Hamor 1615). In the *Generall Historie*, Smith adopts this locution also, except that he says "Priests and their Assistants" (1986 [1624]:103). Beverley's definition of cockarouse as councilor agrees with this earlier use of the word in Strachey and Smith.

Etymology confirms to some extent the trend of the evidence in the colonists' accounts. Geary says that the term "werowance" comes "apparently from *wilaw*-'rich, valuable, precious' (as in Delaware) + *-antesi-* 'exist, get along, have such a manner of life' (as in Fox-Ojibwa-Algonkin *-atesi-*, *-atisi-*, *-adisi-*)" (1991:899). It is cognate with words in other Algonkian languages meaning "rich" or "a rich man, or a man of estimation," or "he is of influence" or "chief" (Barbour 1972:46).[4] A successful warrior and a rich man are not mutually exclusive, and these etymologies in themselves do not preclude our assuming that the Powhatan werowance was simply an outstanding military leader who had thereby achieved considerable political influence and the income that goes with it. The association with wealth is significant, though. Powhatan and his werowances controlled more wealth than did other men; their control of wealth constituted the means to promote life rather than hardship among their people. This function did not cease with the death of a chief but on the contrary became more potent. Even if the chief were, or must be, a noted warrior, the meaning of werowance suggests that his life-giving qualities were more important than his death-dealing ones or, as I argue in connection with sacrifice, that the latter were themselves a means to the former.

Attempts to establish the etymology of cockarouse have so far been less successful, but they are not without value. Although Barbour says that cockarouse was "apparently a Chesapeake area name" and that "the precise derivation is uncertain," he shows its similarity to words in three other Algonkian languages. In two of these it refers to a councilor and in the third to a chief (Barbour 1972:34).[5] As in the case of werowance, the definitions imply an emphasis on governance rather than on warfare. I take up in a later section the military emphasis of the English in describing these two statuses.

Given the etymology of werowance and cockarouse, the various ways in which the English use them, their descriptions of these and other Powhatan social persons, and what we know of other tribes to the south and to the north at that time, the most satisfactory interpretation is that in 1585 and for at least half a century thereafter werowance and cockarouse referred to distinct but not mutually exclusive statuses, ranked with regard to each other and, in the case of the werowance at least, internally as well. The same man might be both but not in the same context. That is, a man who was werowance in his own village was cockarouse in the council of the paramount of his tribe; or he could simply be a cockarouse, either in his own village or in the council of the paramount of his tribe.

The Werowance

In Smith (1986 [1624]:291), we find a summary of the relationship between junior and senior werowances that might come from any anthropologist writing on dual sovereignty: "the younger beares the charge, and the elder the dignitie." This is, in the terms proposed in the Introduction, a complementary opposition between power and authority, respectively. All the evidence we have confirms the werowance's right to command and the execution of those commands by others. Werowances represented the continuity of Powhatan life in the face of the ordinary contingencies of existence. For this reason, they were mummified at death.

The werowance exercised his authority, in part, by judging the accused. We know most about Powhatan's exercise of this function, but there is evidence that lesser werowances acted as judges also. Smith and Strachey call these chiefs "magistrats" as well as kings, commanders, and captains (Smith 1986 [1612]:173; Strachey 1953 [1612]:77), and they liken them to Powhatan in having "power of life and death [over their subjects] at their command" (Smith 1986 [1612]:174; Strachey 1953 [1612]:77). If we take the phrase as Smith's attempt to render the Virginian situation comprehensible in English terms, as I have suggested we must, it becomes evidence of the judicial function of the werowance.

Certainly this was found among the Carolina Algonkians. Harriot reports that "there is punishment ordained for malefactours, as stealers, whoremoongers, and other sortes of wicked doers; some punished with death, some with forfeitures, some with beating, according to the greatnes of the factes," with the implication that the werowance decided which of these, or if any, should be carried out (1972 [1590]:26). The similarity of the Carolina Algonkians to the Virginians justifies the assumption that Powhatan's werowances had a similar obligation. The few relevant comments from the Jamestown colonists support this as well. Archer reports, for instance, that the werowance of Arrohattock himself chased a man of whom the English complained and apparently caused him to be beaten by other men who joined the chase (1910 [1607]:xlviii). From Beverley, we learn that the chief was "Arbiter of all things among them." "They are very severe in punishing ill breeding, of which every Werowance is undisputed Judge, who never fails to lay a rigorous penalty upon it" (Beverley 1947 [1705]:225). He gives an example from Bacon's Rebellion: the werowance had come to set up a treaty with some of the English; one of the men in his party interrupting him, he split the man's skull with his tomahawk and killed him instantly (Beverley 1947 [1705]:225).

The mamanatowick, Powhatan, was possibly the most severe judge among the Powhatan. For this we have independent accounts from both Smith and Spelman. Spelman, indeed, was most forcibly struck by this aspect of Powhatan government, since he says, "my years [ca. 14] and understandinge, made me the less to looke after bycause I thought *th*at Infidels wear lawless yet when I saw sum put to death I asked the cause of ther offence" (1910 [1613]:cx; editors' italics). Spelman reports seeing five executions during his stay among the Indians. Four of these concerned one crime, the murder of a child: the murderers were the child's mother, two people who helped her, and a third who was bribed to keep silent. The other execution was for stealing some copper and beads (presumably shell or bone) from a traveler, "for to steale ther neyburs corne or copper is death" (Spelman 1910 [1613]:cxi).

Spelman describes execution itself also:

> Thos that be conuicted of capitall offences are brought into a
> playne place before ye Kinges [Powhatan's] house when then

he laye, which was at Pomunkeye the chefest house he hath wher one or tow apoynted by the Kinge did bind them hand and foote, which being dunn a great fier was made, Then cam the officer to thos that should dye, and with a shell cutt of[f] ther long locke, which they weare on the leaft side of ther heade, and hangeth that on a bowe before the Kings house Then thos for murther wear Beaten *with* staues till ther bonns weare broken and beinge aliue weare flounge into the fier, the other for robbinge was knockt on yᵉ heade and beinge deade his bodye was burnt. (1910 [1613]:cxi; editors' italics and interpolations)

Spelman's account agrees in the main with Smith's, for whom it is an illustration of his general assertion that the Powhatan "esteemed" their mamanatowick "not only as a king but as halfe a God" (1986 [1612]:174).

> What he commandeth they dare not disobey in the least thing. It is strange to see with what great feare and adoration all these people doe obay this Powhatan. For at his feet they present whatsoever hee commandeth, and at the least frowne of his browe, their greatest spirits will tremble with feare: and no marvell, for he is very terrible and tyrannous in punishing such as offend him.
>
> For example hee caused certaine malefactors to be bound hand and foot, then having of many fires gathered great store of burning coles, they rake these coles round in the forme of a cockpit, and in the midst they cast the offenders to broyle to death. Somtimes he causeth the heads of them that offend him, to be laid upon the altar or sacrificing stone, and one with clubbes beates out their braines. When he would punish any notorious enimie or malefactor, he causeth him to be tied to a tree, and with muscle shels or reeds, the executioner cutteth of his joints one after another, ever casting what they cut of into the fire; then doth he proceed with shels and reeds to case the skinne from his head and face; then doe they rip his belly and so burne him with the tree and all. Thus themselves reported

they executed George Cassen. Their ordinary correction is to beate them with cudgels. Wee have seene a man kneeling on his knees, and at Powhatans command, two men have beat him on the bare skin, till he hath fallen senselesse in a sound, and yet never cry nor complained. (Smith 1986 [1612]:174–175)[6]

Smith's account recalls Archer's report of how the werowance of Arrohattock punished one of his people who had offended the English.[7]

Smith condemns Powhatan as "tyrannous" because Smith takes the form of execution as an expression of the savage egotism of Powhatan himself, for as Smith says, these were punishments for "such as offend him." If this were literally the case, then Powhatan was not a judge but a psychopath. This is, however, an example of seeing license in a chief's actions where one should see obedience to rules; the choice of killing captives is custom's, not the king's (Hocart 1970a:152). What Smith and Strachey represent as the expression of Powhatan's will alone we should understand as the pronouncement of a collective will. This is not evidence of a cruel nature; it is evidence that Powhatan was, as mamanatowick, a judge, responsible for the proper treatment of "malefactours," and we must understand the sentences he handed down as obligatory, not issued at his discretion. The respect in which he was held made him an effective judge, not the reverse, as Smith states.

A singular statement in Strachey is highly suggestive in this context. "We haue observed, how when they would affirme any thing by much earnestnes and triuth, they vse to bynd yt by a kynd of oath, either by the life of the great king, or by pointing vp to the Sun, and clapping the right hand vpon the heart, and sometymes they haue bene vnderstood to sweare by the Manes of their dead father" (Strachey 1953 [1612]:116). This implies an association between the sun itself and Powhatan and between these two and the heart. We do not know what function the Powhatan assigned to the heart; but if they associated it with life (the gesture suggests that they did; see Bragdon 1996:191), then there would be an equivalence: the heart is to one's own life and well-being as the king is to those of the nation or the sun to those of the cosmos. The custom implies also that the king, like the sun, stands for truth; therefore he is a judge. If this were so, he could not be a "tyrant" in the contemporary English sense, at least as far as the Powhatan themselves were concerned. On the contrary, we may suppose that they would consider him derelict if he failed to order such punishment.

The "executions" Spelman and Smith describe were more than the ordained punishment for wrongdoers, however. They constituted a form of sacrifice, as Smith's passing remark that their heads might be laid on a sacrificial stone, the *pawcorance*, suggests. The "executions" follow prescribed rules about means and order. This alone, of course, does not necessarily make a sacrifice of a killing. The method of dealing with the Powhatan criminal is, however, symbolically related to the form of burial for werowances, which I take up in chapter 5. Although we have no direct evidence that the victims were meant as offerings to a spirit, their symbolic connection to chiefly burials, which are manifestly associated with a spirit, makes me think that these victims in their way were intended as offerings and that their deaths were meant to benefit the living who offered them.

The Powhatan treated prisoners of war in the same way, and in fact one early observer of their culture calls the treatment of captives "sacrifice" (Barbour 1969, 1:150). This fact argues that the military importance of the werowance had, in addition to the obvious political motivations, a more profound religious motivation.

As Hocart and Dumézil point out, the king as warrior is structurally equivalent to the king as executioner. Warfare is execution carried on outside the state; in either case, Hocart argues, the king smites the "foes of prosperity" (1970a:157). In both sorts of activity, though, we find the distinction between authority and power maintained. Just as the werowance judged malefactors and ordered their executions, so the most senior werowance would authorize a military maneuver but would take no part in it.

Not every war leader was a werowance. Smith's remark that the leader might be someone "appointed," rather than the werowance, has been cited already. The function of the cockarouse in this regard is considered below. In two descriptions of fighting, both from Smith, it is not clear that the war leader was indeed the, or a, werowance. One of these reports describes a mock battle the Powhatan put on to demonstrate for the English their methods of fighting. They divided themselves into two groups, calling one the Monacan and the other the Powhatan. For officers, each force had "their Captaine" as well as two "Sarjeants" and a "leuitenant" (Smith 1986 [1612]:166–167); in other words, the war leader seems to have had that status for that occasion only. Smith found himself in a real battle like this when he went to Kecoughtan to trade; but again, it is uncertain that the leader was the werowance of Kecoughtan. "Sixtie or seaventie of them, some blacke, some red, some white, some party-coloured, came in a square order, singing and dauncing out of the woods, with their *Okee* (which was an Idoll made of skinnes, stuffed with mosse, all painted and hung with chaines and copper) borne before them: and in this manner, being well armed, with Clubs, Targets, Bowes and Arrowes, they charged the English" (Smith 1986 [1624]:144).

Nevertheless, some werowances did go to war, and they killed people. We have seen that Smith and Strachey equate the werowance with a war leader, and they imply that leading a war party was important if not preeminent in the Powhatan conception of the chief. Evidence besides Smith's and Strachey's glosses on the term "werowance" confirms the military activities of the werowance. The Jesuits' "boy," Alonso, said that Don Luis, the Spaniards' captive werowance, led the Indians' attack on the mission and himself killed one of the missionaries with an arrow and five others with an ax (Lewis and Loomie 1953:110). Wingfield mentions that the werowance of Quiyoughcohannock had been "in the feild against vs" in the summer of 1607 (1910 [1608]:lxxvi). Strachey describes the werowance of Paspahegh as "one of the mightiest and strongest Saluadges that Powhatan had vnder him, and was therefore one of his Champions" (1953 [1612]:67). In each of these cases, however, the warrior-werowance acted as the deputy for someone of yet higher status. As Strachey says, Paspahegh was a subordinate of Powhatan, as was Quiyoughcohannock. Don Luis, it will be remembered, though entitled to the paramount status in his own tribe—possibly the Chiskiac—ceded the status to the younger brother who had been his regent while he was with the Spanish and took a lesser chiefship. Admittedly, we cannot know now whether he massacred the Spanish mission on his own initiative or at the command of his brother(s), but the boy Alonso's bemused report of Luis burying the slain missionary brothers after cleaving their skulls with their own wood-axes—according to one report he wept as well—suggests the latter (Lewis and Loomie 1953:47–48, 119–120, 136).

The most informative passage on the subject is Smith's summary of the discussion between Captain Newport and Powhatan about a joint raid (never undertaken) on the Monacans: "Captaine Nuport would not be seene in it himselfe, being great Werowances, they [Powhatan and Newport] would stay at home, but I, Maister Scrivener, and two of his [Powhatan's] Sonnes, and Opechankanough the King of Pamaunke should have 100. of his men to goe before as though they were hunting; they giving us notise where was the advantage we should kill them. The weomen and young children he wished we should spare, and bring them to him" (1986 [1608]:75). Given Smith's opinions of both principals here, we should imagine this to have been written with heavy irony. Nevertheless, it conveys a separation between authority and power in keeping with much else that we know about werowances. Evidently, Powhatan recognized that the relationship between Newport, on the one hand, and Smith and Scrivener, on the other, was analogous to that between himself and his brother. Opechancanough, Smith, Scrivener, and assorted sons were the effective power to Powhatan's and Newport's authority, and in their turn they would have command over other warriors who would act in effect as beaters for the werowances' hunting.

That Opechancanough was a warrior is plain enough in this passage. We learn, though, that in a different context he delegated this task to his men and waited on the outcome. The circumstance was the capture of Smith in the winter of 1607. Smith reports that "the king of Pamaunck called Opeckankenough with 200 men, invironed me"; they drove Smith into a boggy patch, where being stuck fast he surrendered himself. Then, he says, "they [the warriors] drew me out and led to me to the king" (Smith 1986 [1608]:45–47). We have a clear picture of Opechancanough standing back while his subordinates do the work.

The dialectical hierarchy of the Powhatan that appears in these two passages is confirmed by Powhatan's treatment of Smith himself. Opechancanough, like all werowances, was not absolutely either the authority or the power but assumed a status consistent with the context. He executed commands for his brother within the polity but ordered others within his own tribe. Likewise, in the absence of Newport, whom the Powhatan saw as a werowance, they took Smith as a werowance (Smith 1986 [1612]:248). In Newport's presence, Smith became a person of lower rank—an officer (cockarouse) or a son, or both. Like Opechancanough, Smith did not have an absolute rank in the hierarchy that the Powhatan perceived among the colonists. This, I suggest, is how titles worked among the Powhatan: they were contingent on the company in which one found oneself. This interpretation explains the confusion in the English statements about the status of werowance: sometimes they say he is a king, at other times merely a war leader. Now we see that he could be either but not at the same time.

Powhatan asked that Smith and the others not kill the Monacan women and children but bring them back alive to him. This was usual. "They seldome make warre for lands or goods, but for women and children, and principally for revenge" (Smith 1986 [1612]:165).

"The Weroances, women or Children they put not to death, but keep them Captives" (Strachey 1953 [1612]:109; see Smith 1986 [1612]:166). The examples we have from both the deeper Southeast and the Northeast lead us to expect adoption, slavery, or sacrifice to be the usual fate of captives (Anonymous 1931:253; Hudson 1976:193, 253–255; Kinietz and Voegelin 1939:20–21; Lawson 1709:197; Swanton 1911:124–125, 1929:157; Timberlake 1948:65; Bragdon 1996:226; Morgan 1996:341; Tooker 1991:31–39). The Jamestown colonists, however, say very little about what happened to these people. Smith remarks almost in passing that the captured werowance, women, and children of the Piankatank chief "doe him [Powhatan] service" (1986 [1612]:175), which suggests that they became his slaves and moreover that this was a not unusual fate of such captives.[8] The only other captive werowance we know anything about is John Smith himself, who was adopted as Powhatan's son and given the territory of Capahowosick. I have suggested elsewhere (Williamson 1992) that Powhatan intended by this means to put Smith irrevocably in his debt and thus ensure his subordination— Smith understood none of this, so the stratagem failed—and we might take this as a kind of slavery. But the phrasing of Smith's comment about the Piankatank captives suggests something more like what we are accustomed to think of as slavery: one human being in the control of another, more possession than person. Other than this we have no good evidence for slavery among the Powhatan, although various writers refer to part of the population in terms that leave no doubt as to their inferior, even servile, status. Percy writes that when they first visited Kecoughtan, "the chiefest of them sate all in a rank; the meanest sort brought vs such dainties as they had, and of their bread which they make of their Maiz[e] or Gennea wheat" (1910 [1607]:lxiii; editors' interpolation). In this case, Percy judges the "meanness" of these people's estate by the fact that they wait on the others, but whether they did so as slaves, servants, or commoners acknowledging the superiority of their chiefs is unknown. Beverley says that in the early 18th century there were "people of a

Rank inferiour to the Commons, a sort of Servants among them" (1947 [1705]:226).

Women, children, and the chief became servants, but the fate of a captive common man was sacrifice. The Jamestown colonists usually call it "execution" (and probably among themselves had other terms for it as well). But it seems clear that it was human sacrifice, whether the victim were a "malefactour" or a war captive. In fact, the Powhatan—and perhaps the colonists also—appear to have made no effective distinction between the two. Smith's phrasing in a passage quoted in full earlier is suggestive: "When he would punish any notorious *enimie or malefactor,*" he writes; having described the form of punishment, which he also calls execution, he says, "Thus themselves reported they executed George Cassen" (Smith 1986 [1612]:175; emphasis added). Cassen was one of Smith's companions at the time of his capture (Smith 1986 [1612]:212): he was thus a prisoner of war rather than a thief or murderer in the usual sense. All this confirms Hocart's and Dumézil's views on the equivalence, to a king, of a criminal and a captive: both are enemies of the order the king is bound to maintain.

I conclude, then, that the werowance engaged in warfare for religious as well as for political reasons. Prestige was certainly a motivation for going to war; as Spelman (1910 [1613]:cxiv) says, "And they that kill most of ther enimies are heald the cheafest men amonge them." An ordinary man had this means to achieve renown and influence in his tribe; the status of cockarouse seems to have been at least partly contingent on success in raiding. From what we know about the military activities of the werowance, we may assume that his own prestige depended on it, too. Acquiring captives to be "servants" was another reason for raiding. But the most important reason for the chief engaging in warfare was that a raid or battle provided captives to be sacrificed. Providing the sacrificial victim and by this means ensuring the life of the community are obligations of kings worldwide (see Coomaraswamy 1942:5), and the Powhatan werowances were no exception.

Providing sacrifices was the most important form of gift-giving, itself the most important activity of Powhatan chiefs. The etymology of the word "werowance" implies that for all these Algonkian-speakers, high status and the control of wealth were inseparable. From the first, the comparative affluence of Powhatan chiefs attracted attention, if only because the colonists used the chief as a measure of the wealth of his domain. But we have seen also Strachey's outrage that Powhatan took to himself a great proportion of the products of his people. Strachey accuses him of reducing his subjects to penury to satisfy his own greed and calls him a tyrant.

Taking their cue partly from these sources, some anthropological interpretations (e.g., Feest 1966; Turner 1985:201; Rountree 1989:82; Barker 1992; cf. Gleach 1997:54–55) conclude also that chiefs and their followers were motivated by self-interest alone and that they used religious authority to persuade those less fortunate of the legitimacy of their claims to superiority. In this they may not have been uniformly successful, engendering instead a resentment that led people to hide their valuables from the tax-gatherer (Potter 1993:173). This interpretation seems unrealistic, though. Many ethnographers have remarked, as Lorna Marshall does of the !Kung, that "headmen are as thin as the rest" (1967:38)—any surplus they may achieve, by gift or by garner, must be seen to go to someone else.[9] As Clastres remarks, "Greed and power are incompatible; to be a chief it is necessary to be generous." In an Indian chief, "generosity . . . appears to be more than a duty: it is a bondage" (Clastres 1977:22–23). Here, too, we must ask why the Powhatan should be so markedly different from people in the rest of the Americas—or, rather, whether they are.

Characterizing the polity as a redistributive chiefdom, as many do, is still inadequate. It comes closer to the mark, though, because it recognizes the chief's activities as exchange rather than acquisition and, in doing so, draws attention to the economic function of the werowance without, however, offering an explicit moral assessment of his activities. Such an approach views exchange as a purely economic activity, to be understood only in utilitarian terms: the satisfaction of individual wants or needs, the increase of one's own wealth, the correction of naturally occurring shortages and surpluses. The chief is then primarily an economic actor whose specific function is the distribution, or redistribution, of things that he and his subjects produce or acquire from elsewhere (e.g., Sahlins 1972:130–148). This arrangement, so the argument goes, has practical value for both the society and the chief. It levels most economic inequality—the chief's wealth is obviously an exception—since the chief can compel the fortunate to give to him so that he can give to the less fortunate. By this means he not only maintains his own control over his polity, but he also prevents anyone else attempting a similar form of control. Meanwhile, he in effect buys himself followers with his feasts and his rewards for valor, and he forestalls any material dissatisfactions that could lead to insurrection.

Although chiefship and exchange both have such practical economic and political aspects, this argument is unsatisfactory because it assumes that those practical consequences are the causes of and the reasons for the customs. The relationship between control of wealth and political preeminence is taken to be linear and necessary; whereas it is at least as likely in any given case that the chief controls wealth *because* he is a chief.

Saying this implies nothing about the origins of chiefship, or about any individual's assuming that status, but rather about the reciprocal relation between status and exchange. According to Mauss, "To give is to show one's superiority, to be more, to be higher in rank, *magister*" (1990:74); but Mauss gives temporal primacy neither to giving nor to superiority. If competition is possible, overwhelming generosity allows one to win. If the hierarchy is already established, generosity confirms one's position therein. Gift-giving implies these poles of possibility at every level, from the institution to the individual event, just as political structure moves necessarily between poles of continuity and innovation. It is impossible to know, sometimes even at the event itself, whether structure or event is in the ascendant (see Gledhill 1994:128–129). The most that can be said, of Powhatan werowances at any rate, is that they were—like the contemporary English noble—both politically superior and supremely generous.

In any case, a purely economic interpretation of the chief's liberality is too narrow. Two concepts require attention before we can arrive at an adequate representation of Powhatan chiefs: that of the gift and that of the chief or king.[10] While it is true that each has an economic aspect, this is not their sole nor even their most important raison d'être.

A gift is a " 'total' social phenomenon"; it is simultaneously juridical, religious, aesthetic, political, structural, and economic (Mauss 1990:3, 38, 78–79). Gifts may be "total" in another sense as well, part of what Mauss calls a "*system of total services.*" Such a system includes not just material items and conventional services (e.g., helping someone roof a house) but "banquets, rituals, military services, women, children, dances, festivals, and fairs" (Mauss 1990:5–6), to which we may add parts of persons (e.g., breast milk, semen, blood, organs).

Thus exchange has an importance far beyond the merely utilitarian. There can be no social relationship without an exchange of gifts; likewise, exchange implies a social relationship and provides its index (see Needham 1975:34). People give things to each other not because they have need of each other's possessions—the exchange of gifts rarely leaves either party materially better off than before (Mauss 1990:9, 19, 72)—but because they have need of each other. The gift goes in earnest for the person, or rather the group represented by the person. It is never completely alienable but remains, or retains, a part of the donor. Accepting a gift means accepting whoever gives it also, which is to say the social tie implicit in the offer; the corollary is that to refuse the gift is to refuse the giver (Mauss 1990:11–13, 33). Mauss identifies three obligations of gift-giving: the obligation to give, to identify or maintain a social relationship; the obligation to receive, to agree that the relationship exists and to accept it; and to reciprocate (1990:14, 39). Because accepting a gift means accepting something of the person who gives it—or, better, the group represented by the donor—the recipient incurs a debt to the donor that must be repaid. Symmetrical exchanges, involving sometimes the identical object passed by A to B and then back again, indicate a relationship of equality; asymmetrical ones, by contrast, indicate hierarchy.

The exchanges between a chief and his followers may be shown to conform to these general principles. They are expressions of mutual (social) dependence as well as of hierarchy, part of a system of total services. The economic necessity of chiefly prestations in most cases is nonexistent. Chiefs give things to their people whether the people need them or not, because what is important is that something be given, not the economic value of the gift. Because high status requires unusual generosity, the chief is under the greatest obligation to give lest he lose his prestige. Quantity alone is not the issue, of course, nor is quality per se. Since a gift carries with it something of the donor's personality, a chief's gift confers on its recipient something of the chief's prestige.

Like the gift, the chief or king is himself a total social phenomenon (see Feeley-Harnik 1985:300; Fortes and Evans-Pritchard 1940:16). The political and economic aspects of kingship, which receive such disproportionate attention in anthropology, are only two of its aspects, and they are not clearly distinguishable from the others: juridical, structural, aesthetic, religious. In the king, social particulars dissolve into a general whole. Because he represents, as Mauss says of gifts, "the totality of [his] society and its institutions" (1990:78), the chief can represent his polity politically, whether speaking for those who make it up or confirming its existence as a political entity by his own presence (see Fortes and Evans-Pritchard 1940:16). Like Louis XIV, he *is* his polity. This explains the radical consequence of anything the king does and likewise the restrictions under which he lives (remembering that licentiousness may itself be obligatory). The consequences are more than social, however; they are cosmic.

This is not to deny that a chief is a political actor. The definition of "political" is much contested, but if we say minimally that it is the process of precipitating a following (Wagner 1975; Huber 1980), then it is obvious that a chief must be political at all times. That is, he must be perceived to be doing the right thing, which is to regulate the world, whether in terms of relations among people—settling disputes, suing for peace—or among the elements. The generosity of a chief in providing for the poor is as much a means of regulation as is offering a sacrifice. Nothing he does is without consequence. The men of the Renaissance understood this, which is why they dwelled so minutely on the person and actions of the king, and the Jamestown colonists agreed with the Powhatan on this point.

We can understand neither gifts nor chiefs exclusively in terms of economics or politics nor of both together. The liberality of chiefs represents an intensification of total social phenomena: a person representing a social totality engaging in an activity with the same significance. The wealth of the chief and his distribution of it are alike means by which he confers life and prosperity on his people. Indeed, he really has nothing of "his own" as a private person. Rather, he is the steward of the group's wealth, deploying it on their behalf for their benefit. As a microcosm, everything he does has an effect on the world; by being rich and generous and by living richly, he makes bountiful the macrocosm that he represents (Hocart 1970a:202).

This, rather than simply the quantity of items exchanged or the immediate political consequences of their distribution (much less the threat of violence), explains the superiority of the chief. The gift of life must always be more valuable than anything a lesser person could provide in return. Some return is necessary, otherwise the recipient becomes a slave, which is to say a thing. Commoners are not slaves but persons; therefore they offer tribute to their chief. But they cannot give him life, so they remain minister to his magister (Mauss 1990:74). Nevertheless, the chief remains dependent on his followers, since their obligation to him lasts only so long as they perceive that he observes his obligation to them. In this sense a chief is always "elected," whether or not his position is also inherited.

What are conventionally called the economic activities of Powhatan werowances, like their treatment of prisoners and wrongdoers, must be understood as collective phenomena rather than expressions of individual gratification or promotion. The sum total of the chief's exchanges with his followers, like their ordained executions, was a means by which the chiefs secured the general welfare and thus maintained their status.

The mamanatowick, Powhatan, and presumably all werowances acquired wealth from tribute, trade, and their own labors. Powhatan retained a good deal of this and stored it in his "treasure houses" at Uttamussack in anticipation of his death. We do not know whether the other werowances had similar treasures, but they probably did. Most men, if not all, had such a store, if smaller than a chief's: "Their Corne and (indeed) their Copper, [stone] hatchetts, Howes, beades, perle and most things with them of value according to their owne estymation, they hide one from the knowledge of another in the grownd within the woods, and so keepe them all the yeare, or vntill they haue fitt vse for them, as the Romains did their moneys and treasure" (Strachey 1953 [1612]:115).[11]

The fact that Powhatan's subjects gave him tribute is clear despite Strachey's prejudice, even if we reject (as therefore untrustworthy) his estimate of 80 percent of the people's products. Smith's accounts confirm the custom. He mentions that during his visit to Powhatan shortly after his release, "the King, conducting mee to the River, shewed me his Canowes, and described unto me how hee sent them over the [Chesapeake] Baye, for tribute Beades, and also what Countries paid him Beads, Copper or Skins" (Smith 1986 [1608]:69). Spelman refers in passing to tribute while describing Powhatan's store of treasure. "All the Kings goods and presents *that* are sent him, as ye Cornne. But ye beades or Crowne or Bedd w*hich* ye Kinge of England sent him are in ye gods house at Oropikes" (Spelman 1910 [1613]:cv; editors' italics). Smith's comment that "what others can steale, their King receiveth" (1986 [1612]:81) sounds like a kind of tribute as well, but the little evidence we have suggests that it was not perhaps a serious obligation. In Archer's account of the return of stolen items at Arrohattock, for instance, the booty is still in the hands of the thieves and their comrades, a fact that occasioned no surprise or wrath in the werowance, who witnessed its return to the English (1910 [1607]:xiv). By contrast, Smith reports (1986 [1608]:83) the werowance of Nansemund returning a hatchet that someone had stolen while the English were there.

Strachey's animadversions on Powhatan's rapacity include the information that Powhatan received his tribute from his werowances rather than—or perhaps as well as—from his subjects directly: "he [the werowance of the area] tythes to the great king of all the Commodityes growing in the same, or of what ells his shiere brings forth apperteyning to the Land or Rivers, Corne, beasts, Pearle, Fowle, Fish, Hides, Furrs, Copper, beades, by what meanes soever obteyned, a peremptory rate [the 80 percent] sett downe" (1953 [1612]:63). Strachey then adds something the significance of which he evidently did not understand: "they [the werowances] dare not dresse yt [a skin] and put yt on vntill he [Powhatan] haue seene yt and refused yt" (1953 [1612]:87). Strachey here is using the skin synecdochically for the entire production of the polity. Powhatan did not in fact seize four-fifths of his people's wealth; he was just offered the refusal of it.

So much is confirmed by a passage in Smith in which he contrasts his own acuity with the dullness of Captain Newport, and he means us to understand also why he insists that Powhatan is grasping and untrustworthy. To an anthropologist, though, Newport emerges as the better judge. The occasion was the first meeting between Powhatan and Newport, shortly after Smith's release from captivity. Smith had described Newport in such terms as to make Powhatan recognize that he was Smith's superior (1986 [1608]:57, 75, [1612]:215). Smith and Newport met Powhatan at Werowocomoco, where the mamanatowick entertained them impressively. After ceremonious preliminaries the English wished to trade with their host. According to Smith, Powhatan explicitly refused to trade with Newport like a commoner.[12] He quotes Powhatan as saying, "Captain Newport it is not agreeble with my greatnes in this pedling manner to trade for trifles, and I esteeme you a great werowans. Therefore lay me down all your commodities togither, what I like I will take, and in recompence give you that I thinke fitting their value" (Smith 1986 [1612]:217, [1608]:71). Smith's opinion, which he conveyed to his superior, was that Powhatan's "intent was but to cheat us," a warning to which Newport paid no attention (1986 [1612:217).

Since Smith conveys his ambivalence about the Virginia Indians in many other passages, it is easy to dismiss this contradictory picture of Powhatan as but another instance of it. Smith presents him as both a liberal host and a chiseling trader, an inconsistency in keeping with what he considered the typical Virginia Indian personality: "They are inconstant in everie thing, but what feare constraineth them to keep. Craftie, timerous, quick of apprehension and very ingenuous" (1986 [1612]:160).

Smith, then, interprets his adversary psychologically. But Powhatan's actions are consonant with a collectively held image of chiefly status and its relations to subordinates, particularly in the matter of gift-giving.[13] Just as the show of strength and wealth was obligatory in certain chiefly meetings, so was Powhatan's seeming illiberality in his trade with Smith and Newport, which represents another side of the relationship between Powhatan chiefs. The key lies in Powhatan's statement about the appropriate way for a werowance to trade with him.[14] "Hee seeming to despise the nature of a Merchant, did scorne to sell, but we freely should give him, and he liberally would requite us" (Smith 1986 [1608]:71). Smith is appalled because he inteprets this in terms of the purchase of commodities in Europe, where the seller and the buyer must be mutually wary. Newport, more sympathetic to Powhatan meanings, understands that this is an exchange of gifts and responds accordingly. And indeed, we must take it that the Powhatan had a gift, not a commodity, economy.[15] Powhatan is instructing both Smith and Newport in the etiquette of exchanging gifts with one's social superior—a werowance with the mamanatowick. This, then, is a particular kind of gift exchange: a presentation of tribute and its acknowledgment.

From a comment of Smith's we can infer that the same relationship obtained between a werowance and commoners. After his release from captivity, Smith received the same treatment from the Indians that Powhatan had told Smith was appropriate to himself: "Such acquaintance I had amongst the Indians, and such confidence they had in me, as neare the Fort they would not come till I came to them, every of them calling me by my name, would not sell anything till I had first received their presents, and what they had that I liked, they deferred to my discretion: but after acquaintance, they usually came into the Fort at their pleasure" (Smith 1986 [1608]:61–63).

Because Newport and Smith were English, not Powhatan, and because Smith had already established a pattern of trading English items for corn throughout the James River region, we cannot be sure that it was usual for Powhatan to offer his werowances any more return for their offerings than a part of the offerings themselves, even though he promised to do so for Newport and Smith. But according to Smith and Strachey, the tribute itself was a return for each werowance's territory. "They all [werowances] knoe their severall landes, and habitations, and limits, to fish, fowle, or hunt in, but they hold all of their great Werowance Powhatan, unto whome they pay tribute of skinnes, beades, copper, pearle, deare, turkies, wild beasts and corne" (Smith 1986 [1612]:174; see Strachey 1953 [1612]:63). The very land on which these Indians lived was the gift of Powhatan. A return of some kind was necessary, even though it could never equal the original gift.

Certain of Powhatan's actions made that land fruitful as well, making the gift a double one. Sacrifice is one such, but Spelman reports quite a different ritual that had the same purpose. He says that the "king's," that is, Powhatan's, gardens were sown and reaped not by himself and his family but by all the people together (Spelman 1910 [1613]:cxii).[16] "The setting of ye Kings corne," according to him, took this form:

a day is apoynted wherin great part of ye cuntry people meete
who *with* such diligence worketh as for the most part all y^e
Kinges corne is sett on a daye Aftre w*hi*ch setting the Kinge
takes the croune w*hi*ch ye Kinge of England sent him being
brought him by tow men, and setts it on his heade w*hi*ch
dunn the people goeth about the corne in maner backwardes
for they going before, and the king followinge ther faces are
always toward the Kinge exspectinge when he should flinge
sum beades amonge them w*hi*ch his custum is at that time to
doe makinge thos w*hi*ch had wrought to scramble for them
But to sume he fauors he bids thos *th*at carry his Beades to
call such and such unto him unto whome he giueth beads into
ther hande and this is the greatest curtesey he doth his people
(Strachey 1910 [1613]:cxii; editors' italics)

The purely economic aspects of this are apparent, but they should
not lead us to overlook the symbolic, which was at least as important. This would appear to have been a ritual for maintaining fertility. Spelman is clear that the recipients of this bounty went around
the cornfield backward, followed by Powhatan walking forward and
throwing the beads toward them as they walked. When Spelman
observed him, Powhatan wore the copper crown and red robe sent
him by King James I. So much suggests ritual; but in this context,
Hall's argument that in the deep Southeast beads were structurally
analogous to white body emissions is suggestive. Powhatan circled
his newly planted field symbolically shooting semen all over his subjects, his workers, who faced him just as a woman might face a man
during intercourse. His actions recall the "Bead-Spitter" of southeastern mythology (Swanton 1929:2–7, 126–129, 172–181), who Hall
argues is the southeastern analogue of One Hunahpu, by whose
spittle Blood Woman conceived Hunaphu and Xbalanque, the Hero
Twins of Maya mythology (1989:255; Tedlock 1985:342). But by this
action Powhatan ensured more than the fertility of his own fields
or the fertility of his workers. If he was, metaphorically, his polity,
then his fields were likewise all fields and the fertility of the one

guaranteed that of the others. Thus he not only gave the land to the werowances but made it productive as well.

Powhatan's bestowing pearls and beads in this way is redistribution, since originally they came to him as tribute from various subject tribes. The generic designation is insufficient, though, because assuming that what is valuable is inherently so ignores the particular cultural concepts that the gifts and their distribution express: in this case, fertility and life. The possibility of conferring these in turn expresses and thus maintains hierarchical relationships. The mamanatowick's gifts of pearls and beads, whether broadcast or placed in the hands of favored followers, are an example of gifts from authority to agent among the Powhatan. When Ralph Hamor went as Governor Dale's ambassador to Powhatan to ask for his younger daughter as Dale's wife, Powhatan felt about Hamor's neck for a string of pearls he had given the governor on his arrival with the request that Dale give it to anyone who was his ambassador; otherwise, the man was a runaway from the fort, whom Powhatan was bound to return. The mamanatowick had assumed this obligation following the peace established by the marriage of Pocahontas (Hamor 1615:38–39). Earlier, the English had received from Powhatan strings of pearls—"a greate bracelet, and a chaine of pearle" (that is, a bracelet and necklace of pearls)—together with a formal speech explaining their meaning and "a chaine of pearle" from Opechancanough. Smith says these were overtures for peace between the Powhatan and the English (1986 [1612]:149, 255, [1624]:198). I question this interpretation, though, because this use of pearls is incongruent with everything else reported about gifts of pearls among the Powhatan. It is possible, if not probable, that these signified rather Powhatan's abiding conviction that he was Smith's superior and Smith but his lieutenant.[17]

Another form of "redistribution," which likewise represents more than simply buying political complaisance, is found in the obligation of the werowance or of Powhatan himself to entertain important visitors. In doing so, the chiefs symbolize their people and the collective wealth of the tribes. The welcome they accorded the colonists (at least initially) is that which they provided for any visitor of note. According to Smith,

> If any great commander arrive at the habitation of a Werowance, they spread a mat as the Turkes do a carpet for him to sit upon. Upon an other right opposite they sit themselves. They doe all with a tunable voice of showting bid him welcome. After this doe 2. or more of their chiefest men make an oration, testifying their love. Which they do with such vehemency and so great passions, that they sweate till they drop, and are so out of breath they can scarce speake. So that a man would take them to be exceeding angry or starke mad. Such victuall as they haue, they spend freely, and at night where his lodging is appointed, they set a woman fresh painted red with *Pocones* and oile, to be his bedfellow. (1986 [1612]:167–168)[18]

Beverley's account of the welcoming of visitors is similar, although written a century later (1947 [1705]:188–189). The mats, feasts, and orations that so comforted the colonists, which they compared to the liberality of European and Asian princes, show the visitors to have been, in Powhatan eyes, "notable." In the form of welcome we find also another expression of the relationship between authority and power among the Powhatan. The authority of the chief is clear not only in his representing his chiefdom by such liberality but in ordaining the welcome that was, however, accomplished for the most part by others: the orators and the "bedfellow."

Smith lays great emphasis on the speeches of welcome. We know from various reports that chiefly speech was important. In this the Powhatan conform to Lowie's observation that a "typical American chief" must be among other things a "prolix Polonius" (1967:76); Clastres, enlarging on Lowie, proposes that speech may be as obligatory as generosity for a chief (1977:130). The rules of gift-giving apply to speech as well. Speaking to an acquaintance is obligatory, as is returning such a greeting. Just as a chief gives in the name of his tribe, so also he or his representative speaks in its name. A visiting werowance received a verbal welcome from the entire village through the medium of its chief, representing his political group.

Personal names constitute a special case of speech, and here, too, we find the werowance obliged to make gifts. According to Strachey, a baby boy got his first name from his mother, who thereby expressed her affection for her son. A father might do the same for a daughter, as Powhatan did for Pocahontas. Later the boy's father gave him a second name that reflected the boy's growing skills as a hunter or the like. Still later in his life, the boy, now a man, might do some remarkable act—Strachey mentions a "Strayne of witte" but gives pride of place to military exploits—"the king taking notice of the same, doth then not only in open viewe and solemnely reward him with some Present of Copper, or Chayne of Perle and Beades, but doth then likewise (and which they take for the most emynent and supreme favour) giue him a name answerable to the Attempt" (Strachey 1953 [1612]:113-114). Pearls or beads as a chiefly gift we have encountered already at Powhatan's planting ceremony. Copper was a somewhat different category of gift but no less a statement of hierarchical relations: both Powhatan and subordinate werowances used copper to recruit other chiefs as allies when planning a raid (Strachey 1953 [1612]:68, 107). What distinguishes this particular presentation, Strachey suggests, is the addition of a name, quite as if the werowance were now the recipient's father. At a wedding, according to Spelman, the werowance would take the place of the groom's father if the father were dead. It may be that this act of adding a name formally inducted him into the chief's council as a cockarouse also, but on that point we have no direct evidence.

These facts suggest an asymmetry of gift-giving consonant with the hierarchical relations among the parties to the exchanges. But other evidence suggests a symmetrical exchange of foodstuffs and valuables between superior and subordinate. Powhatan's tribute included everything the people of a tribe produced: "Corne, beasts, Pearle, Fowle, Fish, Hides, Furrs, Copper, beades" (Strachey 1953 [1612]:63). Likewise, Spelman reports that when a werowance visited the house of a subject, his hosts presented him with food or a gift of beads or copper (1910 [1613]:cxiii). Since we find the same kinds of gift given and received between persons of different status, we must assume that hierarchy was expressed in other terms. Relative quantity may have been one of them; quality certainly was, as Strachey notes that "the most rare and delicate of the [fish], and the best and wholsommest of the [Fowle] are now forbidden them [the werowances] and reserved and perserved to Powhatan" (1953 [1612]:92). The circumstances of the giving may also have contributed to the meaning of a gift, a string of beads given ceremoniously in public having had a different meaning from the same kind of string handed over privately in a house. But however these kinds of gift symbolized social relationships, what was most important for the Powhatan was the fact that the means of life were gifts from superiors to subordinates, and any return the subordinate might make would necessarily be insufficient to establish equality.

The affinal exchange obligations of a chief provide an interesting case. Werowances, Powhatan included, had plural wives: "For the Kings have as many weomen as they will, his Subjects two, and most but one" (Smith 1986 [1608]:61; Spelman 1910 [1613]:cvii). The situation is not at all uncommon, and Lévi-Strauss (1967) has suggested that this represents a kind of exchange between the chief or headman and the group as a whole, his provision of security in exchange for the group's provision of wives for economic and other purposes. But it is possible to see in the Powhatan data another sort of pattern, one that is congruent with that already set forth in regard to more obvious items of tribute.

According to Spelman, a chief informed his councilors of his wish to marry. They in turn sought out the most attractive women of the country for his consideration. He chose one from among them and presented to her parents what he considered an appropriate bride-price. Bride-price, in the form of beads and copper, was appropriate for any marriage, but among commoners the woman's father or "kinsfolk," not the suitor, set the amount (Spelman 1910

[1613]:cvii–cviii). The werowance determining the bride-price is similar to Powhatan's style with Captain Newport and suggests that in a chiefly marriage the wife was a form of tribute from his people, for which, as usual, some return must be made. We know little about marriage to the sisters or daughters of chiefs, but we do know that bride-price was appropriate. Hamor states that Powhatan refused the proposal of a marriage between Pocahontas's younger sister and Dale because Powhatan had, in what Hamor says were Powhatan's own words, "sould [her] within these few daies to be wife to a great *Weroance* for two bushels of *Roanoke* . . . and it is true she is already gone with him, three daies iorney from me." Hamor explains that "roanoke" was "a small kinde of beades" (1615:41–42).[19] Strachey does not mention bride-price but says instead that a suitor—a werowance included—made gifts of game or of "Sommer fruictes and berryes" to his intended to show that he could and would look after her as her husband. Having reached an agreement with her parents, he would give the woman some gift of beads or copper as a betrothal gift. Assuming that their mutual affection developed, they were married when the man had built her a house and furnished it with household items such as dishes and mats (Strachey 1953 [1612]:113).

Unlike an ordinary husband, a chief could, or would, send a wife away after a brief period of marriage. "As he [Powhatan] is wearie of his women, hee bestoweth them on those that best deserve them at his hands" (Smith 1986 [1612]:174). Spelman says that as soon as the wife had a child, the werowance sent her away (Spelman does not say where to, but one infers to her parents' house), but he made provision to maintain her and her child "while it is younge." At some point (probably when it was weaned, but the sources do not say how long Powhatan women nursed their babies), he took the child back and gave it into the keeping of someone else—Spelman is vague about this—at which time the young woman was free to marry another (Spelman 1910 [1613]:cviii). According to Strachey, a werowance's first wife could not be divorced or otherwise set aside, but any wives he took thereafter were "(as yt were) mercinary, hired but by Covenaunt and Condicion for a tyme" (1953 [1612]:112). If, however, the chief kept them for more than about a year, he "must ever keepe them how deformed, diseased or vncompanionable soever they maie proue" (Strachey 1953 [1612]:112).

In the custom of setting subsequent wives aside we may have a system of concubinage, or something like the Natchez arrangement whereby the Great Sun married a number of women but set most of them up in households in their own villages rather than bringing them to live with him (Swanton 1911:96). If this was the case, the English obviously misunderstood the "sending away." Undoubtedly, plural marriages, however brief, conferred political benefits, as in the case of Powhatan himself. Smith's statement that Powhatan "bestowed them" on his followers, even if it applies only to Powhatan, suggests another political benefit: the gift of a wife of the mamanatowick to reward a deserving henchman.

Clastres (1977:29–30) rejects the proposition that the chief or headman marrying many more women than any other man in his group is a form of exchange because, he says, the chief can never return sufficient to the group to recompense them for the women they give up (Lévi-Strauss 1967 to the contrary notwithstanding). But in the case of the Powhatan, we seem to have just that: the chief does marry frequently, but few of those wives stay with him—he gives them back to the group. It appears, then, that werowances, including Powhatan, kept not only things in circulation, they also kept women in circulation.

There can be no doubt that gifts received of a chief were more highly valued than gifts from other persons or that the werowance individually made more and larger gifts than anyone else. If this were all, he would be simply a glorified commoner. The argument here, though, is that the Powhatan recognized a qualitative difference between chiefs and commoners, of which the quantitative difference was an expression, and that that difference was the chiefs' ability to convey life, literally, with their gifts. The example of Powhatan casting pearls—or other beads—before his followers best indicates this.

More generally, a werowance's acts of generosity mimic those of the creators. Strachey tells us of two, one called Ahone and one whom he identifies as the Great Hare. Ahone, an otiose divinity, Strachey calls "the good and peceable god"; by his very existence he caused the orderly movements of heavenly bodies, sunshine, the fructification of the earth, and all the good things of life (Strachey 1953 [1612]:89). The Great Hare, according to a myth, created the land and the water; deer for the land and fish for the water; and finally human beings, to whom he gave these for sustenance. Moreover, he caused the original deer, which was killed and eaten by the gods of the four winds, to become many by transforming each of its hairs into a single deer (Strachey 1953 [1612]:102). In other words, both the land and its ability to produce are divine gifts, as is the order of the world. Powhatan imitated these divinities by parceling out the land among his werowances and making it fruitful; very possibly the werowances did the same within their own domains. Moreover, chiefs routinely gave deer and corn as gifts, and the deer, at least, was itself a divine gift to humanity. In imitating gods, the werowance became godlike and conferred with his material gifts the gift of life itself. Thus Strachey came closer to Powhatan ideas than he knew when he claimed to see "sparkles of divinity" in Powhatan.

The parallel between werowance and divinity goes further. Just as Ahone caused and maintained order in the whole world, the werowance maintained it in his role as judge. His warrior aspect is perhaps found in the actions of the Great Hare who, according to the myth, "reproved . . . and droue . . . away" four "Caniball Spirritts," otherwise the four winds, who wished to eat the Hare's newly created humans (Strachey 1953 [1612]:102). "Driving away" is not the same as killing an enemy, but both actions protect the kingdom from chaotic attack.

The responsibility of the werowance to provide and maintain the man or men who were the religious authorities in each tribe represents another form of assurance against catastrophe. The Powhatan called these quiyoughcosoughs. Each territory, or tribe, had at least one resident quiyoughcosough living in a "temple" (Smith 1986 [1612]:169) who was there at the behest of the werowance. Strachey writes, "In every Territory of a Weroance is a Temple and a Priest [quiyoughcosough] peradventure 2. or yet 3. yet happie doth that Weroance accompt himself who can deteyne with him a *Quiyough-quisock* of the best graue luckye well instructed in their misteryes, and beloved of their god and such a one is no lesse honoured then was Dianaes priests at Ephesus for whome they have their more pryvate Temples with Oratories and Chauncells therein according as is the dignity and reverence of the *Quiyoughquisock,* which the Weroane wilbe at charge to build vpon purpose" (1953 [1612]:88). Someone— the werowance, the ordinary people, or both—supplied the resident quiyoughcosough with food as well, since he had no garden and hunted or fished only rarely and as recreation (Whitaker 1613:26; Beverley 1947 [1705]:213). In return, the quiyoughcosough guarded the mummies of deceased werowances and their treasures, cured the sick, identified "malefactours," found game, and shared the governance of the tribe with the chief. The relationship between werowance and quiyoughcosough, which I examine in detail in chapter 5, is the primary form of dual sovereignty found among the Powhatan.

The Powhatan werowance assured his people's well-being and prosperity judicially, economically, socially, and spiritually. He was an aesthetic object, too, covered with pearls, copper, red paint, and sometimes spangles, moving or sitting in a manner intended to excite the admiration and awe of the beholder. He was, in short, the embodiment of his polity, "the totality of society and its institutions" (Mauss 1990:78; see Bragdon 1996:153–155). As Smith says, he was its dignity also. His complementary subordinate was the cockarouse.

The Cockarouse

The colonists translate the term "cockarouse" as "captain," "elder," "councilor," "brave fellow," and possibly "chief man." The etymology, so far as it can be determined, confirms that a cockarouse was a councilor; Smith alone says he was also a "captain" or war leader.

Only three colonial sources use the word "cockarouse": Smith, Strachey, and Beverley. But many sources, including these, use such phrases as "the better sort" or "the chief men." Percy says that when the colonists first visited Kecoughtan, shortly after their arrival in the Chesapeake, "the chiefest of them sate all in a rank; the meanest sort brought vs such dainties as they had" (1910 [1607]:lxiii). Smith's descriptions of Powhatan in state surrounded by his "chiefe men" have been quoted. He mentions noticing during his captivity that "each morning in the coldest frost, the principall [men] to the number of twentie or thirtie, assembled themselves in a round circle, a good distance from the towne, where they told me they there consulted where to hunt the next day" (Smith 1986 [1608]:59). Possibly the "principall" were the same as the "better sort," whom he distinguishes from the rest of the population in that they had better food, finer clothing (of skins, not plant materials, and decorated with paint, copper, or beads; or of woven feathers), and that "before their dinners and suppers, [they] will take the first bit, and cast it in the fire; which is all the grace they are known to use" (Smith 1986 [1612]:152–153, 161, 171). Strachey distinguishes the werowance of Paspahegh from one of his "Cronockoes or chief men," both killed during a skirmish outside Jamestown fort (1953 [1612]:67). Spelman, too, distinguishes the "king" from the "chefe sort" in a passage quoted earlier. In another passage, Strachey refers to the "councellors" whom the werowance consults before undertaking a raid (1953 [1612]:104), and Hamor notes in connection with the diplomatic maneuvers resulting from the capture of Pocahontas that Powhatan "could not without long aduise & delibertion with his Councell, resolue vpon any thing" (1615:6).

Smith reports the Powhatan translation of the Jamestown colonists' social hierarchy: "Captaine Newports greatnesse I had so described, as they conceyved him the chiefe, the rest his children, Officers, and servants" (1986 [1608]:63).[20] This has the potential to tell us about ranks and ranking in Powhatan society. The trick is whether the items in series represent distinct statuses or parallel ways of referring to subordinate status. For reasons that are perhaps apparent already, I prefer the second reading. The "children, Officers, and servants" are variations on the status the English render as cockarouse. We have seen that Smith, a werowance to the Powhatan, was also Newport's "child," and in the projected raid he was to assume the status of "officer" while Newport "stayed at home." Likewise, Powhatan's own sons were to lead this raid with their uncle, Opechancanough, and the English officers. Evidently, Smith and Powhatan's sons, if not Scrivener and Opechancanough, were present at the conference where all this was decided, acting as councilors as well.

What "servant" may mean is not so easily resolved. In some cases it must mean war captives, but in others it referred to cockarouses. We have many instances of people obeying Powhatan's orders. In his account of his abortive execution, Smith says not that Powhatan was about to beat his brains out but that a number of those present in the house prepared to do so. The action followed "a long consultation" (Smith 1986 [1624]:151), implying that the paramount was in council: thus those who leaped to do Powhatan's bidding were also his councilors, or cockarouses. On a later occasion, when a trading party headed by Newport visited Powhatan, Powhatan had dinner sent to the English aboard their boat (they would not spend the night ashore); the next day "sixe or seven of the Kings chiefe men" waded through icy mud to carry Smith to the shore from a stranded canoe (Smith 1986 [1608]:71, 73). Powhatan's sizeable bodyguard might also be considered "servants" in this context, as might Quiyoughcohannock's "train" (Percy 1910 [1608]:lxv).

Indeed, werowances had servants, too. I have already referred to Percy's statement that "the meaner sort" served food to the English at Kecoughtan and to the difficulties of interpreting his meaning. Strachey refers to messengers of the chief coursing through the countryside hitting men on the back to conscript them for military service in a projected raid. Archer describes the werowance of Arrohattock and several of his men chasing another man who had annoyed the English by crowding into their boat in what they took to be a suspicious manner. This posse dealt with the offender out of sight of the English, but as they all returned carrying switches the explorers concluded they had beaten the miscreant (Archer 1910 [1607]:xlviii). High-ranking women had servants, usually themselves women. Archer's description of the werowanqua of Appomattox mentions an "vsher" who went before her with a mat for her to sit on and describes "her woemen attending on her adorned much like her selfe (save they wanted ye Copper)" (1910 [1607]:xlix–l).

If some of these people—the "meaner sort" at Kecoughtan, perhaps—were war captives, and thus servants, still this cannot have been the reason the Powhatan called some of the colonists "servants." Rather, their identification seems to have been based on these men being fairly autonomous, of relatively high status, but subordinate to another man. In this sense, the term "servant" meant one who acted for another, served him, and was thus the <u>executor of his will</u>, the power to his authority. This was also the relationship between werowance and cockarouse and why the "councilor" was also, when necessary, the "servant" or "agent."

This status, too, had its spiritual counterpart: Oke, identified in the Jamestown documents as the most powerful divinity the Powhatan worshipped. Although difficulties attend an understanding of their accounts, which I address in the next chapter, it seems plain that Oke referred among other things to an active, punishing spirit, the complementary opposite of the calm, benevolent Ahone. The parallel to the relationship of werowance and cockarouse is obvious.

How did one become a cockarouse? The colonial accounts suggest two possibilities, which are not mutually exclusive. The cockarouse may have been a junior member of the chief's immediate lineage or a cadet line. Strachey's little history of the dynastic rearrangement at Quiyoughcohannock, for instance, suggests this: the werowance removed for seducing Powhatan's brother's wife and replaced by the very young son of Powhatan and the werowance's own sister, "who [the son] being yet young . . . is for the most parte in the governement of *Chopoke* at *Chowapo* one of Pipscoes brothers" (1953 [1612]:64–65). Pipsco was the demoted werowance; Chawopo was a village or small town near Quiyoughcohannock, at the confluence of the James and Upper Chipoke Creek. "In the government" suggests that an heir to a werowance who was still too young to assume chiefly duties might nevertheless have some sort of advisory role—in fact, be a cockarouse. This might be true not only in this case but also where the incumbent was still alive and governing. It would be a way for the heir to learn how to be werowance in due course, as well as establishing a reputation for himself.

The other possibility is that a cockarouse was a man of ordinary family—possibly what the English call "the meaner sort"—who achieved this status as a result of his great ability, perhaps especially as a warrior. Since many other Indian societies in the deep Southeast accorded the successful warrior high status and political importance (e.g., Anonymous 1931:243; Bossu 1931:258; Galloway 1995:2; Gilbert 1943:318; Gearing 1962; Milfort 1959; Voegelin 1970:17), we should not be surprised to find it among the Powhatan as well. Spelman, as we have seen, says that the warriors with the most enemy dead to their credit were "the cheafest men amonge them" (1910 [1609]:cxiv). Smith suggests the same thing when he says, in the context of describing Powhatan warfare, that cockarouse means "captain." Strachey's report, cited previously, that a werowance honored an outstanding warrior with a gift and a new name likewise conveys an elevation in status from the common—possibly induction into the status of cockarouse. But to insist on this last would be unwarranted.

Beverley's discussion of the status stands out in that he does not list warfare among its criteria. Instead, he says the man must be experienced, have traveled, have some wealth put by, and have demonstrated valor; but the example he gives is hardly warlike: lassoing a sturgeon by the tail and hanging on to it even when it pulls one under water (Beverley 1947 [1705]:147). Finally, the man must have gone through the initiation Beverley calls the huskanaw, which he says was essential for becoming a cockarouse but had virtually no other function. The reason his Powhatan friends gave him for requiring the ritual was, he says, that it made them better judges, since the ritual caused them to forget their kin (Beverley 1947 [1705]:207, 209). The cockarouse in the early 18th century, then, was a councilor and judge only, not a warrior.

The difference between the Jamestown colonists' criteria for being a cockarouse and what Beverley reports is almost certainly due to culture change, evidence of which we have encountered already. In 1607 the werowance was, as we know, both judge and warrior; by 1705 these functions seem to have been divided between the "king," who was the judge, and the werowance, who was the war leader (see Clayton 1965 [1687]:21). A similar separation of functions may well have occurred in the status of cockarouse also. Rather than being both a warrior and a judge's assistant, he was now simply the latter, and the warrior was a separate category of person for whom, however, Beverley does not provide a term.

The cockarouse at the beginning of the 17th century was a notable warrior in the councils of his werowance and ready to execute his commands, whether these were ferrying visitors across frozen mud-flats or knocking their brains out. In addition, he led war parties, either on his own initiative or, more likely, as the representative of his chief. In this capacity he might also, if otherwise of sufficiently high status, organize commoners in some collective endeavor.

Werowance and Cockarouse Related

The werowance and the cockarouse together made up the secular half of Powhatan sovereignty: the werowance the authority for the cockarouse's power. For example, the werowance judged wrong-doers, and the cockarouse carried out his sentence; the werowance planned raids, expecting the cockarouse to lead them; the werowance organized the hospitality of his village, and others entertained the visitors. The structure of this relationship was dialectical, "a series of successive dichotomies or inclusions" (Dumont

1972:106). Most chiefs alternated between commander and agent, depending on the social context in which they found themselves. Thus the councilors to the mamanatowick, Powhatan, included men who were paramount werowances in their own countries (for instance, Opechancanough, "king" of Pamunkey). Their councilors, in turn, included men who were local werowances in the villages of the tribe—included, but not limited to, because the status of cockarouse was achievable as well as heritable. The werowance exemplifies the *gravitas* that Dumézil identifies as a characteristic of priests and priestly kings in Indo-European political organization; while in the cockarouse, who in Smith's phrase "bears the burden," we may identify Dumézil's *celeritas*—junior and usually younger, quicker and more active.

Consonant with his superior status as the authority, the magister, the Powhatan chief was liberal in his gift-giving, by this means not only confirming his right to authority but reestablishing it each time. A summation of the werowance's duties to his followers is found in Powhatan's promise when he adopted Smith to give the English "a Countrie called Capahowasicke . . . Corne, Venison, or what I wanted to feede us" (Smith 1986 [1608]:57); shortly afterward he again said that "the Corne, woemen and Country, should be to us as to his owne people" (Smith 1986 [1608]:67). Gifts of land, food, and women obviously confer and sustain life, but so did the chief's gifts of beads and copper. These were valuable because others wanted them, of course; but in their complementary ways they symbolized life also, as I discuss in chapter 5. The most important thing the chief did in securing the general welfare, though, was providing sacrifices on behalf of his people.

Although the werowance exercised secular authority and lived in most ways like every other Powhatan man, nevertheless his status had more of the sacerdotal about it than had theirs. We know this was so because werowances had the same license as quiyoughcosoughs to approach the most sacred place in the polity, the temples at Uttamussack, which were forbidden to everyone else (Smith 1986

[1612]:170; Strachey 1953 [1612]:95), and because when they died their mummies were kept in the "temple" of their tribe, guarded by quiyoughcosoughs (Smith 1986 [1608]:59, [1612]:169; Strachey 1953 [1612]:94). These authorities say, too, that only the "king" and the "priest" expected to enjoy an afterlife (Smith 1986 [1612]:172; Strachey 1953 [1612]:100).

But, like his sliding secular status, the werowance's sacerdotal status varied also according to context. By comparison with those below him on the hierarchy, he was priestly, but by comparison with the quiyoughcosough he was a secular person much like his subject. The relationship between werowance and quiyoughcosough is the pattern of dual sovereignty, and so I turn next to a consideration of the latter status.

4. *"Priests" and "Conjurors"*

The Roanoke and Jamestown colonists call the religious authority whom these Indians acknowledged "priest" and "conjuror" in English; the Algonkian term they report is "quiyoughcosough" (variously spelled). The colonists were keenly interested in the state of the Indians' souls—quite as interested as they were in their political allegiance and their physical resources—and inquired diligently into their religious ideas and customs. Nonetheless, they leave ambiguous whether "priest" and "conjuror" refer to the same person or to different kinds of religious personage (as was the case, for instance, among northeastern Algonkians; Simmons 1986:43; Bragdon 1996:200) and, if the latter, what distinguished one from the other. The hierarchical relationship between secular and religious authority is variously reported also. This chapter considers the first problem as a prelude to solving the second, which is the substance of the next chapter.

Powhatan Spirits

According to the Jamestown documents, the quiyoughcosough primarily served a being whom the colonists call Oke and in whom they recognized the Devil. Oke (probably pronounced "okee") was one of four principal Powhatan divinities the colonists mention.

One of these divinities seems to have been the Sun (see Swanton 1928). We know only a minimum about the sun's importance in Powhatan life. Strachey's statement that they swore oaths by the sun finds confirmation in other sources as well. Archer mentions that they vowed revenge by pointing to the sun (1910 [1607]:xliv), and Percy says not only that they swore oaths in this way but also that they kept them more faithfully than a Christian. He goes on: "These people haue a great reuerence to the Sunne aboue all other things: at the rising and the setting of the same, they sit downe lifting vp their hands and eyes to the Sunne, making a round Circle on the ground with dried Tobacco; then they began to pray, making many Deuillish gestures, with a Hellish noise, foming at the mouth, staring with their eyes, wagging their heads and hands in such a fashion and deformitie as it was monstrous to behold" (Percy 1910 [1607]:lxxi, see lxxiii).[1] Another important deity was named Ahone. He was "the great god . . . who governes all the world, and makes the Sun to shine, creating the Moone and Starres his Companions, great powers, and which dwell with him, and by whose vertues and Influences, the vnder earth is tempered and brings forth her fruictes according to her seasons . . . the good and peceable god" (Strachey 1953 [1612]:89; see Whitaker 1613:24; Beverley 1947 [1705]:200–201).[2]

A third, perhaps even more significant divinity was called the Great Hare. We know of this being among the Powhatan from a myth that Spelman learned while living among the Potomac (Strachey 1953 [1612]:102; Purchas 1617:954). According to Strachey's version of this myth, the Powhatan recognized five gods: the four Winds and their superior, a "mightie great Hare" living in the East, creator of the land, water, the first people, deer, and fish. Apparently, he introduced some order into the world as well, since Strachey says that the deer were created for people to eat. According to the version in Purchas, the Hare arrived among the Powhatan from some unnamed place and defended them from a "great Serpent" (1617:954). He created deer from the hairs of the single original deer also.

These early sources give no indigenous name or term for this Hare, but he was undoubtedly the Great Hare of the Algonkians. This being was the "spirit of the dawn," the creator, the primal cause, but also the cause of the end of the world. He was master of the cardinal points, that is, the four winds, and also the master of animals, appearing to hunters in dreams to tell them where to find game. He was associated with the east and the north and with the sky or the heavens. As a sky being, he overcame a number of monsters inimical to human existence, particularly the Great Horned Serpent, who had their origins in the water or the underworld. In some areas, the Great Hare was a culture hero and a trickster as well (Brinton 1896:192-198, 235, 255; Leland 1992:208; Willoughby 1935:280; Feest 1986:8-9; *Walam Olum* 1954:42; Hall 1989:262).[3]

Commonly in northeastern and southeastern Indian religions, spirits living underwater or underground complement those of the heavens (Hudson 1976:122-125; Feest 1986:9; Leland 1992:286; Bragdon 1996:184). What we can take as references to infernal spirits among the Powhatan is minimal, however. Purchas's version of the creation myth says that the Great Hare slew a "great serpent" on his arrival in Virginia. This is a myth found among northeastern Algonkians (Brinton 1896:201). The Horned Serpent was a creature of the water, usually malevolent but occasionally with benevolent manifestations; among the Cherokee, for example, he was associated with shamanism (Hudson 1976:167-168). These tribes told stories about a "tie-snake" also, a creature living underwater that bound the unwary in its coils (Swanton 1929:34, 171; Hudson 1976:132). Which, if either, of these appears in the myth Purchas recounts is less important than the fact that the narrative represents a conflict between opposed realms of the cosmos, a spirit of the heavens overcoming a spirit of the underworld. We know also that the Powhatan threw sacrifices into the water as well as leaving them on a stone altar, tossing them into the air, or burning them up. This suggests that they thought of different spirits as inhabiting different elements and directed their offerings appropriately.

The Powhatan told the colonists that they had no need to sacrifice to Ahone: the good things of life would appear simply because he existed. He required no recognition of his bounty, and he was indifferent to what people did (Strachey 1953 [1612]:89). Instead, "All things that were able to do them hurt beyond their prevention, they adore with their kinde of divine worship; as the fire, water, lightning, thunder, our ordinance, peeces, horses, etc. But their chiefe God they worship is the Divell. Him they call *Oke* and serve him more of feare then love" (Smith 1986 [1612]:169). Dealing with this divinity, or divinities, was a primary function of Powhatan religious and secular leaders.

Oke

In his word list, Smith translates the word "Okes" or "Okees" as "Gods" (1986 [1612]:138, [1624]:131). Strachey (M.A. Cantab.) Latinizes the name to "Okeus" and associates it with a material image or idol (1953 [1612]:85, 88, 94) as well as with a spirit (1953 [1612]:95, 97, 99).[4] Barbour characterizes "Oke" as "perhaps the most puzzling word in Smith or Strachey" (1986, 1:138n); he concludes (1972:39, 1986, 1:169n) that the Powhatan borrowed the word from the Iroquoian-speaking Huron, for whom it meant "spirit, with the secondary meaning of medicine man or a person or thing endowed with more than usual talents or power" (Tooker 1991:78n).[5]

The early colonists write of Oke as if the name belonged to one divinity and no other, like Baal or Zeus. Beverley, though, offers a refinement: "They do not look upon it [their idol], as one single Being, but reckon there are many of them of the same nature; they likewise believe, that there are tutelar Deities in every Town" (1947 [1705]:198). It seems likely that "oke" had among the Powhatan the same range of application as it had to the Huron and that it was thus equivalent to *manito* in other Algonkian cultures, *orenda* among the Iroquois (Hewitt 1902), or *wakan* among Siouan speakers (Walker 1991:68–74; Powers 1977:45–47): it referred not to one divinity but to spirits, or to some manifestation of spirit, as Smith's definition suggests.[6]

The English report characteristics of Oke or "the Oke" that are mutually contradictory. Almost always they describe Oke as hideously ugly; but Purchas reports that Powhatan's son-in-law Tomocomo, who accompanied Pocahontas to London and became Purchas's informant, described Oke as appearing "in forme of a personable Virginian, with a long blacke lock on the left side, hanging downe neere to the foote. This is the cause why the Virginians weare these sinister locks" (Purchas 1617:954). A similar description is given by an anonymous writer in 1689, who says that the god of the Virginians "does appear frequently to them, in the shape of a handsome young Indian" (Anonymous 1959 [1689]:235–236). As their appearances differed, so did their nature. The Oke who so exercised the colonists was an active, punitive god associated with the dead and possibly with warfare. The Oke whom Tomocomo and the anonymous writer describe sounds in many ways like the Ahone of Strachey's account, if more involved with human activities: the creator and culture hero, source of all goodness, knower of all things (Purchas 1617:954–955). His appearance suggests that he was one of the many Masters of the Animals found in the Northeast (Feest 1986:8–9; Bragdon 1996:188–190). Possibly he and the punishing Oke were twins, or at any rate brothers, another theme found frequently among cultures of the Northeast. The older twin or brother is the culture hero and sometimes a trickster as well; the younger meets his death at the hands (or fangs) of evil underwater spirits and becomes lord of the dead (Feest 1986:8).

The form of divinity that engrossed the attention of the colonists was that which they found the most diabolical. Consequently, it is this manifestation that we know the most about. Since I have no other name to use, I follow the colonists and refer to him as Oke. The English tell us what this divinity looked like; that he punished wrongdoers with illness and famine; that he caused violent thunderstorms also as punishment; that his devotees could see and converse with him; that he received sacrifices; and that he presided over the land of the dead, inhabited by the spirits of werowances and quiyoughcosoughs, in the west.

Oke conformed closely to the colonists' conception of the Devil. Just as their interpretation of Powhatan chiefs was necessarily colored by their ideas of what was civil, their appreciation of Powhatan divinities and religious observance depended on their ideas of what constituted religion. But in this case they could not represent the culture in positive terms. The truth of their religion was an absolute, not a relative, truth; cultural relativism in this context was unthinkable. They acknowledged two preeminent sacred persons: the triune God, the creator, who was both good and just; and

God's contrary, the Devil, a corruptor, who was neither (see Sharpe 1997:83). When they call Oke the Devil they mean it literally. They still considered revelation a means to religious knowledge, and the Devil revealed himself to mortals just as did God the Father. Although there was debate on the matter (see Hodgen 1964:52), it was thought that these divine beings, to whom the constraints of time and space meant nothing, could reveal themselves to any people on earth. The colonists expected something of the sort in Virginia—this is one reason they inquired closely about Virginian Indian religion—and with, one feels, a certain relief they recognized in the "good god" Ahone a dim apprehension of their God, the true God, imperfectly revealed in Virginia (e.g., Whitaker 1613:24). Unfortunately, the Devil's revelation was clearer and more persuasive, or such was the colonists' interpretation.

What they saw as physical repulsiveness in images of the Oke was consonant with the revolting image of the Devil. Oke caused physical hardships—famine, illness, storms—to the people; likewise, in England, "[theologians] did not deny that devils could do material damage by bringing thunderstorms or by tormenting men and animals with occult diseases" (Thomas 1971:49). The Devil—or his agent, the witch—could possess even innocent people. Whitaker's comments about the shaman indirectly confirm the identification of Oke as the Devil: "Their Priests (whom the [*sic*] call *Quiokosoughs*) are no other but such as our English Witches are. . . . The seruice of their God is answerable to their life, being performed with great feare and attention, and many strange dumb shewes vsed in the same, stretching forth their limbes and straining their bodie, much like to the counterfeit women in *England* who faine themselues bewitched, or possessed of some euill spirit" (1613:24, 26). Witches were thought to have made a pact with the Devil and to have become his servants; in turning deliberately from God, they subverted the proper order of the world and must therefore be rooted out (Sharpe 1997:88). Whitaker would not write, as a modern anthropologist might, of inversions, but he recognized one when he saw it and drew the appropriate conclusion, although in this passage he appears to conflate witches and their victims. Possession, which Whitaker identifies as the primary characteristic of shamanic activity, was not typical of witches but of their victims. It took the form of "fits and trances, the devil speaking through them in a strange voice, . . . vomiting of foreign bodies," and occasionally the victim saw humaniform visions (Sharpe 1997:193–200).

Some writers might temper their condemnation of Powhatan religion with hope that, because the Powhatan seemed already to know God, conversion might proceed easily (e.g., Whitaker 1613:25); others, like Strachey, condemn the whole as past redemption. Either way, they took Virginian religion as a perverted version of their own religion, one that made much of the worst aspects of Christianity and paid insufficient attention to the good and valuable aspects. In such terms we must understand their descriptions.

As a representation of the Devil, the image of Oke seems to have aroused in the colonists the same fascinated horror with which one views a street accident. Most of them emphasize its ugliness, consonant with the moral status of the Prince of Darkness. The mildest description comes from Harriot, who says the images, called *kewas* (pl. *kewasowok*), were "in the formes of men" because "the gods are of humane shape" (1972 [1590]:26); but he says, too, that in the dark corners of the Indians' "temples," *matchicomuck*, where the images were kept, "they shew terrible" (1972 [1590]:Pl. 21).[7] The Jamestown colonists are less restrained. They describe an ugly, "ill-favored" image made usually of wood but sometimes of stuffed skin, painted black and adorned with strings of pearls and copper around the neck and wrists. Whitaker sent an image of Oke "to the counsell in *England,* which is painted vpon one side of a toadstoole, much like vnto a deformed monster" (1613:24). Smith's account of the battle at Kecoughtan mentions a stuffed-skin image, which he calls "their Okee," carried like a standard into the battle, the only reference to such a use of the image (1986 [1624]:144). Some, if not all, of these images were jointed so as to be movable (Beverley 1947 [1705]:197).

The Powhatan, like the Carolina Algonkians, kept the image of Oke in the "temple," which they called a *quioccasan* (Beverley 1947 [1705]:195; compare Carolina Algonkian *quiogozon*, "Royal Tomb or Burial-Place of ther Kings and War-Captains"; Lawson 1967 [1709]:188). Strachey gives us an early description of a quioccasan:

> sometyme 20. foote broad, and a hundred in length, fashioned arbour wise, after their building, having Commonly the dore opening into the east, and at the west end a Spence or Chauncell separated from the body of the Temple with hollow windynges and pillers, whereon stand divers black Images fashioned to the Showlders, with their faces looking downe the Church, and where within their Weroances vpon a kynd of Beare [bier] of Reedes) lye buryed, and vnder them apart in a vault, low in the grownd (as a more secrett thing) vayled with a Matt sitts their Okeus an Image ill-favouredly carved, all black, dressed with Chaynes of Pearle. (1953 [1612]:88–89; see Curry 1999)

These "images fashioned to the showlders" were carved posts, which Harriot likens to nuns (1972 [1590]:64). In John White's watercolors of the Carolina Algonkians, the faces on these posts are pale and reddish, and there are suggestions of white paint as well (cat. 42), suggesting that they presented a lifelike appearance. They seem to have been similar to the carved posts found in the Delaware Big House, in which were "faces, twelve in all, carved on the central post of the house and the wall posts." The Delaware Big House itself was not unlike a Powhatan quioccasan, being rectangular, oriented east-west, with an opening in either end and a fire to the west and to the east of the central post (Tooker 1979:104; Harrington 1921:41, 82–83).

Beverley's description of the quioccasan, based on his surreptitious investigation, shows that much had remained constant in the intervening decades. He says that it seemed from the outside to be a large version of ordinary houses. It was about 18 by 30 feet with a door at one end, plain walls, and a hearth in the middle. The carved posts that Strachey places within the building were in this case in a ring around the house. Similar circles are represented in Harriot, although not surrounding a building. Harriot and Beverley agree that these circles enclosed ritual areas or dance grounds, but they offer no interpretation of the posts (Beverley 1947 [1705]:213; Harriot 1972 [1590]:Pls. 18, 20). They seem not to have been representations of Oke, who lived a retired life. They may have been what Smith calls "images of their kings and Divels," kept in the quioccasan at Uttamussack (1986 [1612]:169), or perhaps of the werowances alone. Inside Beverley's quioccasan were two rooms separated by a partition of mats. The first room comprised about two-thirds of the space and was lit by the smoke hole and the door. The smaller room, in contrast, was "dismal dark," a circumstance that seems to have put the English intruders off temporarily. But they did nerve themselves to go behind it, where they found three rolled mats, secured by sewing, on raised platforms. These they opened and discovered large, presumably human, bones inside one; another held some tomahawks "finely grav'd, and painted"; and the third seemed to be the "idol," although it was in pieces and lacked "the Head and rich Bracelets, which it is usually adorn'd with" (Beverley 1947 [1705]:196–197).

A representation of a Carolina quiogozon (Lawson 1967 [1709]:188) is in Harriot, whose description of chiefly funeral customs reads like those from the Jamestown colonists, except that, according to him and the illustration, the mummies are not wrapped in skins or mats but lie naked within their arch-covered platform. Lawson (1967 [1709]:188), however, says that the bodies were wrapped like those of Virginia chiefs. The platform is itself within a larger structure, probably the quiogozon or quioccasan proper. On the ground before it a priest, identifiable by his cloak, crouches over a fire, and beneath the platform holding the bodies we can make out two crossed skins that form his bed (Harriot 1972 [1590]:Pl. 22). On the left, or to the south if we assume the door to this structure faced the east, is a Kewas or Oke in shadow, guarding the bodies of the werowances. White's original painting, from which this engraving is taken, has some possibly significant differences. He includes the fire but no attendant priest, though the two skins for the priest's bed are under the platform. There is no surrounding building, just the sepulchre. The idol is to the right, not the left, that is, on the north rather than the south; in other words, the engraver has reversed White's painting. This may explain why in this engraving the priest is shown with his left arm exposed, whereas in the engraving of the priest (Harriot 1972 [1590]:Pl. 5) not only is the left arm hidden, but there is no opening in the cloak for it.

The most important quioccasan was at Uttamussack in Pamunkey territory, where "Upon the top of certaine redde sandy hils in the woods, there are 3 great houses filled with images of their kings and Divels and Tombes of their Predecessors. Those houses are neare 60 foot in length built arbor wise after their building. This place they count so holy as that [none] but the Priestes and kings dare come into them" (Smith 1986 [1612]:169–170). Strachey adds that one of these was "a chief holie howse proper to Powhatan" (1953 [1612]:95). Powhatan is reported to have had a "treasure house" at Oropaks that apparently had a similar purpose, even if it were not so important. Spelman, writing after Powhatan had moved there, says that "the great Pawetan . . . hath an Image called Cakeres which most comonly standeth at Yaughtawnoone [in one of yᵉ Kinges houses] or at Oropikes in a house for that purpose and with him are sett all the kings goods and presents that are sent him, as yᵉ Cornne. But yᵉ beades or Crowne or Bedd which yᵉ Kinge of England sent him are in yᵉ gods house at Oropikes, and in their houses are all yᵉ Kinge ancesters and kindred commonly buried [i.e., all together]" (1910 [1613]:cv). The quioccasan as mortuary had its equivalents throughout the deep Southeast. The "bone house" of the Choctaw (Swanton 1931:172), the temple de Soto's men discovered at Cofitacuique (Biedma 1993:230–231), and the mortuaries among the Timucua and the peoples of the Lower Mississippi (Swanton 1987:722, 727–729) are examples. This form of memorial is found at a number of archaeological sites in the Southeast as well (Hall 1989:261, 274–276),

Cahokia and Spiro Mound being among the best known (Emerson 1989:48–49; Brown 1975).

These peoples also maintained a sacred fire, a gift of the Sun, either in the mortuary or in some other sacred structure, a custom the Powhatan likewise observed. As among those peoples, the Powhatan fire was the responsibility of the religious specialists (Strachey 1953 [1612]:95; see Swanton 1928). These, the quiyoughcosoughs, were said to be as ugly as the god they served. Of the earliest colonists, Smith had the best opportunity to observe them, and he writes:

> The ornaments of the chiefe Priest was certain attires for his head made thus. They tooke a dosen or 16 or more snake skins and stuffed them with mosse, and of weesels and other vermine skins a good many. All these they tie by their tailes, so as all their tailes meete in the toppe of their head, like a great Tassell. Round about this Tassell is at it were a crown of feathers, the skins hang round about his head necke and shoulders and in a manner cover his face. The faces of all their Priests are painted as ugly as they can devise . . . (1986 [1612]:170).
>   . . . halfe blacke, halfe red: but all their eyes were painted white, and some red stroakes like Mutchato's ["moustaches"; Barbour], along their cheekes: . . . and then came in three more as ugly as the rest; with red eyes, and white stroakes over their blacke faces. (1986 [1624]:149)

Beverley adds that the quiyoughcosough, whether "priest" or "conjuror," was painted black, like the images. The "priest" presented a frightening appearance altogether. He wore his skin clothing with the fur outside, "falling down in flakes . . . he likewise bedaubs himself in that frightful manner with Paint" (Beverley 1947 [1705]:212). Ordinary people, including the werowance, wore red paint, and the fur of their clothing was inside, next to the skin. The quiyoughcosough had a distinctive haircut as well: his head was shaved except for short bangs stiffened with bear's grease and a short "mohawk" running from his forehead to the nape of his neck (Beverley 1947 [1705]:164–165).

Beverley bases his descriptions in part on Veen's engravings after John White's watercolor paintings of Carolina Algonkian religious persons; he includes copies of the engravings in his own book (1947 [1705]:Tab. 4).[8] One of these paintings White entitles simply "One of their Religious men" (Hulton 1984:Pl. 42); the caption in Harriot adds that the man lived "in the towne of Secota," and Harriot's text calls him a "Priest" (Harriot 1972 [1590]:Pl. 5). The other painting White calls "The Flyer"; in Harriot's book, the picture is called "The Coniurer" (see figs. 4 and 5). Both artists present a great contrast between these men in their dress and in their postures. The "priest" wears a full, short tunic or cloak of skins with the hair outside, hanging from his shoulders to midthigh, covering the left arm and exposing the right. (Both White and Veen show the same arrangement; the engraving is not a reverse of the painting.) The singular haircut that Beverley describes is evident; in addition, the priest has a wispy beard. White's "priest" is clearly an old man. He has a wrinkled, lined face and neck; his ribs and breastbone show through his skin over the top of his garment; his pectoral muscles droop through the armhole; and his right arm and hand show the veins and tendons of age. (Veen's figure does not display these characteristics to any degree.) That White deliberately made the priest look elderly is evident by comparison with his other figures, all but one of which (the "Old Indian Man"; cat. 36) have hard muscles and smooth skin. White's "priest" also personifies gravity. He has both feet on the ground, and he places one hand on a hip and with the other makes a mannered gesture. The fact that this is an English convention, and therefore not certainly Secotan, is irrelevant: White wished to convey the staid deportment of the priest, and he does so. The "flyer" or "conjuror," on the contrary, is a man flying through the air (Hocart 1970b). Veen's engraving of this person, like that of the priest, is a faithful reproduction of White's painting. White makes his conjuror a vigorous muscular man, much younger than the priest. He wears no cloak but instead a waistband with an otter skin tucked in the front that "couereth [his] priuityes" and a bag, possibly a medicine bundle, tucked in the right side. Harriot identifies the black bird above the ear as a "badge of their office"; he says that they wear it "aboue one of their ears," not that it must be over the right ear as it is in the pictures. The bird partly conceals the man's shaven head and the thin "mohawk" along the crest. Unlike the static "priest," the "flyer" seems to be running, with his arms in the air and an anguished expression on his face. He may be dancing (Hulton and Quinn 1964:111; compare the figures in the representations of Indians dancing [cat. 42; Harriot 1972:Pl. 18] and of the village of Secotan [cat. 38; Harriot 1972:Pl. 20]). Thus the artist represents the "strange gestures, . . . often co[n]trarie to nature", of the conjuror in his "enchantments" (Harriot 1972 [1590]:Pl. 11). Together they embody *gravitas* and *celeritas* (Dumézil 1988:33).

Generalizing about the Powhatan either from Beverley, who was writing in the early 18th century, or from Harriot and White, who knew the Carolina Algonkians, requires caution. Beverley, by his own statement, was familiar with the Powhatan, including their religious personages. He says the quiyoughcosough wore black paint, something the Roanoke adventurers neither mention nor represent, and so implies not just that it was a Virginian custom but that he had seen it himself. Since Smith mentions black paint on the "priests" at Uttamussack, we can be sure Beverley is trustworthy on this point. If he describes a mode of dress that appears in paintings over a century old, it is probably safe to assume that a recognizable version of it was still in use when he wrote. Smith states, too, that the Indians whom Raleigh's men encountered were culturally almost indistinguishable from the Powhatan. The conclusion is that the Powhatan quiyoughcosough looked a good deal like the religious persons whom John White painted and therefore very different from the ordinary Powhatan man. Against this, though, is Smith's statement that "the chiefe [priest] differed from the rest in his ornaments, but inferior Priests could hardly be knowne from the common people, but that

Fig. 5. A "Religious Man" (John White). © The British Museum.

Fig. 6. "The Flyer" (John White). © The British Museum.

they had not so many holes in their eares to hang their jewels at"
(1986 [1612]:170).

Smith's account of Powhatan religious observance includes the
statement that "they say they have conference with him" (1986
[1612]:169; see Strachey 1953 [1612]:88). In the context, "they" has to
refer to the Powhatan generally, or at any rate to Powhatan men generally, and not just to quiyoughcosoughs. Tomocomo's description
of the séance with the "good" Oke confirms as much. The quiyoughcosoughs, though, seem to have been the principal mediators with
Oke, specialists in the art. An individual quiyoughcosough might
do this in the open but always in the woods rather than in a village
(Strachey 1953 [1612]:97). A séance, involving several persons, took
place in a quioccasan, the most important of which was at Uttamussack, in Pamunkey territory. Here, according to Strachey, "in

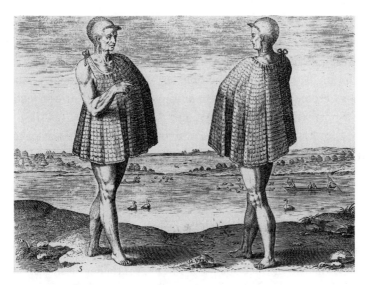

Fig. 7. A "Religious Man" (G. Veen). Courtesy of the Library of Virginia.

Fig. 8. "The Flyer" (G. Veen). Courtesy of the Library of Virginia.

this as the Grecian Nigromancers in their Psychomantie did vse to call vp spiritts either the Priests haue conference and consult indeed with the Deuill and receaue verball answeres" (1953 [1612]:95).

The first, and possibly the only, experience the English had of such a ceremony was the "conjuration" performed in connection with Smith while he was a prisoner for the purpose "(as they reported) to know if any more of his countrymen would arive there, and what he there intended" (Smith 1986 [1612]:170).[9]

> Their . . . Ceremonie I observed was thus: . . . seven of them in the house where I lay [a quioccasan, probably at Uttamussack], each with a rattle began at ten a clocke in the morning to sing about the fire, which they invironed with a Circle of meale, and after, a foote or two from that, at the end of each song, layde downe two or three graines of wheate, continuing this order till they have included sixe or seven hundred in a halfe Circle, and after that two or three more Circles in like maner, a hand bredth from other: That done, at each song, they put betwixt everie three, two or five graines, a little sticke, so counting as an old woman her Pater noster.
>
> One disguised with a great Skinne, his head hung round with little Skinnes of Weasels, and other vermine, with a Crownet of feathers on his head [Strachey mentions a "middle seised Cloke of feathers, much like the old sacrificing garment" over his shoulders as well; 1953 (1612):95], painted as ugly as the divell, at the end of each song will make many signes and demonstrations, with strange and vehement actions; great cakes of Deere suet, Deare, and Tobacco he casteth in the fire [as sacrifices]. Till sixe a clocke in the Evening, their howling would continue ere they would depart. (Smith 1986 [1608]:59)

In 1624 Smith added the information that the "chief priest" was painted black, that they danced around him for a time before settling to their "conjuration," and that they told him that "the circle of meale signified their Country, the circles of corne the bounds of the Sea, and the stickes his Country. They imagined the world to be flat and round, like a trencher; and they in the middest" (1986 [1624]:149–150).

Another account of "conference" comes from Tomocomo, Powhatan's son-in-law. From him, Purchas learned that

> *Okeeus* [the "good" Oke, master of game] doth often appeare to them in His House or Temple: the manner of which apparition is thus. First, foure of their Priests or sacred Persons (of which he said he was one)[10] goe into the House, and by certaine words of a strange language (which he repeated very roundly in my hearing, but the Interpreter vnderstood not a word, nor doe the Common-people)[11] call or coniure this *Okeeus*, who appeareth to them out of the aire, thence comming into the House; and walking vp and down with strange words and gestures, causeth eight more of the principall persons to be called in, all which twelue standing round about him, he prescribes to them what he would haue done. (Purchas 1617:954)

This is similar to Smith's report of the principal men of the village going just outside it every morning to stand in a circle and inquire where the game was so they would know where to hunt that day. The presence of the "principall persons"—this is Smith's phrase also— at these meetings supports the argument made at the end of the previous chapter that the status of werowance had priestly aspects.

Besides seeking counsel from Oke, or the okes, the Powhatan religious cured the sick. Curing may well have required seeking counsel, since they attributed illness to the displeasure of Oke, but on this point we have no direct evidence. We do, however, have some descriptions of curing ceremonies. (Interestingly enough, some of the Powhatan curer's techniques are similar to those reported for "cunning" men and women in England at the same time; Thomas 1971:200–220). Smith writes: "to cure the sick, a man [the context indicates a "priest"] with a Rattle and extreame howling, showting, singing, and such violent gestures, and Anticke actions over the patient will sucke out blood and flegme from the patient out of their unable stomacke, or any diseased place, as no labour will more tire them" (1986 [1608]:59; see 1986 [1612]:168; Strachey 1953 [1612]:111; Anonymous 1959 [1689]:233). Strachey adds that "green wounds" were treated with various herbs, but that a "compound" wound—a broken bone or rupture in addition to a cut or puncture—was beyond their skill to cure. He mentions the use of sweat baths, too, for some ailments (Strachey 1953 [1612]:110–111). Spelman describes something completely different. His "priest" moved slowly and deliberately, "as loith to wake the sicke bodye" during the treatment, having first sprayed water over his arms and chest from his mouth. The curer shook his rattle gently over the body, massaged the ailing part, and then aspersed the body while mumbling over it. Spelman mentions sucking only in connection with treating a wound, which the curer first cut until it bled and afterward covered with a powdered root, possibly puccoon (Spelman 1910 [1613]:cix–cx).

The reported "howling" of the curer, together with the colonists' emphasis on the contortions, "antics," howling, sweating, and the like in the activities of the quiyoughcosough generally, seems to confirm the importance of spirit possession in Powhatan religious observance.[12] There are the wild actions of the "flyer" in the Outer Banks, the "Deuillish gestures, with a Hellish noise" that Percy describes in sun worship, and the "broken sentences . . . [and] starts and strange passions" of the quiyoughcosoughs when they performed the ceremony for Smith. Whitaker mentions the quiyoughcosoughs "stretching forth their limbes and straining their bodie" (1613:25–26). Strachey describes the solitary quiyoughcosough in the woods seeking a vision with "howling and with such paines and strayned accions as the neighbour places eccoe agayne of the same, and themselues are all in a sweat and over wearyed" (1953 [1612]:97). An anonymous account says that the "conjurors" "raise storms, or divert clouds from one place to another and make them fall where they will. This they do by drawing circles, and muttering words, by making a dreadful howling and using strange gestures and various rites, upon which the wind ariseth etc" (Anonymous 1959 [1689]:232).

Spirit possession and "conference" with a divinity argue that the quiyoughcosough was a shaman. Such a conclusion is hardly startling, since most North American Indian religious were shamanic. Nevertheless, it is as well to be cautious since the English, although aware of trance, never say clearly that the Powhatan experienced such a state. One of the two English terms they use to refer to shamans, "conjuror," accords perfectly with this interpretation, but the other, "priest," would seem to contradict it. I take up this problem in the next section.

The word "quiyoughcosough" meant more than "shaman" or even "priest" or "conjuror," however. Smith says that it means "Pettie Gods, and their affinities" (1986 [1612]:139), or, more specifically, "a superiour power they worship; . . . one they have for chief sacrifices, which also they call *Quiyoughquosick*" (1986 [1608]:59). Purchas writes of "their *Oke* or Diuell, and their other *Quiyough-cosughes,* or gods" (1617:953; see Smith 1986 [1612]:172). Strachey and Whitaker confirm Smith's identification of shamans and spirits (Strachey 1953 [1612]:100; Whitaker 1613:24, 26). According to Geary, "Smith's *quiyoukosuck* seems to be a plural, although the English plural ending *-es* was added to it; it seems to be for *kwayax-kwesaki* 'those who are upright, honest', in other words 'the just, or righteous'" (1991:888; see Barbour 1972:42, 1986, 1:139n).[13]

If the quiyoughcosoughs were just, so, too, was Oke. The reiterated references to Oke's ugliness may represent an English outrage more moral than aesthetic, but it is equally possible that the Powhatan intended the image to be frightening. Oke punished wrongdoing; in fact, Smith goes so far as to say that if it were not for this spirit the Powhatan would constantly steal from each other (1986 [1612]:160), and Strachey adds, "nor let any man doubt but that the devill cann reveale an offence actually committed" (1953 [1612]:76). Strachey likens him to the Roman god Jove or Jupiter, "a god of ill omen for whom Romulus erected a temple on Capitoline Hill" (Wright and Freund 1953:88n). "Only the displeased Okeus looking into all mens accions and examyning the same according to the severe Scale of Iustice, punisheth them with stormes, and thunderclaps, stirrs vp warre and makes their women falce vnto them" (Strachey 1953 [1612]:89). Strachey had not read Dumézil, of course, any more than had his sovereign. But his association of Romulus and Jove with Oke, the just agent of correction, is telling.

Smith implies an indigenous distinction between oke and quiyoughcosough such that the former refers to a greater divinity and the latter to those of lesser status. Strachey's identifying quiyoughcosoughs as "their other godds [i.e., besides 'their Okeus']" (1953 [1612]:99), would seem to confirm this. Apparently, the Powhatan recognized a hierarchy in the spirit world analogous to that in their social world (or, better, the other way around). Oke and quiyoughco-sough were related as superior to inferior, authority to power, remote to at hand, general to specific, werowance to cockarouse, cockarouse to commoner. This interpretation suggests the logic of applying the same term to both the spirit and the human medium: together they mediate Oke and the rest of humanity.

"Priests" or "Conjurors" or Both

The Jamestown colonists give us one Powhatan word, "quiyoughcosough," for the shaman, but they use two English terms to refer to these men: "priest" and "conjuror." Sometimes they present them as two distinct statuses, as in White's paintings of the Carolina Algonkians. Other accounts read as if the terms were interchangeable. This confusion is analogous to that over the titles werowance and cockarouse and may be sorted out in similar fashion, with the difference, already identified, that the English were not prepared to be as tolerant of paganism as they were even of supposed tyranny, and their comments about Powhatan religion and religious persons are almost entirely interpretations rather than reports.

Since it appears that most, if not all, Powhatan men were capable of achieving contact with spirits through trance, an initial consideration should be whether there was indeed any separate status of "priest" or "conjuror" among the Virginia Algonkians—as there clearly was among the Carolina Algonkians and also among the Algonkians of southern New England (Bragdon 1996:200–201; Simmons 1946:41) — or whether the English applied these terms to anyone entranced, perhaps following an indigenous usage of the word quiyoughcosough. This would be a logical, if not necessary, application if the word meant simply "petty god" or "divine agent." But all the evidence indicates that this was a status distinct from others, including what in modern terms we would call the laity. We might look no further than Strachey's vigorous fulminations against the quiyoughcosoughs, which show clearly that they constituted a category of person, not of consciousness (1953 [1612]:89, 90, 94); Whitaker likewise directed his scathing denunciation at a status, not a state (1613:24, 26). But if these be set aside as insufficiently objective, we have more acceptable evidence as well. Smith's earliest report includes the statement, "one they have for chief sacrifices, which also they call *Quiyoughquosick*"; in this he also describes for the first time the "chief priest" at Uttamussack (1986 [1608]:59). The colonists say that the huskanaw, the initiation of boys, produced "priests and conjurors," again arguing a distinct status. Smith and Strachey report that the Powhatan accorded no souls a life after death except those of "their Werowances and Priestes which they also esteeme *Quiyoughcosughes*" (Smith 1986 [1612]:172; Strachey 1953 [1612]:100). Virtually all the colonists, including Beverley, write that the chief adviser to the werowance was the quiyoughcosough, and most say that he was the chief's superior. This matter I take up in the next chapter.

If quiyoughcosough was a recognized Powhatan status, why did the English in effect translate it as both "priest" and "conjuror" (as well as "pettie gods, and their affinities," as Smith does)? On the face of it, these two terms refer to very different kinds of religious activity. Modern anthropology not only distinguishes priest from shaman but opposes them as mediate to immediate, controlled to wild, Apollonian to Dionysian, *gravitas* to *celeritas*. Yet some of the Jamestown accounts make no distinction between the priest and the conjuror, while others show a great difference between them.

To the English themselves, though, there was a difference in the terms. A priest belonged to and represented an established church in his parish, which he served; he was subordinate to the rest of the Church hierarchy, including canons, deans, bishops, archbishops, and (in the Catholic Church) cardinals and the pope. For most people in the Church, he was the means of access to God, since such access was possible only through the Church. The priest was, or should have been, the representative of divine order in the world.

To find the term in the writings of English Protestants about a savage people provokes reflection. Pertinent to this problem is the English Reformation idea of the local religious authority. The difference of opinion regarding the constitution of congregations and the relationship of the congregation to its leader was motivated by the same concerns over which James I and the Parliament argued, namely, whether authority was legitimately conferred from above or below and whether authority and obedience to authority were necessary to social order. The Church of England was organized hierarchically like the Catholic Church but with the major difference that its head was the English monarch, not the pope. The Church appointed its parish clergy, most commonly by a system of patronage by which a property owner, usually one of the laity, recommended a candidate to the bishop, who confirmed the choice pretty much automatically (Hill 1980:65). Parishioners had thus no control whatsoever in the choice, retention, or dismissal of the incumbent, to whom, however, they owed tithes and from whom they had to accept punishments for a variety of infractions (e.g., working on Sunday or fornication, whether on Sunday or not) (Hill 1980:63). Presbyterians and Puritans alike objected to this arrangement. They argued that authority was conferred by those under its constraint, and thus they insisted on the election of ministers whose tenure was contingent on the will of the congregation (Davies 1970:59–60). They were also more willing than the Anglicans to allow that access to God was possible outside the organization of the Church.

To one of Puritan or Presbyterian convictions, the Anglican divine was more popish than Christian and properly called a priest. Nevertheless, the Anglicans distinguished their clergy from the priests of Rome on several grounds, which they shared with other Protestants.[14] Fundamental to the definition of the clergyman was the identification of doctrinal authority: the possibilities included tradition, scripture, reason, and "guidance of the Holy Spirit." Tradition was acceptable so long as it included only the first five centuries of Christianity. The elaborations of the Roman Catholic Church were ruled out as tending farther and farther away from, rather than closer to, the teachings of Christ. Scripture was important because it was the word of God: contact with the word in itself, even through the medium of print, would make a person godly. Protestants took the view that unless the participants knew what God promised with the sacraments, they were meaningless. Thus the reformed Church emphasized both literacy for the laity (at least for the men, although for a brief period educating women was considered equally important; Stone 1979:142) and the translation of the Bible into modern languages. A result of the emphasis on the word was that the clergyman ceased to be a mechanical dispenser of Communion bread and wine, a mechanical means to absolution, and became an expounder of doctrine and exhorter to moral action. The sermon, not Communion, was the central part of a Protestant service. Even in the hierarchical Anglican Church, the insistence that each man could and should understand what he was doing — and impart as much as was good for them to his wife, children, and servants — meant that this was a more democratic body than was a Romish congregation.

The head of an English Protestant congregation in the early 17th century was a minister, a parson, a vicar — not a priest, except to those inimical to his brand of Protestantism. The use of the word for Powhatan religious persons conveys the colonists' disapproval, then, but we were aware of that anyway. Even this necessarily brief summary of attitudes to the clergy shows us some further implications:

the quiyoughcosough was a "priest" because he was imposed on his "congregation" from above (chosen by the werowance), because he was incomprehensible to the laity, and because his activities smacked of magic rather than genuine religion. In this last we find perhaps the most important reason for the colonists' terminology. Generally speaking, Protestants condemned all Catholics as magicians, and the clergy were the worst magicians of all (Thomas 1971:68). The medieval Church sought to separate magic from religion, condemning the former; but in popular thought, the magus and the priest were hard to tell apart. Because he was literate, the priest could read charms and spells as well as the Gospels, and as he invoked Christ during the sacrament he could invoke other spiritual beings as well (Thomas 1971:274). Like the Powhatan shaman, priests before the Reformation had been asked to undertake, with the help of the saints, nonecclesiastical chores such as finding stolen items and identifying thieves, controlling the weather, and assuring the fertility of animals (Thomas 1971:218, 32, 29). To the Protestants, such powers were magical, not divine. Whether they condemn the quiyoughcosough as a Roman magician or as a witch, the Jamestown colonists saw him as the Devil's agent.

The conjuror was equally contemnable, and for the same reasons, but the term carries with it a sense of lesser powers, lesser influence. A priest might be called, as a way of denigration, a "conjuror" (Thomas 1971:69); the ordinary "conjuror" was never called a priest. The word "conjuror" comes from the Latin "sworn together," a meaning in use as late as 1596; it referred to the equal parties to a contract. But the sense of the term was extended to include a spirit as one of the parties, and it came to mean "to call upon, constrain (a devil or spirit) to appear to do one's bidding, by the invocation of some sacred name or the use of some 'spell.'" This usage is found as early as 1535 and continued for almost 200 years (*OED s.v.* "conjure"). During the reign of Elizabeth I, conjuration, in the second sense, had enjoyed royal tolerance, if not favor; but the English as a whole were at best ambivalent about conjuration (French 1972; Yates

1969, 1972, 1979). In its humbler, popular sense, the term "conjuror" was equivalent to "cunning man," "wise woman," "witch"—"good" witches in this case—and the like, who promised to cure the sick, discover lost and stolen items, reveal thieves, tell fortunes, divine the future, and counter witchcraft (Thomas 1971:179; Sharpe 1997:66-67). As with the priest, we find in the functions of the conjuror in England a close parallel to the responsibilities of the quiyoughco-sough—or some of them—in Virginia. The fact remains, though, that to orthodox Protestants no sort of magical activity was acceptable, because it was the Devil's work.

Both terms the colonists use to translate quiyoughcosough express condemnation, a fact that should occasion no surprise. The Powhatan were not Christians but instead seemed to worship the Devil, an allegiance no good Christian could approve. We are left with the question, though, why the colonists thought it appropriate to use both terms rather than only one, and a reasonable answer is that there were not one but two kinds of religious status among the Powhatan. For one thing, in England, priest and conjuror were related hierarchically, the former encompassing the latter. The documents, however, either equate the two or leave it unclear in what their distinction consists. In the Southeast, it was not uncommon for at least two categories of religious practitioner to be recognized (Early 2000:132; Gilbert 1943:321, 336; Swanton 1989:774, 778, 2000:614; Milanich 2000:7), and as we have seen among the Carolina Algonkians, the "priest" and the "conjuror" obviously differed from each other in form and movement. But Harriot's commentary does not clearly identify any differences in their religious activities. He says that the priests were "notable enchaunters" and that the conjurors, whom he also calls "jugglers," were "verye familiar with deuils, of whome they enquier what their enemys doe, or other suche thinges" (Harriot 1972 [1590]:Pls. 5, 11; see Hulton 1984:182, Pls. 42, 49), suggesting but not confirming that the conjuror used trance and the priest did not. More apparent is the distinction in age, on which I have commented earlier.

Smith likewise appears to distinguish between priests and conjurors. His statement that "when they intend any warres, the Werowances usually have the advice of their Priests and Conjurers, and their Allies and ancient friends; but chiefely the Priestes determine their resolution" (Smith 1986 [1612]:165), may be taken to refer to two kinds of religious adviser, the priest and the conjuror, the former having the greater weight in deliberations. Alternatively, the phrase "priests and conjurors" may have been merely a rhetorical device, like "Medes and Persians," that is actually pleonastic; hence the use of the word "priests" alone in the final clause. Smith uses the word "priest" alone when discussing Uttamussack, first saying that "this place they count so holy as that but the Priestes and kings dare come into them" and next that "in this place commonly is resident 7 Priests." But he then says that these seven priests performed the "conjuration" over him when he was a captive (Smith 1986 [1612]:169–170). He almost never uses the word "conjuror" by itself. If there was any indigenous distinction between the two, it must appear from Smith's usage that "conjuror" was a subcategory of "priest."

As we would expect, Strachey repeats much of what Smith says about quiyoughcosoughs and, like Smith, seems to make a distinction between the status of "priest" and "conjuror." He repeats the report that the Chickahominy were governed by their "priests" rather than by a werowance and in a later passage says that "conjurors" discovered thieves (Strachey 1953 [1612]:69, 76; see Smith 1986 [1612]:160; this is one place where the word appears alone). In themselves, these comments suggest that the "priest" was a magisterial figure, concerned with the workings of the tribe as a whole, while the "conjuror" was concerned with individuals and their difficulties—more like a policeman—an executive rather than a judge or legislator. Such an interpretation finds support in Strachey's statements that "their Priests . . . doe at all tymes . . . absolutely governe and direct the Weroances or Lords of Countryes in all their accions" (1953 [1612]:89) and that only "priests" and werowances may come to the main quioccasan at Uttamussack. Strachey sends us back to square one, though, when he refers in the same breath, as it were, to the "7 Priests" at this place as "these Coniurers," telling us that they "have conference and consult indeed with the Deuill and receaue verball answeres" (1953 [1612]:89, 95, 96).

The accounts of two other early colonists present us with yet different usages that suggest there was no indigenous distinction between a "priest" and a "conjuror." Spelman uses these words interchangeably, saying at one point "yow must understand that for ye most part they worship ye diuell, *which* ye coniurers who are ther preests, can make apeare unto them at ther pleasuer," and at another referring to "ther preests *which* are ther coniurers" (1910 [1613]:cv, cix; editors' italics). Whitaker does not use the word "conjuror" at all; he translates quiyoughcosough as "priest" (1613:24, 26).

The later colonial accounts clearly distinguish the "priest" from the "conjuror." An anonymous writer identifies the conjuror as the most knowledgeable man among the Indians, capable of divining the intentions of enemies (except for the English) and of affecting the weather; the priest was the curer (Anonymous 1959 [1689]:232-233). Beverley is equally specific. His account includes an illustration that combines the engravings of the "religious man" and the "flyer" from Harriot's report—Beverley identifies these as the "Priest" and "Conjurer," respectively—as well as a representation of a huskanaw pen. Beverley's verbal descriptions of these two men follow Harriot's to some degree, but they seem to be based on personal observation as well (1947 [1705]:164-165, 212). He distinguishes likewise between the statuses in terms of their activities. In the rituals in the quioccasan, the "chief Conjurer" manipulates the image of Oke from behind the screen, while the "Priest of authority" stands among the assembly "to keep them from being too inquisitive" (Beverley 1947 [1705]:198). The conjuror performed the *pauwaw* (powwow), for which he appeared in public attired as in Veen's drawing and "with an air of Haste, or else in some Convulsive posture, that seems to strain all the faculties, like the *Sybils*" (Beverley

1947 [1705]:212). The priest apparently rarely appeared in public, and when he did his object was to arouse people's respect by his fearsome aspect (Beverley 1947 [1705]:212). Beverley's language, as he describes these men, implies a contrast as great as that which we see in White's and Veen's illustrations from the Outer Banks.

Nevertheless, Beverley also suggests, in other passages, an identification between the two: "The Priests and Conjurers have a great sway in every Nation. Their words are looked upon as Oracles, and consequently are of great weight among the common people"; even more to the point (if unnecessarily cynical), "the Conjurer is a Partner with the Priest, not only in the Cheat, but in the advantages of it, and sometimes they officiate for one another" (1947 [1705]:201–202, 212, see 212–213).

These seemingly contradictory accounts may be resolved into a coherent pattern that is also consistent with everything else we know or understand about the Powhatan. I suggested earlier that the "affinities" of Smith's translation—or definition—of "quiyoughcosough" refers to the human agents of his "Pettie Gods," themselves evidently agents of yet more remote divinities. In the evidence adduced here, the "priest" and the "conjuror" appear as complementary modes of agency. This interpretation explains the Powhatan having a single term for their religious persons and the colonists' persistent use of two terms as glosses for that term and their choice of terms. For them, as for the Powhatan, "priest" and "conjuror" were complementary.

All quiyoughcosoughs practiced trance and divination and possibly curing as well. The distinction between the priestly and the conjuring quiyoughcosough was, as John White's paintings convey, the difference between *gravitas* and *celeritas,* or between *seniores* and *iuniores* (Dumézil 1988:41–44). The "priest" counseled the werowance; he lived a retired life as guardian of chiefly mummies, and it may be (although here the evidence is thin) that his trance behavior was comparatively restrained.[15] We know less about the "conjuror" specifically, a fact that in itself suggests his subordinate status.

His admission to the counsels of the chiefs, the degree of his familiarity with those who were not shamans, and the nature of his trance behavior are all unknowns. The scanty evidence we have, though, makes him appear the complementary opposite of the "priest" in all these regards.

We cannot know today on what the distinction between the priest and the conjuror was based, although age seems a reasonable criterion. White's paintings certainly suggest that. The quiyoughcosough was valued for his knowledge as well as his skill (Beverley 1947 [1705]:213), and presumably an older shaman was reckoned wiser than a younger one. An alternative possible distinction is according to the divinity one served, the "priest" serving the greater spirit and the "conjuror" the lesser one. Or the relationship of authority to power found in the spiritual world may have been mirrored in that between "priest" and "conjuror," the "priest" being the master and the "conjuror" his agent.

Given the evidence, the question of which of these interpretations is correct cannot be answered definitively. The lack of resolution is less important than the fact that within the category of quiyoughcosough there were two complementary modes of serving the spirits: one was antic, junior, ministerial; the other grave, senior, magisterial.

We can take this further and say that the opposition was also that between the quick and the dead. In some sense this was true. The Powhatan shaman was a dead man, socially speaking, but possibly the "priestly" shamans were more dead than the "conjuring" ones. The fact that the colonists report the "priests," but not "conjurors," taking care of the mummies of werowances in the quioccasan is suggestive if slender evidence. The description of curing that most sources give us suggests the conjuror performed it rather than the priest—Spelman's account is always an exception—allying the conjuror more with the living than the dead. But there, of course, we are being tautologous.

5. Dual Sovereignty in Tidewater Virginia

Quiyoughcosough and Werowance

The relationship between quiyoughcosough and werowance in aboriginal Virginia was that between spiritual authority and mundane power, the chiefs submitting to the direction of the shamans. As a dyarchy, it is analogous to that between, on the one hand, werowance and cockarouse and, on the other, what we may for convenience call "priest" and "conjurer"; thus it is a more inclusive expression of the principle of dyarchy.

The Jamestown colonists are very clear that the quiyoughcosough directed the werowance on what to do. Strachey says that "they [the priests] doe at all tymes . . . absolutely governe and direct the Weroances or Lords of Countryes in all their accions" (1953 [1612]:89). He provides instances, attributing the increasing tensions between colonists and Indians to the authority of the "Quiyough-quisocks or Prophetts." He contends that they prevented the werowances from forming friendships with the English and that they urged the chiefs to drive the English out, both on pain of Oke's extreme displeasure. He assures his readers that Powhatan, at the urging of the shamans, caused the massacre of the Lost Colony at Roanoke, even though he had no provocation from them to do so (Strachey 1953 [1612]:89–91). This may have been in response to a prophesy "that his Priests told him, how that from the *Chesapeack* Bay a Nation should arise, which should dissolue and giue end to his Empier" (Strachey 1953 [1612]:104).

Strachey's evidence makes a strong case for the superiority of the quiyoughcosough over the werowance. Smith presents a similar hierarchical relationship, although he implies that it operated only in martial contexts: "When they intend any warres, the Werowances usually have the advise of their Priests and Conjurers, and their Allies and ancient friends; but chiefely the Priestes determine their resolution" (1986 [1612]:165). The first part of this statement makes it sound as if the chiefs proposed and the shamans approved, but the latter part says that the priests make the decisions. Strachey is clearer on his matter, as he often is; he rewrites Smith's statement to read, "When they intend any warrs, the Weroances vsually advise with their Priests or Coniurers, their Allies and best trusted Councellors and Freindes, but commonly the Priests haue the resulting voice, and determyne therefore their resolucions" (1953 [1612]:104). Likewise, Whitaker writes, "They stand in great awe of their *Quiokosoughs* or Priests. . . . At his command they make warre and peace, neither doe they any thing of moment without him" (1613:26). Nearly a century later, Beverley was reporting the same: "The Priests and Conjurers have a great sway in every Nation. Their words are looked upon as Oracles, and consequently are of great weight among the common people." "The Priests and Conjurers are also [i.e., besides the "kings" and "queens"] of great Authority, the people having recourse to them for Counsel and Direction, upon all occasions" (1947 [1705]:201, 226).[1]

These passages show that the quiyoughcosough gave permission for, if he did not initiate, activities such as going to war or arranging peace, besides discovering lost items, locating game, curing, regulating the weather, and appeasing Oke otherwise as necessary. What is less clear is who proposed what to whom. Did the werowance invariably formulate plans or identify difficulties and ask the quiyoughcosough for permission or relief, or did he wait passively until his superior told him what to do? Smith, commenting on the virtues of the werowance of Quiyoughcohannock, provides part of an answer to this question. Quiyoughcohannock's "devotion, apprehension, and good disposition, much exceeded any in those Countries, who though we could not as yet prevaile withall to forsake his false Gods, yet this he did beleeve that our God as much exceeded theirs, as our Gunnes did their Bowes and Arrows and many times did send to the president [i.e., Smith], at James towne, men with presents, in-treating them to pray to his God for raine, for his Gods would not send him any" (Smith 1986 [1612]:172, see also 266). Evidently, it was usual for a werowance to send for his quiyoughcosough when any pressing matter arose. This need not mean that the quiyough-cosough always awaited requests from his werowance, but it does suggest that communications between them went in two directions. It also shows the werowance seeing to the welfare of his tribe, ask-ing a religious authority to intercede with his own divinities on the tribe's behalf. The "presents" mentioned may have been just that—none of the authors specifies their nature—but possibly they were meant to be sacrificed by the recipient. If so, Quiyoughcohannock would have been acting in a common kingly role, that of supplier of sacrifices to the priests (see Dumézil 1973:112, 1988:61).

The argument so far has presented Powhatan sovereignty as a dyarchy, dual rule by a religious authority and a secular power. The werowance had some sacerdotal qualities, however, as well as being a warrior and a judge, so it is necessary to ask whether this was not in fact a monarchy with all the sovereign functions combined in one person.[2] The werowance alone among secular persons could visit the primary quioccasan at Uttamussack; to everyone else it was forbidden. Presumably, he had comparatively free access to other quioccasans as well, particularly that of his own tribe. Ordinary people apparently could approach these places but not actually go in. Whitaker describes villagers approaching the shaman's "cottage" and leaving, at a little distance, provisions for him which he collected as necessary (1613:26). The fact that only chiefs and shamans were thought to have immortal souls further identifies the chief with the shaman, while his being placed in the temple after his death com-pletes the identification of the two.

Although these facts show that the chief was more like a shaman than his people were, they do not in themselves make him into a monarch. He was undoubtedly the shaman's agent, not his equal, in any sort of decision-making. His complete transformation into a purely spiritual figure occurred only after his death; his life and appearance were very like those of his subjects, while those of the shaman were opposite in every regard. The werowance cannot be called a true monarch because he was not the sole ruler of his tribe. His status is another example of the dialectical hierarchy that characterized the whole of Powhatan society. Just as a secular man might be both werowance and cockarouse, depending on the social context, so a paramount werowance might be also a comparatively priestly or shamanic figure by contrast to his subjects.

Powhatan was an exception. That might be expected from his having had a number of different titles, none of which his werowances seem to have shared. In many ways he was like his subordinate werowances on a grander scale, but the evidence suggests that he was also a more sacred person than they. Spelman tells us that "as *with* the great Pawetan he hath an Image called Cakeres *which* most comonly standeth at Youghtawnoone [*in one of ye Kinges houses*] or at Oropikes in a house for the purpose and w*ith* him are sett all the Kings goods and presents *that* are sent him, as ye Cornne" (1910 [1613]:cv; editors' italics and interpolations).[3] Spelman distinguishes these houses from another house, also at Oropaks, which was Powhatan's treasure house and in which his ancestors were kept. It was, in other words, a quioccasan, whereas the house with the "Cakeres" was where Powhatan lived. We have no report of any other werowance keeping a religious image in his house. Smith's observation that "their principall Temple or place of superstition is at Uttamussack at Pamaunke, neare unto which is a house Temple or place of Powhatans" (1986 [1612]:169) likewise suggests that there was not much difference between Powhatan's house and a temple. It was built next to the most important quioccasan of the Powhatan, which only chiefs and priests could visit with impunity and in which, Smith implies, rituals for the benefit of the entire polity were carried out. That a chief could live so close to such a place, like one of its inhabiting shamans, suggests his own comparatively spiritual nature.

Powhatan's title of mamanatowick probably indicates this also. This is another word for which I have been unable to find a modern translation. (Strachey's translation, "great king," is not informative.) But its resemblance to *manito* (pl. *manitowok*), "sacred," in other Angonkian cultures is unmistakable and likewise to Ojibwa *mamand-*, "wonderful, miraculous," and especially *mamana-*, referring to "Indian jugglery" (Geary 1991:889), or shamanism. The literal meaning of this word may be lost to us, but it surely referred to the preeminence of the titleholder in spiritual activities. When Smith and Strachey say that the Powhatan regarded their paramount chief as "halfe a God," it is not Elizabethan bombast but a statement of fact. The evidence for such an opinion, though meager, is consistent. Powhatan, the mamanatowick, the wonderful shaman, was accorded semidivine status among his people. As the priestly king of his polity, the monarch, he represented its unity; his subordinate werowances, less spiritual and more of the world, managed practical business within their localities, as his agents.

The Powhatan dyarchy, like dual sovereignty everywhere, was more than a political structure, indeed more than a politico-religious structure. It expressed in itself, and thus exemplified, the totality of symbolic classification in Powhatan culture. A thorough comprehension of the relationship of authority to power requires the identification of Powhatan symbolic categories and of their relationships to each other. By this means we discover a consistent association among authority and masculinity, the west, the elevated, the right hand, desiccation, sterility, stasis, black, the spiritual, and death; and among power and femininity, the east, the nether, the left hand, moisture, fertility, change, white, the mundane, and life. Men in general and chiefs in particular stood midway between these poles, being both male and female, death-dealing and fertilizing, authoritative and powerful according to context. At the extreme masculine end stood the shaman, opposed at the extreme feminine end by women in general.

The Huskanaw

A convenient point of departure for this analysis is the ritual of initiation that produced, among other social actors, the quiyoughco-sough.[4] Beverley alone among the colonial writers calls this ritual a huskanaw. According to Gerard, this word comes from "*uskinaweu,* 'he has a new body,' said of a youth who had reached the age of virility" (1907:94) or perhaps one who had undergone a rite of passage. Barbour (1980:154n) relates the Powhatan word to the Massachusetts "*wuskenoo,*" which meant literally " 'he is young,' and referred to puberty ceremonies." Although Siebert does not discuss the term "huskanaw" (Strachey's word list, which forms the basis for his analysis, does not include it), his analysis of a term meaning "new" is similar. Strachey gives the word as "*uscautewh,*" which he translates as "it is fair." Siebert prefers a translation "it is new, young," and compares it to Cree /oska·tisiw/ "he is youthful, a young person" and to /oska·w/, /oska·yiwa·w/ "it is new" (1975:362).

The first, perhaps the only, English witness of the Powhatan ritual was William White, who went to live with the Quiyoughco-hannock in 1608 during a lean period at James Fort and who "seems to have told his story personally to Samuel Purchas sometime before 1614" (Barbour 1980:148);[5] Purchas published it in his *Pilgrimage* (in Barbour 1969 [1614]). For purposes of this discussion, the abbreviated version in Smith is adequate:

> In some part of the Country they have yearely a sacrifice of children. Such a one was at Quiyoughcohanock some 10 miles from James Towne and thus performed. Fifteene of the properest young boyes, between 10 and 15 yeares of age they painted white. Having brought them forth the people spent the forenoone in dancing and singing about them with rattles. In the afternoone they put those children to the roote of a tree. By them all the men stood in a guard, every one having a Bastinado in his hand, made of reeds bound together. This made a lane betweene them all along, through which there were ap-

pointed 5 young men to fetch these children: so every one of the five went through the guard to fetch a child each after other by turnes, the guard fearelesly beating them with their Bastinadoes, and they patiently enduring and receaving all, defending the children with their naked bodies from the unmercifull blowes that pay them soundly though the children escape. All this while the women weepe and crie out very passionately, providing mats, skinnes, mosse, and drie wood, as things fitting their childrens funerals. After the children were thus passed the guard, the guard tore down the trees, branches, and boughs, with such violence that they rent the body, and made wreathes for their heads, or bedecked their haire with the leaves. What else was done with the children, was not seene, but they were all cast on a heape, in a valley as dead, where they made a great feast for al the company. The Werowance being demanded the meaning of this sacrifice, answered that the children were not al dead, but that the *Oke* or Divell did sucke the blood from their left breast, who chanced to be his by lot, till they were dead, but the rest were kept in the wildernesse by the yong men till nine moneths were expired, during which time they must not converse with any, and of these were made their Priests and Conjurers. This sacrifice they held to bee so necessarie, that if they should omit it, their *Oke* or Divel and all their other *Quiyoughcosughes* which are their other Gods, would let them have no Deare, Turkies, Corne, nor fish, and yet besides, hee would make a great slaughter amongst them. (1986 [1612]:171–172)[6]

Today we recognize—as indeed the English did in the years following this early encounter—that this was an initiation and not a sacrifice. Other accounts make it clear that all Powhatan boys went through this in order to receive a vision, which seems to have been necessary to participate in adult life. For some few of them, this vision would reveal the shaman's vocation; the remainder would return to ordinary society as proper men after a period corresponding to the length of human gestation.

In this description, we can identify several of the symbolic oppositions listed previously: wilderness and the settled areas, high and low, spiritual and mundane, male and female, right and left, senior and junior, black and white, death and life. As this way of listing them suggests, these oppositions were analogous. Thus we find only boys among the initiates — apparently women, or girls, did not engage in spiritual contact — and the ritual is conducted by men. The boys' introduction to spiritual connection took place in the wilderness, not in a village. For the purpose they were painted white, presumably to highlight their transition to the spiritual state, which was marked by black — Smith says that the initiates were afterward called "black boys" (1986 [1624]:124). The women acted as if their sons were dying, and indeed some of them did die, but socially rather than physically. Those whom Oke chose as his agents he "killed" by sucking the blood from their left breasts.[7] That they were afterward classified with the dead rather than the living I infer from the fact that a shaman's life was the inverse of an ordinary man's. He lived in the wilderness; pursued no productive economic activities; remained unmarried and apparently childless; wore his clothing inside-out; painted himself black instead of red or white; shaved his head but sometimes wore a beard; and had as his dwelling a sepulchre in which the figure of Oke, lord of the afterworld, was also kept.

He was also the most male person in Powhatan society, distinguished from ordinary men, who were both male and female, and from women, who were entirely female. Demonstration of this conclusion requires an excursion into Powhatan notions of gender, which I begin with a discussion of Powhatan women. These ideas in turn may be related to other aspects of the Powhatan world.

Powhatan Women

The Jamestown colonists paid little attention (in print, anyway) to the women of their new domain. What they describe represents them as little different, save in appearance, from the women they had left in England. The nature and status of English women, especially English wives, at that time were much debated by contemporaries (Amussen 1988:182; Gowing 1996:5-6, 25), as indeed they are today among historians. It is safe to say, though, that ideally English wives were subordinate to their husbands in the same way as a subject was subordinate to the king. Cooperation rather than domination characterized both kinds of relationship, which were recognized as expressions of the same cosmic principle (Sharpe 1989:7; Brown 1996:15; but cf. Stone 1979:109-111). The wife—or the child, for that matter—was obedient to her husband or father in return for due guidance, support, and representation (Amussen 1988:38; Brown 1996:31). Likewise, the wife had the same right and obligation to counsel her husband as the subject had to counsel or petition the king, and the husband had the corresponding obligation to solicit and to take advice (Amussen 1988:42, 47). Women were neither mindless drudges nor chattel, nor were they expected to be; on the contrary, the good husband made his wife an extension of himself, his agent, sharing his heart and his will. She was the husband's second-in-command rather than a servant (Laslett 1971:2; Amussen 1988:39, 41; Gowing 1996:25; Brown 1996:24; Stone 1979:137).

It would be a mistake, as Amussen points out (1988:3; see Gowing 1996:5-6, 25), to conclude that because women were ideally subject to their husbands all women were automatically subordinate to all men. In fact, as these writers remind us, rank was ultimately more important than gender, as it usually is; we have seen that the Jamestown colonists found nothing anomalous about the sight of a Powhatan woman of high status commanding men of lower rank to her service. But the colonists also thought it entirely proper that brothers and sons should take precedence over sisters and daughters in the succession to chiefship.

In England, wifely subordination meant deferring to one's husband, keeping quiet, and above all being sexually chaste. It did not mean forfeiture of one's status as a person, nor did it mean drudgery or economic alienation. Legally, women enjoyed a number of rights, although they ceased to be legal individuals at marriage and their husbands were responsible for their crimes (Amussen

Fig. 9. A young woman. Courtesy of the Library of Virginia.

1988:70, 50). They could testify in court; sue for defamation or separation; inherit, own, and bequeath property; and receive wages (though they were paid half what a man earned) (Amussen 1988:61, 70–72; Gowing 1996:30; MacFarlane 1986:263; Stone 1965:633, 1979:72, 137). Women, even married women, worked at a variety of occupations in both urban and rural settings, and although there were differences between the two settings, the general rule was that women worked indoors or close to the house and men worked outdoors (Amussen 1988:68). In an urban setting, the men were more likely to earn and the women to disburse (Amussen 1988:68), but poorer women especially might sell cheeses in the market, knit, or take service in an inn or private house (Gowing 1996:14). On farms, "women were responsible for the house, the dairy, the brewhouse, poultry and the kitchen garden; men were responsible for livestock and field crops" (Amussen 1988:68). Women were usually the marketers, too, both buying and selling as part of their primary responsibility of keeping house (Amussen 1988:68–69; Gowing 1996:14; Peters 1997:332); such activities might be of considerable importance to the economic well-being of the household at this period (Brown 1997:24).

With these ideas of the proper relationship between women and men the English must have felt themselves at home, so to speak, with Powhatan women, who were also subordinate to their fathers and husbands. Powhatan courtship seems to have been initiated by the prospective groom, who made gifts of food and valuables to his intended. Apparently she had the right of refusal, but neither she nor her mother had anything to say about the size of the bride-price, which was agreed between her father and her suitor (Strachey 1953 [1612]:112; Spelman 1910 [1613]:cvii; but see Smith 1986 [1612]:235).

> The cerimony is thus The parents bringes ther daughter betwene them (if hir parents be deade then sume of hir kinsfolke, or whom it pleaseth ye king to apoynt (for ye man goes not unto any place to be maried But ye woman is brought to him wher he dwelleth). At hir cumminge to him, hir father or cheefe frends[8] ioynes the hands togither and then ye father or cheef frend of ye man Bringeth a longe stringe of Beades and measuringe his armes leangth thereof doth breake it ouer ye hands of thos *th*at are to be married while ther handes be ioyned together, and giues it unto ye womans father or him *that* bring hir, And so w*ith* much mirth and feastinge they go togither (Spelman 1910 [1613]:cvii; editors' italics)

Strachey confirms the virilocal rule of postmarital residence, adding that the groom married only after he had built a house for the couple to live in. The bride might eventually inherit this, as Spelman says that the husband left it to his favorite wife on his death (Strachey 1953 [1612]:112; Spelman 1910 [1613]:cx). The breaking of the string of beads over the couple's hands in order to present it to the bride's father would appear to be a ritual of separation from her father's society with corresponding incorporation into her husband's.[9] So although the bride could veto a suitor, she was otherwise at the disposition of the male principals: her father and the groom.

The custom of providing important visitors to Powhatan villages with "a woman fresh painted red with *Pocones* and oile, to be his bedfellow" (Smith 1986 [1612]:73) likewise argues a subordination of women to men, in this case to the werowance of the village. Even if the women themselves volunteered such service, which seems not unlikely given Strachey's and Beverley's observations on Powhatan women's sexual freedom, the English perceived this as a gift from the chief, not from the women. In this as in everything else, the women were agents of their superiors.

The subordination of Powhatan women must not be taken to mean that they were culturally insignificant, though, any more than were contemporary English women. Like them, Powhatan women were economically important and in similar ways. The division of labor was such that the women attended almost exclusively to gardening, while hunting and fishing were men's activities. The gardening cycle began with someone—probably the men—preparing a site by slash-and-burn in one year and then in the following year clearing away the dead and burned wood. Women planted with a digging-stick, placing four corn kernels and two beans in each hole; they and their children cultivated and harvested the crop (Smith 1986 [1612]:157–158, 162). Smith admired the "industry of their women": "The men bestowe their times in fishing, hunting, wars and such manlike exercises, scorning to be seene in any woman-like exercise, which is the cause that the women be verie painefull and the men often idle. The women and children do the rest of the worke. They make mats, baskets, pots, morters, pound their corne, make their bread, prepare their victuals, plant their corne, gather their corne, beare al kind of burdens and such like" (1986 [1612]:162). Although none of the sources says so, it seems probable that women made the striking feather cloaks (Rountree 1998:18), one of which Strachey saw a werowance's wife wearing when he called one morning (Strachey 1953 [1612]:65).

English disapproval of these women's labors (e.g., Percy 1910 [1607]:lxix; Strachey 1953 [1612]:81) was due not to their having to work, nor even to the kinds of work they did, but to their having to work so hard. Drudgery was not considered women's natural lot in England, and the colonists thought reprehensible what they took to be the idleness of the men, which was contrary to English expectations of a husband. Their neglecting their domestic duties for the gentlemanly occupations of hunting and fishing was, moreover, presumptuous, since they were not gentlemen (Axtell 1981). To the colonists, then, the economic relationship between Powhatan spouses appeared analogous to that between a tyrant and his people: the natural superior, whose obligation was to support as well as guide, acting instead only in his own interests and leaving his natural helpmeet to shoulder alone every sort of burden, including himself.

But even as they condemn, however mildly, these accounts provide us with material to see that this was not a parasitic relationship, as Smith implies (cf. Rountree 1998:20); it was a division of labor, a collaboration. Men fished, but women spun the thread that made their nets and lines. Men formed hunting parties in winter, but women carried and erected the mat-covered houses to which they returned to be warmed and fed (Smith 1986 [1612]:163–164; Spelman 1910 [1613]:cvi–cvii). According to Strachey, the hunters were successful because their mothers had taught them how to shoot (1953 [1612]:113). Men cleared gardens, and women planted them. The women provided the vegetable component of the Powhatan diet and the men the animal. Women cooked and served whatever was available to eat (Smith 1986 [1612]:162, [1608]:65; Percy 1910 [1607]:lxix; Archer 1910 [1607]:xliv; Spelman 1910 [1613]:cxiii). They processed all sorts of raw materials—shells, copper, skins, feathers, reeds—into culturally recognizable and useful items— ornaments, clothing, housing, even the mats on which werowances sat in state. They were the barbers for the Powhatan (Smith 1986 [1612]:160; Strachey 1953 [1612]:73; Purchas 1617:956), which for men, at least, was crucial to any sort of success, as their asymmetrical haircuts made them pleasing to the gamekeeping Oke. Women were also the artists for their own extensive tattooing (Strachey 1953 [1612]:73). Any achievement thus represented, on many levels, a collaboration of the sexes, presumably realized in the joint efforts of the wife and husband since, as Smith says, "Each household knoweth their owne lands and gardens, and most live of their owne labours" (1986 [1612]:160).

Even this brief survey of the activities of Powhatan women reveals a consistent pattern in the relations between women and men such that men initiate and women carry on. It is a syntagmatic relationship (Huber 1980:49) analogous to that between shaman and chief and between a chief and his subjects, or more specifically between a chief and his cockarouse and, in turn, between the cockarouse and his chief's subjects. As in the relationships between men of different ranks, the wife was subordinate to her husband in that she carried out tasks that he authorized and in some cases only when he authorized them. But she was not impotent, any more than the cockarouse or the common man; on the contrary, she was the power, the effective cause, in the household.

Other activities of women show them in the same syntagmatic relationship with men. Politically and diplomatically, we find women acting as agents for their male relatives: a werowance's sister, for instance, would head a village in her brother's tribe; in 1656 the widow of the last werowance of Pamunkey assumed the leadership of the entire tribe, representing it to the English officials for nearly 30 years (McCartney 1989). The most famous example of a woman acting politically is Pocahontas's rescue of Smith, which though unique for dramatic detail is still but one of several reports of women acting in a political capacity. She herself is reported to have come in the winter of 1608 to James Fort at her father's request to plead for the release of some Indians held captive there (Smith 1986 [1608]:93). Women were present at Powhatan's councils and presumably at those of lesser werowances as well, although we do not know what they did there. Opechancanough, unable or unwilling to meet Smith and Newport when they first visited Werowocomoco, sent his daughter as an ambassador to the captains with the message that her father was lame and wished them to come to him (Smith 1986 [1608]:75). When Powhatan attempted what Smith took to be an assassination of Smith and his party during a visit to the Pamunkey, Powhatan left Smith in his house with "2 or 3 of his women [wives] talking with the Captaine, whilst he secretly fled, and his men as secretlie beset the house" (Smith 1986 [1612]:249). In late 1608 the colonists captured the werowance of Paspahegh (whom Strachey praised as one of Powhatan's "champions") and kept him prisoner for some days. "Daily this kings wives children, and people, came to visit him with presents, which hee liberally bestowed to make his peace" (Smith 1986 [1612]:260). The evidence, though not as detailed as we would wish, allows the legitimate inference that it was usual for a man to enroll his female relatives in his political activities. One other example deserves mention in this context, although it is not certain on whose behalf the women were acting. Several women lured an Englishman, George Cawson or Casson, into a house at Appocant, where he was captured and afterward sacrificed (Strachey 1953 [1612]:60; Strachey does not call this a sacrifice, but William White does; see below).

That women enjoyed such responsibility argues, contra what Smith implies, that the Powhatan regarded women as moral beings, an inference supported by the fact that women could be punished for breaking laws and for other peccadilloes. (In this they differed from their English sisters.) We have seen that Powhatan caused the execution of a woman for murdering her baby. Spelman tells us that the Potomac chief at Pasptanzie, with whom he was living at the time, knocked out one of his (i.e., the chief's) wives for beating Spelman during his absence (1910 [1613]:cviii). We have rather more information on the consequences to women of breaches of sexual morality, doubtless because chastity was of defining importance to English female morality at that time (Gowing 1996; Amussen 1988:117, 130;

Brown 1997:27–28). In the *Generall Historie,* Smith describes Powhatan's punishment of an errant wife: "And he made a woman for playing the whore, sit upon a great stone, on her bare breech twentyfoure houres, only with corne and water, every three dayes, till nine dayes were past, yet he loved her exceedingly" (1986 [1624]:128). Elsewhere Smith says that a woman must obtain the permission of her husband before having intimate relations with other men (1986 [1612]:160), which Strachey—the more reliable writer on such subjects—corroborates: "They are people most voluptious, yet the women very Carefull, not to be suspected of dishonestie without the leave of their husbandes, but he giving his consent, they . . . may embrace the acquaintance of any Straunger for nothing" (1953 [1612]:112–113). "Playing the whore" meant sexual congress without such permission rather than selling one's wares. This is perhaps a startling example of the authority-power relationship between husband and wife, but it is an example nevertheless.

The Powhatan marital relationship was an expression on a domestic scale of the general principle of dual sovereignty, which also informed the relations between quiyoughcosough and werowance, werowance and cockarouse, and these chiefly or subchiefly persons and ordinary Powhatan men. It remains to be demonstrated that the hierarchical relationship was gendered throughout, however, since the fact that husbands commanded wives may not be taken as evidence that all subordinates were female to all superiors. Study of the Powhatan economy and environment in cultural terms confirms that there was a consistent association of maleness and authority, femaleness and power, and that these were related conceptually to the physical environment and the activities that took place there.

Moral Topography

The association of women with sessile food resources and men with mobile ones has been remarked so often in anthropology that one may almost take it for granted. The significance of these activities for the people engaged in them is not, however, something we can assume. (Among the Powhatan, the important aspect of food was not its mobility but whether acquiring it involved bloodshed.) Nor can we assume that subsistence activities occur as and where they do because of ecological constraints. The location of Powhatan gardens and villages in the eastern part of their domain may be explained in such practical terms: the soils there are sandy, not clay like those in the west, and easier to work with a digging-stick. But such practical explaining is fallacious (see Sahlins 1976). The horticultural success of the Monacan to the west of the Powhatan demonstrates that Indian technology was more than equal to the demands of that terrain. We must question, too, how much of what constitutes the environment of a culture is genuinely "natural" and, by implication, the cause of cultural forms. It would appear that the reverse is true. Cronon (1983) demonstrates that in New England at the time of English colonizing, the "natural" landscape of the Algonkians there was in effect a well-tended garden organized to encourage the growth of useful plants and animals and to discourage those they considered without value. The same sorts of practices appear to have been in effect in Virginia as well. A simple ecological explanation for Powhatan cultural phenomena, then, will not do. The locations of Powhatan villages and gardens, like the importance of gardening and the nature of the feminine, are alike culturally motivated and may be understood only in cultural terms.

The Powhatan practiced horticulture where they did because they associated the east with life and generation and the west with their opposites. Women gardened and men hunted because life and generation were female attributes, and death and dissolution were male ones. In one of its aspects, Powhatan topography represented a gradation between the two poles. The division of labor and the consequent pooling of resources (for example, in meals or dress) constituted a union of these extremes.

Of the spatial categories of Powhatan territory—high and low, central and peripheral, east and west—the last is the most salient in the Jamestown documents. The "temple," or quioccasan, illustrates this well; like temples everywhere, it was a microcosm. The east-west orientation of the building conforms to the Powhatan association of the east with creation, light, and life and the west with darkness and death. Entering the quioccasan one moved from east to west, from light to darkness, from known and predictable to arcane and dangerous, from mundane to spiritual, from life to death.[10] The perpetual fire, which in the deep Southeast was a gift of the sun and was its facsimile (Hudson 1976:126; Swanton 1928), represented life. The Great Hare, the creator of the world, lived in the east, according to the myth Strachey recorded. (The myth is recounted below.) Oke, on the contrary, lived in the west and ruled the dead (Smith 1986 [1612]:169, 172); the early sources also identify him as a master of game, which was created in order to be killed. Among the spirits of the dead were the werowances, whose mummified bodies lay beyond a screen or interior wall at the west end of the building, well away from light and life.

The economy of the Powhatan conformed to these cosmic principles: producing food without killing in the east, producing food by means of killing—that is, hunting—in the west. Warfare was also primarily a thing of the west, since the most serious enemies of the Powhatan lived in the Piedmont and the mountains. The opposition between life—gardening—and death—hunting and homicide—is not absolutely clear-cut, admittedly, since the Powhatan did hunt and raid during the summer as well as the winter. On the other hand, gardening in the winter (especially four centuries ago, when the winters were much colder than now) was clearly impossible. But there does seem to have been a decided shift in economic emphasis from one half of the year to the other, and those emphases are congruent with what they told the English of their cosmology: the cast was the source of life, the west the abode of the dead.

Powhatan gender hierarchy conforms to this cosmic ordering also. In the east, social groups, including families, lived in villages where women cultivated gardens. In the surrounding light forest, maintained by the Powhatan, men, including the chief, hunted. Farther away in the wilderness, equivalent to the west, the Powhatan erected quioccasans to shelter their shamans and their dead chiefs. That the Powhatan associated the west with wild(er)ness emerges from the descriptions we have of the peoples to the west of the Piedmont: "all confederats with the Monacans, though many different in language [i.e., mutually incomprehensible, unlike the various Powhatan tribes], and be very barbarous living for the most part of wild beasts and fruits" (Smith 1986 [1612]:165). This is not a report of Smith's own observations, note, but rather of the Powhatan conception of their western neighbors. The Monacan and the other peoples of the Piedmont were actually settled agriculturalists living in large towns and raising burial mounds (Hantman 1990). Powhatan women were lively: they produced life without killing. Shamans were moribund: their housemates were mummies, and they brought forth no living thing—they had no children and grew no food. In between we find the secular men of different ranks whose relationship to the moral topography of their land, and to the opposition of life and death, was ambiguous: they moved between the village and the wilderness for their activities, and the highest-ranking could even approach the house of the dead with impunity; they produced children; and they produced food, but mostly by killing it first. Their killing of the enemy in warfare was equally, we may suppose, a means to preserve life, if only indirectly.

The argument so far, then, is that the Powhatan associated the west, wilderness, death, and masculinity and opposed them to the east, settlement, life, and femininity. The subsistence activities of ordinary Powhatan men represent a mediation of these extremes, since they both killed and produced food and did so in an area neither truly settled nor truly wild. They were categorically both male and female (Williamson 1979). This ambiguity of gender corresponds exactly to ambiguity of status; that is, a man's gender (distinct from his sex; secular Powhatan men, so far as we know, were always heterosexual) was contingent on the social context in which he found himself. As a husband, he was male; as a subject, he was female to his chief's masculinity. The chief was in turn female to his superior shaman's masculinity. We find a consistent association of male with authority and female with power.

The puissant wife bringing gardens to life would seem, though, to be at odds with the argument advanced above that werowances in general and Powhatan in particular maintained their superior status by securing to their followers the means of life, which bounty no amount of tribute, itself dependent on those means, could ever equal. What I have been calling the liveliness of women, which is to say their power to bring into being, consisted not in providing the means to life but in realizing the potential of those means; it is another expression of the syntagmatic relationship between female and male. Domestic gardening re-created on a small scale the relationship between chief and commoner, including the cosmic fertilizing of the mamanatowick. A woman, with her children, planted, cultivated, and harvested the gardens her husband had cleared; these were his fields, not hers, since postmarital residence was virilocal. Men cleared land apportioned them by the werowance, who himself was lord of a territory at the pleasure of Powhatan. At each level the agent caused the potential of the land to be realized further, until the ultimate realization: the women's harvesting of crops.

The prominence of the east-west opposition in the colonial accounts, together with Smith's statement that the Powhatan thought the world was flat (1986 [1624]:150), suggests that, unlike both the southeastern Indians and the New England Algonkians (Hudson 1976:122–147; Bragdon 1996:191–194) the Powhatan assigned little significance to a cosmic dichotomy between high and low. But there are intimations that they recognized such an opposition and gave it importance both spiritual and mundane.

Sun worship argues an importance attached to an upper world, as does the location of Ahone. Strachey's description of celestial powers who ruled with Ahone has been quoted earlier. True, it reads like an occultist tract (see Yates 1979), but we need not therefore dismiss it out of hand as evidence that the Powhatan recognized a number of spirits living in the heavens, even if they had not the powers or virtues Strachey attributes to them. The burning of sacrifices, and of tobacco on important occasions, implies a notion of powers above, since smoke is frequently seen as a mediator between the human world and the spiritual. Percy describes the shamans at Nansemund hurling firebrands into the air to bring on rain that would render useless the guns of the English attacking the town (1922 [1612]:277), again suggesting some spirit above who might come to the Indians' aid. (The spirit did not, and the English sacked the town.)

Evidence for corresponding spirits of the lower world is even less satisfactory. Sacrifices into water must have been meant for some recipient, but the English identify the recipient only as "Oke" and equate him with the punishing ruler of the afterworld, who they say lived in the west, not in the water. We have no explicit statement, either, that there were subterranean spirits among the Powhatan, but Smith's description of the "chief priest's" headdress may indicate that they had such spirits. This headdress included the skins of "Weasels and other vermine" and "a dosen or 16 or more snake skins," stuffed with moss, with a circle of feathers around the top. Neither Smith nor his comrades say anything about Powhatan classification of animals (nor even whether they had one), so we cannot be certain that they shared the common southeastern idea that snakes and "vermin" were creatures of the underworld and birds of the upper world (Hudson 1976:128), but it is a possibility. Moss, with which the skins were stuffed, was used in a child's funeral (Smith 1986 [1612]:172; Strachey 1953 [1612]:99; also White 1969 [1614]: 147–149)—how it was used no one tells us—and it is probable that children were buried, since commoner adults were. The shaman's headdress would then have been a mediation between the upper, represented by the feathers, and the lower, represented by the skins stuffed with moss—not inconsistent with the meaning of the form of the ritual, which represented the Powhatan as the center of the world—but with greater emphasis on the lower. It is difficult, though, to reconcile the characteristics of the Powhatan shaman (which included authority and sterility) with the madness, disorder, and fertility associated with the underworld in the deep Southeast (Hudson 1976:128). It is possible the "vermine" and snakes did represent the nether regions but that the Powhatan accorded them another set of meanings.

As with the east-west distinction, the spiritual importance of relative elevation had its social analogue. Powhatan in state sat above everyone else, elevated on what Smith calls both a throne and a bedstead (and it may have served Powhatan as both) piled high with mats and embroidered pillows. Other werowances may have had similar arrangements within their houses, but we know nothing about those. Although no werowance, not even Powhatan, is reported to have been carried about in a litter like the Natchez Great Sun, Smith's story of how Powhatan caused "sixe or seven of the [his] chiefe men" to wade through icy mud to carry Smith out of a stranded canoe (Smith 1986 [1608]:71, 73) may be evidence that this was occasionally done. Strachey mentions, too, that Pipsco's glamorous wife had herself carried ashore from her canoe, although other women and girls waded ashore (1953 [1612]:65). And all werowances were elevated at death, when their mummies were placed on the platform in the quioccasan.

Just as they have comparatively little to say about Powhatan spirits of the below, the colonists tell us almost nothing about any corresponding social significance of depth underground or underwater. The most obvious is the burial of ordinary Powhatan: "For their ordinary burials they digge a deep hole in the earth with sharpe stakes and the corpes being lapped in skins and mats with their jewels, they lay them upon sticks in the ground, and so cover them with earth. The buriall ended, the women being painted all their faces with black cole and oile, doe sit 24 howers in the houses mourning and lamenting by turnes, with such yelling and howling as may expresse their great passions" (Smith 1986 [1612]:169). In death, the werowance and his subjects lay at physical extremes from a median that was the earth's surface.[11]

The Powhatan buried their valuables for security, too, but this appears to have been done as a practical necessity rather than with the expectation that subterranean spirits would protect them from theft. But the valuables themselves, with the exception of furs, originated either underground or underwater; it may be their place of origin at least contributed to their value, if it was not the cause of it.

Besides beads and copper, Powhatan men are reported to have worn a great variety of things on their heads and in holes in their earlobes, including garter snakes (living), rats (dead), feathers or even the whole skin of a bird, and "the hand of their enemy dryed" (Smith 1986 [1612]:161). Anyone wearing a full complement of these items must have represented the whole world, east and west, wet and dry, life and death, below and above and in the middle.

Although we could wish for better evidence on the point, the Powhatan seem to have made an association between elevation and the spiritual: Powhatan was more sacerdotal than his subordinates, just as he was more often physically higher than they; the deceased werowance on his bier was likewise in a spiritual state not shared by his living colleagues or by his subjects living or dead. Thus we find that relative elevation, like orientation to east and west, was a metaphor for social status. The further west, conceptually speaking, the more male and the more authoritative, which is to say the higher in elevation; contrariwise, the more easterly, the more female and the more powerful, which is to say lower in elevation. The association of high with west and low with east is, of course, consonant with the facts of Powhatan physical topography, the land at sea level in the east and rising as one moves west to the Appalachian Mountains.

Both these spatial distinctions may be related yet more generally to an opposition between wet and dry. The lower elevations in the east are bounded by the sea or tidal rivers, while the higher areas are comparatively dry. The same distinction appears in the third mode of spatial ordering evident in the Jamestown documents: center and periphery.

This is most obvious in Powhatan ritual, which took the form of a circle with a center. The circle of posts with carved heads in or around the quioccasan and the circle of men around the initiates, themselves encircling a tree, at a huskanaw have been mentioned. William White also describes the men conducting the huskanaw lying in a circle around the boys after they were removed to the nearby valley, and he says that the men's dancing took the form of two contrary circles of four men abreast (1969 [1614]:148–149).

Almost no ritual was complete without a dance. Strachey writes that the Powhatan danced so often that it seemed to be as necessary to them as meat and drink. They would dance to welcome visitors, to plead for relief from some general hardship, or to celebrate a victory or the harvest. On these occasions they would

> make a great fier in the howse or feildes, and all to sing and daunce about yt in a ring . . . , sometymes fashioning themselues in twoo Companies, keeping a great Cercuyt, one Company daunceth one waie and the other the Contrary . . . , certayne men going before with either of them a Rattle, other following in the midst, and the rest of the trayne of both wings in order 4. and 4. and in the Reare certayne of the Chiefest young men with long Switches in their handes to keepe them in their places: after all which followes the Governour or Weroance himself in a more slowe or sollemne measure, stopping, and daucing, and all singing very tunable. (Strachey 1953 [1612]:96, see 86; Smith 1986 [1612]:170; Harriot 1972 [1590]:Pls. 17, 19)

Other observers confirm Strachey's description. Smith saw what he calls a "maskarado" performed in a field near Powhatan's lodging, in which about 30 young women in male attire "with most hellish cries, and shouts rushing from amongst the trees, cast themselves in a ring about the fire, singing, and daucing with excellent ill varietie, oft falling into their infernall passions, and then solemnely againe to sing, and daunce" (1986 [1612]:236; see Lawson 1967 [1709]:44–45). Percy describes a dance of welcome at Kecoughtan: "After they had feasted vs, they shewed vs, in welcome, their manner of dancing, which was in this fashion. One of the Sauages standing in the midst singing, beating one hand against another; all the rest dancing about him, shouting, howling, and stamping against the ground, with many Anticke tricks and faces, making noise like so many Wolues or Deuils" (1910 [1607]:lxiv).

Percy also mentions that sun worship included "making a round Circle on the ground with dried Tobacco" (1910 [1607]:lxxi); this is similar to the circles constructed during the so-called divination or conjuration performed over Smith when he was captive. There the shamans made several concentric circles on the floor of the cabin, taking the fire as the center point. First, there was a circle of cornmeal around the fire made by the "chief priest" alone; then, farther out, there were two circles of corn kernels made by all the shamans in turn, put down three or more at a time in little heaps between songs and speeches (which Smith does not translate); finally, they put specially prepared sticks between the heaps of corn. They explained to him that "the circle of meale signified their Country, the circles of corne the bounds of the Sea, and the stickes his Country. They imagined the world to be flat and round, like a trencher, and they in the middest" (Smith 1986 [1624]:150). This sort of "map making" appears to have been typical not only of Powhatan but of southeastern Indian cartography in general, as Waselkov argues persuasively (1989a).

Given this sort of evidence, including a nice piece of native exegesis, it would be surprising if we found no corresponding classification in Powhatan daily life. Indeed, Gleach concludes that the opposition between inside and outside is the principal, and perhaps the only, categorical distinction informing Powhatan conceptual order. His understanding of Powhatan dual sovereignty is couched in these terms, too. He calls the superior the "inside" chief and the subordinate the "outside" chief and argues that they were, respectively, a peace chief and a war chief (Gleach 1997:56–57, 142–143).

Although the argument that the subordinate was "outside" and the superior "inside" is valid, this conclusion does not take into account the associations of direction and elevation that the Powhatan clearly found at least equally important. (Calling the superior a peace chief and the subordinate a war chief is also overly simplistic.) Smith's report of the meaning of his conjuration shows us that the three forms of classification may be mapped on to each other, so that the linear asymmetry of directional classification was converted to a circular asymmetry and vice versa. The periphery, which the shamans, who explain the ritual, identified as the sea, was equivalent to the east and the nether regions and thus also to settlement, fertility, the feminine, and power; the center, therefore, was equivalent to the west and the higher regions, the wilderness, sterility, the masculine, and authority. The chief shaman's putting down the central circle in the diagram confirms this, as does the central location of the man clapping his hands to provide the beat for a dance. The werowance wearing a circular headdress, as at least two of them are reported to have done, should probably be added to this list.

A center-periphery (or as Gleach would prefer an inside-outside) dichotomy seems evident in the relation of Powhatan villages to the surrounding country, too. Some villages had palisades, which are usually—and reasonably—taken to be a form of military defense; but they are also to be understood as a way of separating the settled from the wild. Other villages were without physical definition, but the conceptual boundary was nevertheless there. Visitors might not enter until the werowance had emerged into the liminal space round the village and provided a suitable welcome, including orations and food. Only then were the visitors incorporated into the village and free to enter. The shift from settled horticultural village, through open woodland hunting-ground, to wilderness—a transition that corresponded to a shift from east to west—also corresponded to a move from center to periphery; from that outer limit one might, traveling in a line, move toward another center, which was another village. Politically, we may conceive of Powhatan territory as a series of such circles.

But the structure has to be understood as a fractal, the same relationships obtaining proportionately at every level of magnitude. The conjuration over Smith shows us that Tsenacommacoh was the center of the world. Within that realm the inherited tribes were a center for the whole polity. As one moved from there, Powhatan's influence became progressively weaker until disappearing altogether. The limit of his realm was not a fixed political boundary, as it would be today; instead, it was the limit of his ability to conquer or to influence, either directly or through agents. Each of the constituent tribes likewise had a center, the village in which the principal werowance lived. The center was opposed to the other villages of the tribe, which were conceptually classed with the wild; but each of these was itself a settled center surrounded by increasing degrees of wilderness.

In each village, we find the irreducible minimum of social organization, the household, centered on its fire like a ritual or a dance. The household fire was tended by the wife, who could not allow it go to out for fear of bringing "bad luck" on her family (Strachey 1953 [1612]:115). She thus carried out on a domestic level one of the important duties of the quiyoughcosough in his quioccasan. These structures, too, were center points; at least, Smith's account of his conjuration suggests that. They were the inverse of the political centers, the dark or mystical side of the Powhatan cosmos: centers of spiritual authority that waned and waxed again as one moved through the wilderness from one to another. Authority became converted to power progressively as one moved from the temple through tended open forest to gardens and into the village. But arriving at the domestic hearth, one found one's self again at a site of spiritual communication, so that although one had moved in a line one had come full circle.

Although we can see that the Powhatan could, and did, transform linear asymmetry—east-west and high-low—into a circular asymmetry and back again, there is an inherent difference between the two sorts of classification. East-west and high-low are of necessity relative, not absolute, distinctions. Powhatan social hierarchy, which was generically ambiguous but specifically definite, exhibited the same relativity. Even the quiyoughcosough, socially the ultimate authority, was himself but an agent of his spirits, the medium for their communications with ordinary people. A center, on the contrary, is absolute, or so it would seem, and if we equate authority with an absolute center, we cast serious doubt on the previous arguments. But the Powhatan recognized a number of centers, some of them subsuming others in a sliding scale that replicated, or was replicated by, the social relations of the principal persons in each. All aspects of Powhatan spatial classification were consonant with all aspects of their social classification.

One purpose of this analysis has been to demonstrate that dual sovereignty among the Powhatan, as elsewhere in the world, was a summary expression of fundamental classifying principles. As we have seen, the principles by which they ordered space they also applied to the definition of social status and social relations. We could at this point consider the demonstration sufficient and leave it at that. But spacial organization is but one aspect of Powhatan culture, and the analysis would be incomplete without a consideration of other equally significant aspects that also have a bearing on the nature of Powhatan sovereignty. These include cuisine and curing, sacrifice and funerals, gifts, and colors.

What is common to all these and allows us to identify the associations among them is a distinction between wet and dry. We have seen that moisture, in the form of the sea, was associated with the east and low elevation and thus with the feminine, fertility, and power. It was also the outermost boundary of the world and as such presumably had an absolute association with these qualities. Its contrary—at least in the "conjuration" Smith observed—was the desiccating fire, which we find at the center of all sorts of circles and which may have had just such an absolute association with masculinity, the west, sterility, and authority. Thus the common theme of moist or dry in cooking, curing, and the other aspects of Powhatan culture proceeds from the fact that these qualities of wet and dry encompassed all the others. They alone most closely approached the absolute, if they did not achieve it. Much if not all of Powhatan culture represents a dialectic of wetting and drying, which seems to have been a means to regulate and to balance these qualities in all aspects of their world.

Powhatan Cuisine

Both in its methods and its substance, Powhatan cuisine represents such a dialectic. Powhatan women did most of the cooking, a responsibility consonant with their role as the main transformers of raw materials into the culturally useful. Our only illustrations of cooking and eating come from Harriot (1972 [1590]), but the Jamestown colonists report similar methods among the Powhatan. In an engraving entitled "The browyllinge of their fishe ouer the flame," two fish lie on a hurdle, laid on four posts over a fire, and two more fish are propped on sticks stuck in the ground close to the fire. On one side of the hurdle a man holds a two-pronged utensil to turn the fish, and on the other another man approaches with a fresh supply of fish in a bark container. The companion picture shows the other major method of food preparation, boiling. They boiled "fruite, flesh, and fish" together, and in the engraving we can see the end of an ear of corn and a fishhead breaking the surface of the bubbling water. An oddly dressed woman seems to be about to stir the contents with a spoon, while a man fans the flames below.[12] The representation of a meal shows a man and woman sitting opposite each other (in what appear to be singularly immodest postures) on a mat on the ground with a dish or basket of something that is probably hominy—Harriot tells us that "their meate is Mayz sodden"—between them.[13] Various examples of foodstuffs—a fish, walnut, corn, clam, and possibly a squid—lie along the front of the mat, together with a large gourd, probably for water. According to Harriot, people usually ate in large groups rather than in pairs, but the men and the women were on opposite sides of the food as shown in the engraving (Harriot 1972 [1590]:Pls.13, 15, 16; also Spelman 1910 [1613]:cxiii).

Smith, Strachey, and Archer all mention that the Virginians boiled foods—corn, fish, meat, and some wild foods such as acorns and berries (Smith 1986 [1612]:151-163, [1624]:108-117; Strachey 1953 [1612]:80-81; Archer 1910 [1607]:xliii). Roasting, either over an open fire or in an oven, was another common cooking method. They cooked fish and meats on a hurdle in the same way as the Carolina Algonkians; Beverley (1947 [1705]:178) calls this "barbecuing" (he implies, erroneously, that it was a Powhatan term). But unlike the Carolinians, they also dried foods of many kinds either over a slow fire or in the sun, thus preserving them for some months or even years.[14] Tuckahoe root was roasted in an oven made of "oke leaves and ferne" and covered with earth, over which they kept a fire burning for 24 hours. Although Smith says that "raw it is no better then poison," it was a staple in the summer (Smith 1986 [1612]:153-154).

What was roast or dried might be boiled as well and usually was. At Arrohattock, the werowance gave the James River explorers "a Deare roasted; which according to their Custome they seethed againe" (Archer 1910 [1607]:xlii-xliii, xlviii). Smith lists a number of foods the Powhatan dried and then mixed with water, sometimes pounding them first. The treatment of nuts is typical. These were first "dryed to keepe," then pounded between stones, dried again, pounded again in a mortar until fine, and then poured into water to separate the shells from the meats. The result was a white milky liquid called *pawcohiscora*, which they stored for later consumption (Smith 1986 [1612]:152). According to Percy, "bread"-making also involved drying, wetting, and then redrying: "The manner of baking of bread is thus. After they pound their wheat [maize] into flowre, with hote water they make it into paste, and worke it into round balls and Cakes; then they put it into a pot of seething water: when it is sod throughly, they lay it on a smooth stone, where they harden it as well as in an Ouen" (1910 [1607]:lxix).

Fig. 10. Two people at a meal. Courtesy of the Library of Virginia.

Fig. 11. Boiling food. Courtesy of the Library of Virginia.

Beverley says that while the Powhatan cooked hominy and meat or fish in the same pot, "they never serve up different sorts of Victuals in one Dish; as Roast and Boyl'd, Fish and Flesh; but always serve them in several Vessels" (1947 [1705]:178). This implies a distinction between roast and boiled, made presumably on the basis of the last treatment the food had received and more generally between dry and wet.

Curing Ailments

The relation between wet and dry suggested by Powhatan cooking is found in their treatment of ailments also. The reported practices suggest that it aimed at restoring a balance between moist and dry in the patient. Medicinal roots (e.g., *wighsacan*) were treated the same way as foodstuffs, being dried first and then added to water, if for internal use, or moistened to make a paste, if for external use. The highly valued puccoon root was made into a salve in this way. If instead of water they added oil, made either from bear grease or acorns, it became the red paint with which Powhatan painted their heads and shoulders in order, so they said, to preserve their health and to moderate the effects of extreme temperatures. These treatments added moisture to the person, either externally or internally. Other treatments removed it. The sweat house that Strachey mentions is an obvious example. Another is the cure for a painful joint, for which one inserted a piece of wood about the size of a matchstick at the site of the pain and burned it down to the skin. The running sore that resulted let out the misery (Beverley 1947 [1705]:217). The annual use of wighsacan as a purge purified by dehydration. The conjuror's cure involved both wetting and drying, since the physician first sprayed the patient with water and then sucked the blood containing the illness from the body. Likewise, physicians would cauterize wounds by heating reeds to the burning point and then applying them over thin, wet leather to the ailing joint (Beverley 1947 [1705]:217).

The aim of Powhatan medicine, to establish a balance between extremes of dry and wet in the body, replicates the combination of wet and dry in Powhatan cuisine. This is so whether we consider the preparation of food diachronically, with alternate soaking and desiccation, or synchronically, with the regulation of wet and dried foods in the same dish. Powhatan cooking methods strongly resemble the forms of sacrifice described by the colonists; indeed, their whole structure of sacrifice depended on the opposition between wet and dry and regulating the relations between them.

Sacrifice

Sacrifice was, besides trance, the major mode of communication between mundane and spiritual among the Powhatan. Like curing and cooking, the means and manner of sacrifice express a distinction between wet and dry; the symbolic meanings of sacrificial forms reiterate the whole range of oppositions set out previously, including that between authority and power. The means of sacrifice included immolation in fire, on stone, or in water; its matter included pearls, shell beads, tobacco, deer suet and blood, puccoon, copper, and human life. In the rituals of sacrifice we can identify, too, a color symbolism that was important in daily life also.

The Powhatan offered a variety of sacrifices, usually to ward off or lessen divine punishments but also in thanksgiving. The quiyoughcosough, the "priest," made the "chief sacrifices" (Smith 1986 [1608]:59), but any man could and did sacrifice on a number of other occasions. We may judge the importance of sacrifice from its function of ordering the world in the myth that Strachey and Purchas recount. According to Strachey's version, the Great Hare, the Creator,

> conceaved with himself how to people this great world, and with what kynd of Creatures, and yt is true (said he [Iopassus of Potomac, the narrator]) that at length he divised and made divers men and women and made provision for them to be kept vp yet for a while in a great bag, now there were certayne spirritts, which he described to be like great Giants, which came to the Hares dwelling place (being towards the rising of the Sun and hadd perseveraunce of the men and women, which

he had put into that great bag, and they would haue had them to eate, but the godlike Hare reproved those Caniball Spirritts and droue them awaie. . . . the old man went on, and said, how that godlike hare made the water and the fish therein and the land and a great deare, which should feed vpon the land, at which assembled the other 4. gods envious hereat, from the east the west from the north the sowth and with hunting poles kild this deare drest him, and after they had feasted with him departed againe east west north and sowth, at which the other god in despight of this their mallice to him, tooke all the haires of the slayne deare and spredd them vpon the earth with many powerfull wordes and charmes whereby every haire became a deare and then he opened the great bag, wherein the men and the women were, and placed them vpon the earth, a man and a woman in one Country and a man and a woman in another country, and so the world tooke his first begynning of mankynd (1953 [1612]:102)

Purchas's version, which is shorter and seems rather to summarize a narrative than to reproduce it, differs somewhat in its details, but it makes the same point. He says that the Great Hare came into Virginia from some other place (unidentified). The Hare "first made men," after which he "preserued them from a great Serpent." Then "two other Hares came thither, that Hare for their entertainment [i.e., to feast them] killed a Deere, which was then the only Deere that was, and strewing the haires of that Deeres hide, euery haire prooued a Deere" (Purchas 1617:954). According to this myth, the killing of a deer brought about both fecundity and social order. Powhatan sacrifice at the time of contact aimed most generally at repeating this feat, producing life from death.

More immediate purposes of sacrifice were to avert or dispel divine anger and to offer thanksgiving. "Before their dinners and suppers the better sort will take the first bit, and cast it in the fire, which is all the grace they are known to use" (Smith 1986 [1612]:171). Anyone who passed the "chief holie howse proper to Powhatan"

(Strachey 1953 [1612]:95) at Uttamussack, except a werowance or a quiyoughcosough, must make an offering of beads or copper in the water to Oke or suffer his displeasure (Smith 1986 [1612]:169–170). In severe thunderstorms, not uncommon during the summer in Tidewater Virginia, the conjuror threw some valuable item such as tobacco, puccoon, or copper into the river to calm the wrath of Oke (Smith 1986 [1608]:59, [1612]:171; Strachey 1953 [1612]:98). According to Beverley, who provides the only indigenous explanation of these actions, sacrifices in water were appropriate because the Powhatan saw in the eternally running water of rivers a metaphor for the permanence of divinity (1947 [1705]:213).

The Powhatan attributed the same permanence to stone, and so they erected stone altars called pawcorances at various places, especially where any memorable thing had happened.[15] Indeed, the altar stones were partly mnemonic and partly educational as well as sacrificial (Smith 1986 [1612]:171; Purchas 1906 [1625]:451; Beverley 1947 [1705]:213). Pawcorances could be used by anyone, not just quiyoughcosoughs, but we do not know for certain who received these particular sacrifices. The Powhatan offered sacrifice at a pawcorance when they returned from a raid or a hunt "and upon many other occasions," adds Smith unhelpfully (1986 [1612]:171), but he may be referring to the commencement of any activity, for which Beverley says a sacrifice was appropriate, and to first-fruits offerings (1947 [1705]:210, 202). Offerings included "blood, deare suet, and Tobacco" (Smith 1986 [1612]:171). Smith does not say what sort of blood, although his context makes it sound as if deer, not human, blood is meant.

It may have been human blood, though, since Smith mentions as a form of punishment one that he presumably knew at firsthand: having one's brains beaten out on a "sacrificing stone" (1986 [1612]:175). Other colonists mention human sacrifice as well, although he is the only one to mention this form. William White, to whom we are indebted for knowledge of the huskanaw, describes what he calls the sacrifice to "the Diuell" of an Englishman, George

Cassen or Casson (Purchas 1617:953), and Strachey writes, "not only their owne children but Straungers are sometymes sacryficed vnto [Oke]" (1953 [1612]:89). Whether or not the Powhatan had a hierarchy of sacrifice, human sacrifice had to be highly significant, not necessarily because it involved killing a human but because it was more consequential than the other kinds. Those, according to the colonial accounts, addressed specific, short-term situations such as a storm or a successful raid or harvest. Human sacrifice secured general well-being over the long term. Although no direct statement to this effect occurs in the original sources, nevertheless we can arrive at this conclusion by an analysis of what they do tell us.

The colonial accounts mention three kinds of immolation for humans among the Powhatan: dashing out the brains, burning alive, and dismemberment followed by burning. (Humans were apparently not thrown into the water as sacrifices.) Each of these represents a special case of another kind of activity.

The suggestion that Powhatan's treatment of prisoners of war and of "malefactours" in his own domain were analogous forms of defending the realm finds support in the ceremonial beating out of brains, which repeated the action of a warrior on a raid. Smith observed Powhatan's warriors pretending to do this during the mock battle that they enacted for the colonists' "pleasure" (1986 [1612]:166); Spelman also mentions its occurrence during a real battle he saw between the Potomac and "Masomeck" (1910 [1613]:cxiv). In describing the "execution" of criminals, he tells us that before they were killed "cam the officer . . . , and *with* a shell cutt of[f] ther long locke, *wh*ich they weare on the leaft side of ther heade" (1910 [1613]:cxi; editors' italics and interpolation). This preliminary tonsure was likewise imposed on prisoners of war before their dispatch. Powhatan secular men wore their hair asymmetrically, very long on the left and short on the right. As I have shown elsewhere (Williamson 1979), the form of haircut among Powhatan reflected the wearer's status as male or female, dead or alive. Married women wore their hair long; shamans shaved their heads. Ordinary men were both male and female and consequently wore their hair both short and long. Logically, then, cutting the long hair off removed the feminine aspect of the culprit. Assuming an association between death and the spiritual, it made him also a more fitting gift to offer (masculine) divinity—a sacrifice.[16] Smith says that those who "displeased" Powhatan merited death by bludgeoning, and he distinguishes these from the "notorious enimie." He thus implies that these victims were Powhatan's subjects. The similarities adduced here prompt the suggestion that they had done something so heinous as to make them seem non- or anti-Powhatan.

The custom of casting victims into the fire involved tying the captive to a tree, not far from which was a large fire in a pit. A person Smith identifies as the "executioner" cut off parts of the victim's body at the joints one at a time, throwing each part into the fire as it was removed. Then, while the victim was made to watch, his head and face were flayed piecemeal and the skin burned; the innards were then pulled out and thrown into the fire.[17] Finally, the remains of the body and the tree were burned together in the pit (Smith 1986 [1612]:175; Strachey 1953 [1612]:60; Spelman 1910 [1613]:cxi).

What appears to have been a short version of this ritual, in which the victim was simply flung into a large fire or pit of coals, is reported by Smith (1986 [1612]:174; see Spelman 1910 [1613]:cxi; Purchas 1617:956). What made one form more acceptable than another on any given occasion is something we cannot now discover, since Smith refers to the victims in both cases as "malefactors." One would imagine the duration to have been proportionate to the severity of the crime, but the choice may have been a matter of expediency.

Smith conveys that the ferocity of this treatment proceeded directly from Powhatan's egotistical (that is, "savage") rage at being "offended." Following Hocart (1970a:152), I prefer to understand these actions as obligatory on the part of Powhatan. I take them to have been formalized actions, too—not, that is, the result of anyone's extemporaneous invention. The formality of an execution does not in itself warrant calling the event a sacrifice, and none of these writers explicitly calls this treatment by that term. My doing so rests partly on other documentary evidence. Percy and White give us accounts of almost identical killings, which they call sacrifices. White's, indeed, is about the death of Cassen: "sacrificed, as they [the English] thought, to the Diuell, being stripped naked, and bound to two stakes, with his backe against a great fire; then did they rippe him and burne his bowels, and dried his flesh to the bones, which they kept aboue ground in a by-roome" (1969 [1614]:150). Percy describes the later immolation of Captain Ratcliffe, who had gone to Powhatan to trade. Having cut off and killed most or all of Ratcliffe's men, Powhatan's men surprised the captain and "bownd [him] unto a tree naked wth a fyer before And by woemen his fleshe was skraped from his bones wth mussell shelles and befre his face throwne into the fyer. And so for want of circumspection miserably [per]ished" (Percy 1922 [1612]:266). Earlier, according to Percy, the Indians at Nansemond had captured two English messengers and said afterward that "they [the messengers] weare sacrifysed And thatt their Braynes weare cutt and skraped outt of their heades wth mussell shelles" (1922 [1612]:263). There seems little doubt that the "sacrifices" described in these passages belong to the same category as the "executions" described by Smith and other colonists, even though these victims were prisoners of war and the others were criminals.

Sacrifice in water and in fire take to extremes Powhatan methods of cooking, suggesting the possibility, following de Heusch (1985:17–22), that they were intended to provide divine feasts. Such an interpretation allows us to see the sacrificer feeding the divinity as an analogue of the wife feeding her husband, the hierarchy in both cases the same. A difficulty with this interpretation arises when we look at what was actually sacrificed in what medium. Sacrifices cast into fire were certainly edible: deer suet, blood, a part of a meal. Human victims would appear to have been associated with the "edible" category, although on what grounds we cannot be sure today. There is no evidence (cf. Sheehan 1980:46) that the Powhatan were cannibals; indeed, Wingfield writes with apparent relief that on 6 September 1607 "*Paspaheigh* sent vs a boy that was run from vs. This was the first assurance of his peace with vs; besides wee found them no Canyballs" (1910 [1608]:lxxvii). The myth Strachey recounts suggests that the Powhatan found the consumption of human beings objectionable even among divinities. Nevertheless, the mythic juxtaposition of the first people and the first deer reiterates the identification between them suggested by the forms of sacrifice. What went into the water was, on the contrary, inedible: pearls, shell beads, puccoon, and copper. Tobacco, ambiguously edible, could be immolated in either.

There is nothing to suggest that the Powhatan thought that their spirits in any sense ate any of the items sacrificed to them. Thus taking forms of sacrifice as extremes of cooking, something intended to prepare a meal fit for the gods, would appear in this case to be questionable. But the distinction between the dry and the wet does obtain; together with an understanding of the color symbolism, it allows us to make sense of the variety of Powhatan sacrificial ritual described in the documents.

The Powhatan valued running water and stone as symbols of permanence, and therefore they offered sacrifices there. The value of fire, the third sacrificial medium, seems to have been that it was the means by which the wet-dry dialectic was achieved. They used fire to transform the state of a thing from wet to dry or the reverse in almost any context where such a change was desirable (cooking, relieving a sore joint, and so on). In cases where things were dried in the sun—like food and corpses—the fire and the sun were analogous. Other ritual uses of fire confirm this. In Smith's "conjuration," the shamans explicitly identified the ceremonial fire with the Powhatan as a whole, and presumably the same symbolism informed the central placing of a fire during dances. We have seen, too, that the Powhatan saw as analogous the heart, the mamanatowick (Powhatan), and the sun—as the heart was to one's own life and honor, so Powhatan was to the society and the sun was to the world as a whole. We know from Percy's account of morning sun worship that a circle was appropriate for addressing that divinity (1910 [1607]:lxxi, lxxiii). It needs no great feat of imagination to see the central fire as a figuration of the central sun (see Hudson 1976:126; Swanton 1928; Gleach 1997).

The transforming virtue of fire is apparent in the dispatch of an "offender" who was burned to death, whether or not he was dismembered first, since he was rendered dry ash by the operation. But we also find it in the treatment of a dead werowance, of which it was the inversion; this practice also confirms the association of the sun with fire as well as that between authority and desiccation. We know quite a bit about the funerals of chiefs. In England at that time, the heraldic funeral was the subject of considerable elaboration, and the colonists' interest in Powhatan deposition of the dead arose as much from a desire to assess their degree of civility as from concern about whether they understood that the soul was immortal. It was usual for a noble English corpse to be eviscerated and embalmed; the organs were deposited in a separate urn and the body wrapped in a cere-cloth or winding-sheet (the necessity of this last is evident in the fact that even the poorest corpse had a winding-sheet). Coffins at this period were rare and confined to a few of the very wealthy. Coffined or not, the body was borne to the cemetery on a wooden bier in a procession whose length and ostentation proclaimed the social importance of the deceased. Black cloth for mourning hangings and dress was usual for both sexes (Bland 1986; Gittings 1984; Litten 1991).

Although their methods differed, the English and the Powhatan were alike in wishing to preserve the bodies of their high-ranking dead, and much (though certainly not all) that the Powhatan did in this regard must have reassured the colonists. According to Smith, "Their [chiefs'] bodies are first bowelled, then dryed upon hurdles till they bee verie dry, and so about the most of their jointes and necke they hang bracelets or chaines of copper, pearle, and such like, as they use to weare, their inwards they stuffe with copper beads and covered with a skin, hatchets and such trash. Then lappe they them very carefully in white skins and so rowle them in mats for their winding sheetes. And in the Tombe which is an arch made of mats, they lay them orderly. What remaineth of this kinde of wealth their kings have, they set at their feet in baskets" (1986 [1612]:169).

Strachey provides much the same information, but there are some differences worth noting. He says that the flesh was scraped from the bones as soon as death occurred; flesh and bones were dried separately, after which the flesh was put into "little potts (like the ancyent vrnes)"; he mentions that the Powhatan did not use any of the materials the ancients used to mummify their dead (he seems to have had the Egyptians in mind). To the collection of valuables stored with the deceased he adds "his Apooke [tobacco] and Pipe, and any one toy which in his life, he held most deere in his fancy," and he includes pearls and beads as well as copper in the abdominal filling (Strachey 1953 [1612]:94). Beverley reports similar customs in the early 18th century: first, they flayed the body carefully, making the incisions at the back of the body. Then they scraped the flesh off the bones but left the ligaments so that the skeleton remained articulated. Both flesh and bones were dried in the sun. They put the skeleton back into its skin, filled out the depressions with fine white sand, and sewed the skin together so that the body looked as if it were still intact. They put the dried flesh into a basket that they placed at the feet of the body (Beverley 1947 [1705]:214; see Anonymous 1959 [1689]:231–232).[18]

The resulting mummy was placed on a platform at the west end of the quioccasan next to those of its predecessors, in the care of the quiyoughcosoughs of the tribe. The preservation of the body, its being filled with valuables, and its placement in a religious structure dedicated to a spirit who, we know from other contexts, maintained the flow of life-giving resources for the Powhatan all suggest that even in death the werowances were held to be a source of life. In this they had the same function as human sacrifices.

The treatment of a deceased chief and the most elaborate form of human sacrifice are mutual inversions. The rituals exposed a body in which the fluids were still present to the parching action of the fire or the sun but with opposite results. The funeral preparation began with a dead body from which the skin and entrails were carefully removed and preserved; the skeleton was articulated; the entrails were replaced with valuables; and the body was preserved in a state as lifelike as Powhatan technology could achieve. The related form of sacrifice began with a living body from which the skin was removed haphazardly and burned, the joints disarticulated and burned, and the entrails ripped out and burned; finally, the entire body was destroyed by burning.[19]

These opposed treatments reiterate the fact that a chief and a prisoner were at opposite ends of a spectrum in Powhatan society. What is perhaps not immediately clear, though, is that these practices contributed to the prosperity of those in between, beyond the well-known fact that sacrifice is a common means of ensuring well-being (Hubert and Mauss 1964; Evans-Pritchard 1956; de Heusch 1985; Dumézil 1988). The consumption by fire of a prisoner's body has parallels in other Powhatan cultural practices, such as making salt ash (Smith 1986 [1624]:77; Beverley 1947 [1705]:180) or hollowing logs to make canoes (Harriot 1972 [1590]:Pl. 13; Smith 1986 [1612]:163). The clearing of gardens by burning is more obviously connected to the sacrifice: both were part of a cycle of destruction and renewed growth, burning a garden to yield new plant life, burning a human to yield new human life. We find burning in more ceremonial activities as well: making offerings before meals or smoking tobacco to signify friendship (Archer 1910 [1607]:xliii, l; Percy 1910 [1607]:xlvi; Beverley 1947 [1705]:1868; Hamor 1615:39). Tobacco was burned as an offering to divinities also: Smith says that during the conjuration held during his captivity, the "chief priest" threw "great cakes of Deere suet, Deare, and Tobacco" into the fire in the center of the house (1986 [1608]:59; see Harriot 1972 [1590]:16).

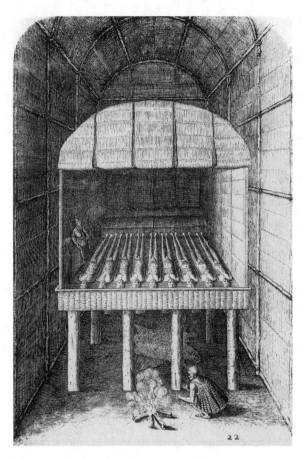

Fig. 12. Carolina Algonkian tomb with mummies.
Courtesy of the Library of Virginia.

We hardly need Beverley's observation that the Powhatan valued stone for its permanence to understand the reason for the desiccation of an organic substance. If dried foods lasted the Powhatan longer than fresh and provided sustenance in lean times, a dried chief was intended to last forever and provide life for his people. As Hertz points out, a primary intention of funerals is to render the body of the deceased in an immutable, and therefore pure, state, whether by allowing decomposition, by cremation, or by (as in this case) mummification (Hertz 1960). The method chosen reflects ideas about, among others, the relationship of the dead to the living. For the Powhatan, a mummified chief seems to have signified, and therefore ensured, the continuity of their polity, much as the Shilluk king symbolizes a transcendent eternal kingdom (Evans-Pritchard 1962). The body remained in the quioccasan because the werowance became after death even more closely associated with the spirits than he had been in life (see Hocart 1970a); thus he became even more important as a conduit of spiritual power to his subjects. This explains, in part, the custom of filling the abdominal cavity with valuables, a reference to the idea that the best things in life came out of the (living) chief's own body as ossified semen.

The idea that death is necessary to produce life is common in native American cosmology, and we should not be surprised to find it among the Powhatan. Mummification and cremation represent two ways—one linear, one cyclical—to ensure continuity, that is, a balance in moist and dry. The desiccated chief was nevertheless still alive—at least, his spirit was—and he was a conduit of benefits from the western spiritual abode to the land of the living. The desiccated sacrifice was as dead as a garden patch before it is sown and in the same way would bring about a renewal of life, part of the endless cycle of destruction and renaissance.

This interpretation is suggested by the descriptions of these rituals, but without taking into consideration other Powhatan ritual forms, it remains but tentative. All these rituals acquired their meanings by reference to each other as well as to other aspects of Powhatan collective experience. Thus in order to be conclusive we must consider what is known of other Powhatan sacrificial forms as well: sacrifices into water and on pawcorances, in which the appropriate gifts were usually Powhatan valuables and the blood or fat of deer. The distinction between wet and dry that I have identified in other contexts is at work in these rituals, too, but their consequences were somewhat different, as the permanence of stone or of running water is different from that of coals or ash.

Sacrifices in water were for purposes such as stopping a thunder-storm or appeasing the anger of Oke; we may regard these as the same, since the anger probably took the form of a thunderstorm. An appeal in water, then, was made to the punishing aspect of Oke, which is to say the executive power of the spirit. This agrees with the oppositions laid out so far. The exercise of such power is necessarily short-lived, suggesting a further association between moist and the temporary. Beverley, we have seen, says that the Powhatan revered rivers because of their permanence. That was a Heraclitan perma-nence, though. Generically rivers go on forever, but specifically they change constantly. There is a logic about offering into a river a sac-rifice intended to avert or change some unpleasant condition. This may not have been the Powhatan logic, but it is a reasonable inter-pretation of the facts.

Offerings into water and into fire sought to balance moist and dry by bringing their extremes into contact. Water offerings were pri-marily hard and imperishable, and they were designed to reduce the amount of water. Fire offerings were perishable, and they may have been a supplication against drought. Nonhuman sacrifices made on pawcorances represent a mediation of these extremes.[20] Although Smith is vague on the point, it appears that these altar stones re-ceived blood and deer fat following the successful conclusion of some activity such as a raid or a hunt. They were, in other words, sites of thanksgiving rather than places to avert danger, and thus they referred to conditions that the Powhatan hoped would persist forever. But they could not take them for granted; they explained their morality and their obligation to initiate their sons in terms of avoiding the anger of Oke and the consequent withdrawal of game and other means to life, and misfortunes such as drought were held to be due to divine wrath at human wrongdoing. In hopes of averting these, and so perpetuating a desirable condition, they made offerings on permanent altar stones, the markers for their collective memory.

The pawcorance was probably the most immediate representation to ordinary Powhatan of the presence of spirits among them. They were set up anywhere that spirit seemed to have manifested itself to humans; thus they were not restricted to sacred spots, or rather any spot might become a locus of spiritual presence. Ordinary Powhatan seem to have sacrificed on them relatively frequently in association with routine activities. These offerings reproduced the colors, but not the imperishability, of offerings into water, suggesting that they addressed something temporary. The offerings were neither burned nor sodden but left to decay by natural means, mediating the extremes of other sacrifices. A raised stone, derived from the western uplands—natural stone is nonexistent in Tidewater—represented the spiritual, male, permanent, and authoritative; but since it might be found in the village or near a garden and was covered occasionally by substances liquid with putrefaction, it mediated the more momentous and extreme sacrifices just as ordinary Powhatan men mediated extremes of authority and power and male and female.

Color Classification among the Powhatan

The substances offered in these sacrifices express the same relationship between wet and dry, and thus between other complementary oppositions in Powhatan culture, that we find in the elements to which they were consigned. Copper, and probably puccoon, came from the western mountains, as did stone for hatchet blades and pawcorances; pearls and shells came from the eastern waters. But these things were also colored red, white, or black. The colors of these objects were significant not only in a sacrificial context but in ordinary life as well (see Miller and Hamell 1986; Lankford 1992).

The symbolism of this color triad is consonant with the oppositions discussed so far.[21] Most obviously, there was an association between white and the sea and between red and the land or the mountains. But the color classification is more complex than this, and not only because this association ignores the importance of black. The Powhatan assigned meanings to colors alone, but they regarded combinations of colors—white and red, black and red—as yet more significant. Black was the color appropriate to spirits and spiritual communion; it represented permanence, the static and predictable, and authority—characteristics of Dumézil's *gravitas*. White belonged to the mundane, to civil activity of a peaceful nature, to change and short-term relationships, and to power—characteristics of *celeritas*. Red most usually appeared in association with one or the other and took its meaning from that context. Thus Powhatan color symbolism was consonant with dual sovereignty, both proceeding from the same cultural principles and expressing them.

White figures largely in Powhatan ornament, mostly in the form of strings of shell, bone, or pearl beads but also in paint and in white bird down on the head or the body. The strings of beads and the down appear to have been necessary for both men and women at council meetings (e.g., Smith 1986 [1624]:150), but everyone also wore beads in one form or another as part of their daily attire. The Powhatan used white paint alone only infrequently. Probably the most significant use was in the huskanaw, where the initiates were painted white for the first part of the ceremony. The shamans at the "divination" over Smith during his captivity included white in their face-paint, as did the warriors who attacked the English at Kecoughtan and the women who performed the "maskarado" that took Smith aback so (Smith 1986 [1624]:149, 144, [1612]:236).

Usually the Powhatan painted their heads and shoulders red with a mixture of puccoon root and oil. All ordinary adult persons, and possibly children as well, wore this daily. The shamans, warriors, and dancers included some red in their face-paint. Two werowances are described as wearing a headdress that included red-painted "deer hair": Percy, for instance, writes that the werowance of Quiyoughcohannock wore a "Crown of Deares Haire colloured red, in fashion of a Rose fastened about his knot of haire, and a great Plate of Copper on the other side of his head" (1910 [1607]:lxv; see also Archer 1910 [1607]:xliii). Most of the figures in John White's watercolors, incidentally, show no body paint; apparently the Carolina Algonkians had a different attitude to body ornament.

The most important red substance to the Powhatan was neither paint nor puccoon but copper. They seem never to have used it for tools but rather for ornament and gifts, as they used pearls and beads. Unlike the white ornaments, copper seems to have been a prerogative almost exclusively of men. A man was expected to provide his wife with copper as well as beads, but the Jamestown documents mention only three women—the "quene" of Appomattox and a couple of werowances' wives—actually wearing any copper. Men, on the contrary, habitually wore quite a lot of copper. As a gift, copper seems most often to have been used by a werowance to enlist the aid of allies in staging a raid. We may conclude from this that among the Virginians copper was gender-marked as male, which is suggested also by the fact that the werowance of Quiyoughcohannock wore his copper on the right (i.e., male) side of his head and his red-dyed deerskin on the left (i.e., female) side. As a male substance, copper was bound up with warfare in a way that puccoon was not.[22]

Black receives comparatively little mention in the Jamestown documents, perhaps because its use was more restricted than that of either white or red. Black valuables, for instance, are difficult to identify. Possibly stone items such as hatchet blades and pawcorances fell into this category. The stone hatchet blades may have been as highly valued as copper; iron hatchets were among the most frequently pilfered items from James Fort. Whether they were genuinely black or not, altars and even hatchets figure in ritual contexts where black was the most appropriate color. Thus including them in a category of black valuables is not inconsistent with other Powhatan usage.

Only slightly less obscure in the accounts are strings of black pearls. Strachey says that the blackened pearls in Virginia resulted from the Indians roasting the oysters in the fire before determining if there were pearls within.[23] He does not tell us much about these items, making his observation in passing, as an example of the failure of the Indians to develop and profit by the valuables in their country: "Lastly that the Lakes haue Perles, yt cannot be doubted for we our selues haue seene many Chaynes and braceletts worne by the people, and we haue found plenty of them in the Sepulchers of their kings though discoloured by burning the Oysters in the Fier" (Strachey (1953 [1612]:132). His observation is dubious not just because it expresses an English mercantile point of view but, more important, because (with this possible exception) descriptions of living Powhatan say that they wore white pearls, not black. (White's Carolina Algonkians, however, are shown with black or blue beads, which may be pearls; cats. 45, 50, 51, 52.) Evidently, they usually inspected their oysters for pearls before roasting them. The blackening, then, was intentional. Although the passage is ambiguous, I take it to mean that such black pearls were found only in the sepulchres of the werowances.

This interpretation accords with much else that we know about the use of black. The image of Oke was painted black (though hung with chains of white pearl and copper), and we find black paint also on the shamans at Smith's conjuration, on warriors, and on the women who performed the masquerade. Beverley reports that quiyoughcosoughs painted themselves black just as ordinary Powhatan painted themselves red. At the ritual that effected Smith's adoption, which occurred in a quioccasan rather than a dwelling, "Powhatan more like a devill then a man with some two hundred more as blacke as himselfe, came unto him and told him now they were friends" (Smith 1986 [1624]:151). Mourning women painted their faces black with charcoal and oil. (The colonists do not mention men mourning.) Black was important in the huskanaw as well. The men who participated in the huskanaw were painted black or wore black-painted accoutrements, and Smith calls the boys who went through this ritual "black-boyes," even though they were initially painted white, presumably because the ritual moved them from a state of religious ignorance, signified by the white paint, to revelation, signified by black paint (Smith 1986:124–125). Among northern Algonkians, at least, a black face indicates that one is seeking spiritual guidance or blessing (e.g., Bragdon 1996:143; Landes 1971:3–5; Densmore 1929:71; see Harrington 1921:83; Simmons 1986:39), and the huskanaw involved, if it was not primarily, a vision quest.

This evidence indicates that black represented the spiritual, including the spirits of the dead, and thus it represented death also. In most of the contexts cited here the association is obvious. In the case of the black-painted warriors, we know that an image of Oke was carried into battle on that occasion (Smith 1986 [1624]:144). If the "maskarado" of the women was a thanksgiving dance addressed to spirits, that would account for their black paint as well.

Smith and Strachey both say that the black paint of mourning women was made by combining powdered charcoal with oil, and presumably all black paint was made this way. According to Strachey's word list, the word for black, *mahcatawaiuwh*, is closely related to, if not derived from, the word for "cole of fier," *mahcatois* (1953 [1612]:177, 184; see Siebert 1975:317, 325). This suggests a strong similarity between the paint of those in spiritual communion and the burning to ash of important sacrifices. The humans so immolated were blackened even more thoroughly than their sacrificers and by something like the same agent.

Black paint must be associated with things dry because it was derived from charcoal, because it was associated with the spiritual westerly landward elevated side of Powhatan territory, and because it was opposed to white. The white items the Powhatan valued came from the water and from the east (most of them seem to have been made on the Eastern Shore), associated with life and renewal but also with the mundane rather than the spiritual. The uses reported for white items confirm these associations. The use of white to signify the initiates' lack of spiritual experience in the huskanaw is obvious. The striking presence of white ornament on persons gathered for an occasion of state, evidently much more obvious than for ordinary wear, suggests that white distinguished the occasion as civil or mundane rather than spiritual. We can make a similar observation about the circumstances in which white beads alone were used: a man separating his son's bride from her family and Powhatan (and perhaps any werowance) rewarding his gardeners, restoring relations with a subordinate, or establishing the legitimacy of his envoy. In the case of the huskanaw, white stands against black; in these cases, though, it stands against red. The white beads that a man's father gave to the father of his new daughter-in-law should be distinguished from the bride-price his son had given her family, which consisted of copper as well as beads. After Powhatan showered his workers with white beads, he rewarded certain of his bravest warriors individually with presents of beads and of copper. And if pearls were the medium by which a chief insisted on the submission of troublesome subordinates, copper persuaded others to follow him — or his agent — into conflict.

Red, then, seems to have been associated with the mundane along with white. But red is often if not necessarily a symbol with ambiguous meaning (Turner 1967:80–81), and it seems to have been among the Powhatan, too. Black and white were clearly opposites, but red was associated with both peaceful pursuits and with warfare, with the social and the spiritual. Moreover, it was usually paired with either white or black, making it opposed to its pair's opposite in that context. Thus in battles and rituals we find black combined with red and, to a much lesser degree, with white, whereas on occasions of state white and red were the dominant colors. John White's handsome "Indian in Body Paint" (cat. 52) has a thin line of white paint along the edges of the larger areas of red paint, and White's text identifies it as paint for "generall huntings or Solemne feasts," not for warfare.

An association black = spiritual and white/red = mundane is, however, insufficient to account for all the facts, since, among other things, white and red figured in certain kinds of sacrifice as well as in what the English call the "trash" stuffed into the abdomen of a chiefly mummy.[24] To say instead that black represented permanence and red and white represented change allows us to explain all these uses, spiritual and mundane. The black-colored spirit Oke was associated with dead persons of authority, whose bodies were desiccated and unchanging, like their stone altars (which were a means to preserving the memory of the past as well as places of sacrifice).

Authority itself constitutes a kind of stasis; it is one aspect of Dumézil's *gravitas,* that is, law and order, regularity and the predictable. The mummified chiefs and shamans in the conceptual center of each Powhatan territory, their souls with the eternal Oke, represented the quintessence of permanence. Like the coal-based black paint, the mummies resulted from the action of fire or of the sun, which fire imitated. The spirit Oke received blackened sacrifices because they, too, had been transmuted beyond mutability. And the motive for these sacrifices was to ensure long-term stability.

Power, the complement of authority, is an aspect of Dumézil's *celeritas;* it involves change and contingency, which is to say action. The colors appropriate to these, white or red and white in combination, are also the colors of a living body capable of action. (No causal relationship is proposed here, since it is as likely that the Powhatan considered that a body was active because it was red as that they cherished red because it characterized active bodies.) We have seen how this principle was applied in sacrifice, where red and white gifts addressed the powerful punishing aspect of Oke. In the context of the mundane, red and white likewise signified action and therefore the contingent and transitory. Consistently the Powhatan used red and white for persons and for social situations, both of which are contingent and temporary however much we may at times wish it otherwise. The red and white ornament proper for a Powhatan council meeting was congruent with the inherent instability of political relations and the unpredictable consequences of political action. The bride-price of copper and white beads was appropriate to a relationship whose initiation and termination were matters of choice and chance. Copper made temporary allies of those who accepted it; the werowance's red deer-hair and copper headdress identified the current occupant of a social status; the fertilizing white beads scattered after ritual planting marked a stage in the agricultural cycle.

The combination in the quioccasan of red and white ornaments with a preponderance of black may be understood in these terms as well. Although a repository for the dead and a house for spirits, the quioccasan also had a perpetual fire and a doorway facing east. It retained, that is, a connection to the lively contingent world, for which it was the conduit of spiritual benefits. Like Powhatan persons, its nature must be understood as part of a continuum, not as something absolute. The valuables included in the body of the chiefly mummy may have been intended to ensure the continued existence of the spirit. It may be going too far to say that they represented a kind of posthumous pregnancy; nevertheless, the image is not inapt if the reason for mummification was to guarantee that the werowance, even static in death, provided the means of life and action for his people.

Dual Sovereignty as a Total Social Phenomenon

The black-painted quiyoughcosough and the red-crowned werowance with his strings of white beads embodied Powhatan cultural categories. The relationship of authority to power, or dual sovereignty, that they represented informed and expressed categorical relations in every other aspect of the Powhatan world.

All hierarchical relationships in Powhatan society were expressions of this principle. Any pair of statuses displayed the same structure: the superior was always the authority, and he was more spiritual, more masculine, and physically higher than the subordinate, who was always the power, the more mundane, the more feminine, and physically lower. Although a status, as an abstraction, had a constant place within the hierarchy as a whole, its relevance to any given person depended on the social context. The only exceptions in human society were the commoner wife, who was always subordinate, female, and endowed with power; and the shaman, who was always superior, male, and endowed with authority. And even he was subservient and female in comparison to the spirits he served, indicating that the principle of sliding status extended beyond human social relations.

Identification of this principle allows us to understand the reason for the confusion among the colonists about these relationships and in consequence to make sense of their contradictory accounts. It permits the reconstruction of precontact Powhatan social organization and social functioning. But it takes us even further, because this principle was itself only one expression of basic Powhatan cultural ideas about the nature and workings of the world as a whole. Their hierarchy must be understood primarily as a way for them to be in harmony with the cosmos. It was not, in other words, conceived of as a means for the dominant to deprive the subordinate of autonomy or wealth or anything else, and it does not seem to have operated like that either. Therefore we find a consonance among the hierarchical relationships, cosmology, geography, subsistence, wealth, gender, reproduction, social relations, relations with spirits, the yearly cycle, the cycle of life. The dialectic of status is the same as the dialectic of moist and sere and thus the annual shift from farming to hunting, from low elevation to high, from mundane to spiritual, from east to west, and so on. Powhatan culture was based on a principle of ordered alternation, the shaman and the chief between them ensuring the order. Their hierarchy is simply the form in which it has been made most obvious to us today. But comprehension of the full dimensions of Powhatan dual sovereignty requires a study of the whole culture, which likewise is incomprehensible without an understanding of the relations of sovereignty.

6. Conclusion

The use of colonial documents to re-create earlier forms of radically changed cultures is an established practice in anthropology. By this means, modern scholars have been able to identify cultural characteristics (e.g., modes of subsistence, forms of housing, physical appearance) and to show their distribution through space and, with the help of archaeology, through time. This kind of information has been used to develop hypotheses about such problems as the relation of cultural forms to environment and the identification of diffusion and independent invention in cultural change. More recently, interest has shifted from these questions to the evolution of hierarchical societies and the consequences of colonial intrusion, and whether and how the two may be related. This represents a change not just of focus but of the understanding of culture, since instead of producing a laundry list of cultural "traits" it tries to understand something of the integration of the culture into a whole. The present analysis demonstrates that it is possible to retrieve a very considerable amount of information about meaning and cultural integration from colonial sources. Dumézil's insistence that "the system is truly inherent in the material" (1988:17) is justified here as well.

Having recognized that dual sovereignty was present among the Powhatan at the time of contact with the English (and very likely well before that), we may consider the variety of forms and manifestations of this relationship in the rest of the continent. Dyarchy was present in the deep Southeast, as we have seen. In the Southwest, we find an opposition between the peace chief, the "inside" or "village" chief, who exercises authority, and the war chief, the "outside" chief, who arbitrates people's disputes and organizes them in warfare. The opposition between a peace chief, who is superior, and a war chief, who is subordinate, is found in the Plains and the Great

Lakes regions as well. The relationship between shaman and chief on the Northwest Coast is different again (but these cultures have as much in common with those of the Pacific as they have with the rest of native North America). Among the northeastern Iroquoians and Algonkians, the relationship between the sachem and the war chief, later called the Pine Tree Chief, may be called a dyarchy also.

This very superficial survey suggests some of the possibilities for further analysis. The examples available in native North America may be connected historically, as are those from Indo-European cultures, but it is a different history played out in different physical circumstances, which in itself may prove informative.

The value of such an extensive study goes beyond simply adding instances of the form to a list already, one might have said, sufficiently long. The present study, for example, confirms Needham's almost casual observation (1980:89) that while a complementarity between authority and power is global, and may indeed be universal, neither of these constructs is logically (i.e., necessarily) related to any other complementary pair. The present analysis demonstrates that the spiritual or mystical need not always be associated with the feminine, nor the political—commonly equated with power—with the masculine. In the Powhatan case, the spiritual has authority over the mundane in every case; in other cultural examples (e.g., the Atoni; Cunningham 1973) the reverse is true, and the spiritual comes under the control of the worldly. All sorts of permutations and transformations in these relations are to be expected, and common instances as well as rare ones deserve attention and explanation.

So much would be true even if we considered merely the form of governance in each case; but, as I have tried to show, the principle of dual sovereignty is found in every sort of Powhatan social relationship that we can reconstruct. That the principle was so thoroughly influential among the Powhatan provokes several hypotheses, the most obvious of which is whether it might not be equally pervasive in every culture whose governance takes the form of dual sovereignty. As this analysis shows, regarding the household or the family as a miniature kingdom puts the vexed question of gender hierarchy in a very different light. As a corollary, we may ask whether some intimation of dual sovereignty might be found among so-called egalitarian groups such as the Inuit or the sub-Arctic Athapaskans. Anticipating a positive answer, I propose that the most obvious dyarchies, those characteristic of hierarchical societies, do not constitute a cultural form in and of themselves requiring a separate category of "theory" for their understanding; on the contrary, they are one example of a usual way of ordering social relationships of any kind.

The assumption that all social relationships are relations of power is commonplace; the proposal that they are also examples, on different scales, of dyarchy would appear to be but a restatement of that assumption and therefore pointless. I would resist such an interpretation, however. Dyarchy is not conceived as a relationship between two persons in a contest for control over one another but a complementarity in which one acts as the power for the other, who makes legitimate the exercise of that power. How any particular instance of the relationship is worked out in practice is partly a matter of contingency, but ultimately it must have reference to the ideal structure and realize it.

The idea that all social relationships are power relationships is to be resisted also because of its implicit assumption that "power" means, that it must mean, coercive control over others. The definition may hold for Europe and its colonial offspring, but the native cultures of the Americas demonstrate repeatedly that, to them, power has (or had) no such significance. The same may be said of the precolonial cultures of Indonesia, Micronesia, and Polynesia, all characterized by rank-ordering of greater or lesser involution and in all of which power is the complement of authority and refers to the efficacy of its possessor.

The greatest value of the study of dual sovereignty is that it demonstrates so clearly that authority is as necessary to effective governance as is power. Modern politics and political discourse, however, concentrate on power, which they understand as control, to the exclusion of authority, so that leaders are no longer said to assume authority; instead, they come into power. This way of thinking has distressing consequences. It has become difficult, if not impossible, to construe any hierarchical relationship at all in terms other than power and coercion, whether real or implied. One result of this frame of mind is that such relationships do in fact become relations of power. This is not simply to say that one party controls the other and that since power is supposed to be limited, the subordinate party automatically loses some or all autonomy. More profound is that the parties to the relationship themselves think that it is a power relationship, the superior being constrained to compel and to expect resistance and the subordinate to expect compulsion and so to resent and resist the encroachment on liberty. The exercise of legitimate authority, such as that possessed by an African king, a university professor, a parent, is perceived to offer such encroachment and results in intervention by democratic governments, boards of inquiry, or social services.

None of this is to deny that persons in authority do abuse it. The relation between authority and power is easily defined in the abstract, but in practice distinguishing one from the other can be difficult. If we define "power" as "efficacy," then any authority who gives orders effectively may be said to have some power; likewise, any executive who successfully organizes labor in carrying out such orders may be said to have some authority. Drawing the line between the two is difficult not just for an observer but also for those constrained by these ambiguous concepts. But the fact that in practice there will be differences of opinion regarding the use and abuse of authority should not lead us to dismiss the notion out of hand. On the contrary, it has great value analytically because people who make such charges have an idea of authority against which they test specific actions. It is thus necessary to our understanding of action in such a society.

But there is still the by now universal problem of the conflation of authority with power. The history of colonialism provides numerous examples of this. Whether through ignorance or willfully, colonial forces ignored local distinctions and relations between authority and power, conscripting now one and now another to act as either or both and blurring a distinction that is difficult to maintain in the best of circumstances. The colonials themselves provided a model of a government at odds with the governed rather than in alliance with them. While it would be an oversimplification to insist that these factors are the sole causes of postcolonial instability, still they must be taken into account. The conception of a dyarchy is that authority may ordain, and no more; power may agree or refuse. The conflation of the two means that authority may not only ordain but require, leaving the supposed power, the executor, impotent— an end that the ordaining body may have intended. The resulting resentment and rebellion, however regrettable, are understandable.

Recognition that authority and power are separate qualities with different functions, obligations, and rights would revolutionize how we study society and the society we study.

Notes

Introduction

1. Rountree's book on Powhatan culture (1989) and Gleach's on Powhatan warfare (1997) are exceptions.

2. Most of the scholars who do recognize the possibility of cultural bias in these accounts offer no suggestions as to what it was. Swanton, writing about chiefs in the Southeast, says, "In spite of a natural tendency to exaggerate the power and state of Indian chiefs in agreement with ideas of the kingship prevailing in contemporary Europe" (1987:647). But one would like to know what those ideas were. See also, for example, Lurie (1959:38), Rountree (1989:115, 146), Dent (1995:216). Kupperman (1980) is much more thoroughgoing than these writers in her identification of English cultural assumptions about social relations and social status in the early Virginia documents. Gleach (1997) provides considerable information about military theory and practice in Europe, but otherwise he does not say much about English culture at that time.

3. Indeed, in a collection of papers, *The Anthropology of Power: Ethnographic Studies from Asia, Oceania, and the New World* (Fogelson and Adams 1977), all those pertaining to North America regard power as the (usually supernatural) ability to accomplish rather than as domination over other people.

4. Needham's examples are, besides the Shilluk, the Nyakyusa, Gurage, Meru, Purum, Karo, Lamet, Kachin, and the people of the Ryukyu Islands of Japan (1980). To this list may be added numerous examples from native North and Meso-America, including (besides the Southeast, which I discuss below), the Winnebago, Navajo, Hopi, Zuni, Kwakiutl, Maya, Aztec, and possibly Teotihuacán. The Pacific Islands, including Papua New Guinea, provide other examples. Feeley-Harnick (1985)

discusses additional cases from Africa and from Southeast Asia.

5. Misnumbered §37. Sir Edwin Sandys, a son of an archbishop of York under Elizabeth I, was a most influential treasurer of the Virginia Company from 1618 until its dissolution in 1624. His younger brother, George, became one of the governors of the colony (Davis 1955:44; Craven 1932).

6. Although tobacco is a native American domesticate, Craven includes it in this list because at the time of which he writes, the Spanish had begun to grow it in Spain and had established a monopoly on its sale in Europe.

7. Hakluyt was probably overly optimistic about the ease of Atlantic passage, possibly dangerously so. "The perils of the Atlantic passage impressed themselves vividly on all who contemplated it and unforgettably upon all who undertook it, whether in the seventeenth or the eighteenth centuries" (Zuckerman 1995:118). Voyages to Jamestown were no exception: the first, which set out in December 1606, was "kept six weekes in the sight of England" by contrary winds, a delay that almost cost them the life of their minister; it experienced at least one more serious storm off the coast of Virginia (Smith 1986 [1612]:204–205). The third supply, which left England in May of 1609, encountered a hurricane that separated the ship carrying the arriving governor, Sir Thomas Gates, and Sir George Somers, Captain Newport, and William Strachey (among others) from the others, who gave them up for dead until they reached Virginia in two ships they had constructed while shipwrecked on Bermuda (Strachey 1906 [1610]; Smith 1986 [1612]:268; Archer 1906 [1609]).

8. The distinction that Craven makes, while valid in the sense that today it needs to be made, is nevertheless anachronistic. As Kevin Sharpe observes, "what we would delineate as 'private interest,' distinct from and in confrontation with public roles and duties, was not accepted in early modern England"

(1989:13). The Virginia Company must necessarily operate in the interest of the commonweal.

9. As Craven (among others) has described, the Virginia Company underwent reorganization in 1609, 1612, and 1618 before it was finally dissolved by the Crown in 1624; the reorganizations were at least in part responses to changing conditions in Virginia as well as in London (Craven 1932, 1957, 1970). The original organization of the company, rather than its subsequent history, is most pertinent to the subject of this book, so I do not pursue this topic in any detail.

10. As this event was important not only to the colonists (or else, I assume, they would not have bothered to report it) but also to any attempt to understand political relations among Powhatan tribes and between the tribes and the sovereign, I discuss it in greater detail below. Although several accounts mention it, they do not all agree on who the ambassadors were, which day they came, or which tribes they identified as either friendly or inimical.

11. Waselkov (1989a) has a good assessment of the importance of Powhatan cartography to the success of Smith's endeavor.

12. Morgan (1996:14) identifies these Indians with the Iroquois. Jefferson, however, locates them west of the Powhatan and the Iroquoian-speaking Nottoway and Meherrin (who occupied territory south of the James River) and distinguishes them from the Siouan-speaking Manahoac who lived in the northern piedmont of Virginia; he says that their territory went as far as the Great Lakes (1832:98). If that were so, though, their presence in canoes on what was probably the Susquehanna River seems odd. Barbour (1986, 1:230n) says simply that they "spoke an Iroquoian language," which is the soundest conclusion. Morgan's identification (though it may in some sense be correct) must be viewed with reserve, given the date of the encounter, the multiplicity of Iroquoian-speaking groups in the region, and the extensive social disruption that occurred there between 1608 and the late 19th century.

13. Smith obviously thought the paramount ungenerous in the extreme; in fact, this is but one passage in which he so represents him. But Smith did, or would, not reckon with the idea of divine kingship (or semidivine, anyway). If, as Smith said elsewhere, the Powhatan really did esteem the paramount as "halfe a god" (1986 [1612]:174), how much more valuable must even his old shoes have been than the richest crown offered by a committee of mortals? Smith's comment on Powhatan's prestige may have been, like much that he wrote, intended ironically; but as I show below, he was in fact correct.

14. Elsewhere (Williamson 1992), I have suggested that the emphasis historians have placed on the relationship between Pocahontas and Smith is misguided because it diverts attention from the relationship between Smith and her father, which was really the crux of the success or failure of the Jamestown Colony. The evidence does strongly suggest that Powhatan saw in Smith a very powerful rival to his own sovereignty and that he so regarded him simply because of his personal characteristics. This particular incident may have given Smith more influence in the polity than Powhatan had at that time. Whether or not that were so, it is notable that this miraculous action had much more effect on the Indians than all of Smith's military rampages.

15. Tuckahoe is the green arrow arum (Barbour 1986, 1:153n). In the summer, when the even the green corn was not yet ready to harvest, this was a staple in the diet (Smith 1986 [1612]:153–154).

16. Although this phrase may allude to Ham seeing the nakedness of Noah, with attendant misfortune for his descendants, its main point is that the werowance of Nansemond was not materially in a class with Martin, who had arms and armor at his disposal (see Kupperman 1980:39–41, 2000:49); thus the attack was cowardly and unbecoming. No adult Powhatan was literally naked, and certainly no chief was.

17. The paramount, known today as Powhatan, took this name from a tribe and a territory where he was born and raised but in which he was not living in 1607. He had other titles and a proper name besides. The possible relationship among personal names, territorial names, and chiefly titles I explore in the next chapter.

18. To a modern reader, Barbour's would appear to be an understatement. Punishments ranged from being deprived of a day's rations (e.g., for missing daily divine service once) to flogging (missing such service twice, fornication, breaking or stealing a tool), losing one's ears (stealing food in the course of preparing it for the common mess), serving in the galleys (the same, second and third offense; missing daily divine worship three times), court-martial (failing to keep a clean house or to sweep the street in front of it), to death (failure to attend Sunday services three times; committing rape, sodomy, or adultery; robbing the colony's store; criticizing the government three times). It is desirable, though, to put this in some sort of contemporary context. By 1612 the cracks in English society that were to result in the Civil War were already apparent (Wrightson 1982; Underdown 1985; Sharpe 1989), and nowhere more than in religious matters where disputes between Puritans and Anglicans grew increasingly acrimonious. Nor was James I himself a popular figure, for a number of reasons. Whether cause or consequence, official censorship increased during his reign and that of his son, Charles I (Hill 1980:81–83; Patterson 1984; but see Sharpe 1989:9). The "Lawes," with their emphasis on religious conformity and unquestioning obedience to authority, appear to aim at countering these tendencies as they were manifest in the colony.

19. I have found no source that explains this choice of name. It may have been aesthetic. But given the penchant among both Renaissance Englishmen and the Powhatan for symbolic representation (see Girouard 1978:86–87), this is unlikely. Almost

certainly it refers to the succor the biblical Rebecca gave to Abraham's servant, who went to her people seeking a wife for Abraham's son, Isaac (Genesis 24).

20. Most extensively, Rountree (1989, 1990, 1993); other recent scholars include Dent (1995), Fausz (1985), Feest (1966, 1969), Gleach (1997), Lurie (1959), McCary and Barka (1977), Potter (1989, 1993), and Turner (1985). In a previous generation of anthropologists, Kroeber (1939), Lowie (1967), Mook (1943, 1944), Mooney (1907), Speck (1924, 1928), Swanton (1935, 1952, 1987), and Wissler (1938) all discuss the Powhatan, usually in terms of their culture-area associations.

21. For the Monacans (Manacam), see Jefferson 1832; Bushnell 1931, 1933, 1940; Swanton 1935; Hantman 1990.

22. In his analysis of the symbolic meaning of Mississippian mounds, Knight makes the important point that the so-called disappearance of mounds in the Southeast should rather "be seen as merely a change of emphasis within an unbroken ritual tradition" (1989:280). I am suggesting that the same principle applies geographically as well as temporally.

23. For this summary I have relied on Milfort (1959) and Swanton (2000) for information about the Creek; for the Caddo, Early (2000); for the Choctaw, Swanton (1931), Galloway (1995), Bossu (1931), and Anonymous (1931); for the Chickasaw, Gibson (1971); for the Cherokee, Gilbert (1943), Fogelson (1977), and Timberlake (1948); for the Natchez and Taensa, Swanton (1911); and for the Timucua, Milanich (2000). In addition, as general sources I have used the accounts of Biedma (1993), Rangel (1993), and the "Gentleman from Elvas" (Elvas 1993) among Soto's companions; and Hudson (1976) and Swanton (1987, 1998). Translations from the French of Bossu and Anonymous are mine.

24. The situation described by Bragdon (1996) appears to have been somewhat different. With the possible (but not probable) exception of the Narragansett, there appears to have been no

separation of functions into a "peace" and a "war" chief; on the other hand, there were a number of religious statuses all of which appear to have been subordinate to that of sachem (e.g., Bragdon 1996:143, 148, 205–206, 214–216), although Bragdon herself does not couch her discussion in these terms.

1. The Realm of Powhatan

1. As will appear, both men and women could be chiefs among the Powhatan; in relation to their subordinates, however, chiefs were always gendered male.

2. Beverley's report of village sizes is different from those of the first colonists. Smith (1986 [1612]:162) and Strachey (1953 [1612]:77–78) say that the Powhatan lived in small villages consisting of between 2 and 100 scattered houses, though most were smaller rather than larger. By 1705 English settlements, English warfare, and English microbes had combined to re-duce and concentrate the population in a settlement pattern different from the aboriginal one.

3. This contradicts both Smith's statement that war parties always spared women, children, and werowances (1986 [1612]:166), and Strachey's own statement to the same effect (1953 [1612]:109). The possible fate of such prisoners is discussed below.

4. *Matchacomoco* is found (in various spellings) in Harriot, Smith, and Strachey as well as in Beverley. Harriot writes that the "Mathicomuck" or "Mathicomuck" was the "temple" among the coastal Algonkians of what is now North Caro-lina (1972 [1590]:26). Geary suggests that " 'Place of suppli-cation' . . . seems to be the meaning" (1991:889). Strachey's word list includes the entry "*A great Howse*—Machacammac" (1953 [1612]:188), on which Geary (1953) does not comment, unfortunately. Barbour writes that the element "-comoco" means "enclosure, house" (1972:34). In the passage cited here, Beverley uses the word in the sense of "a meeting" as well as of "a meetinghouse."

5. Probably the country of the Tuscaroras in North Carolina; these Indians later joined the Five nations to make the sixth element of the Iroquois confederation. [Eds.]
6. Monahassano is a form of the word Yeseng, the native name of a Siouan tribe living at that time in the region of Bedford and Buckingham Counties. [Eds.]
7. Rountree (1989:9–15) provides a good summary of current ideas concerning the "fringe" and "core" areas of Powhatan's polity; see also Potter (1993:19).
8. We encounter some confusion about these embassies. The time-table according to Archer, Smith, and Wingfield is as follows:

14 June	two Indians visit, set out political situation, promise help	Archer
21 June	Opechancanough sends peaceful embassy to fort	Smith
25 June	embassy from Powhatan saying he would ensure peace with Paspaheigh & Tappahannock	Wingfield
3 July	embassy from Pamunkey Indians bringing a deer for the President (Wingfield)	Wingfield
[?] shortly after 3 July	deer sent Wingfield from Powhatan	Wingfield

Barbour, in a note to Smith's statement about the 21 June visit (1986, 1:100n), writes, "Wingfield independently testified that the Indian came from Opechancanough, not Powhatan, on June 25, not June 21, 'with the worde of peace.'" The basis for Barbour's saying that Wingfield credited Opechancanough with this friendly gesture is not clear, but Smith and

Wingfield may be reporting the same visit. In any case, as we shall see, Powhatan and Opechancanough were the same person in this sort of context.

9. To concede this does not, though, force us to agree that Powhatan or his subordinate werowances were the absolute rulers that the English accounts suggest, since conquest implies nothing about the political relations within either the conquering group nor the vanquished.

10. For example, Strachey 1953 [1612]:61; but that inquiry appears to have been motivated more by prurience than politics.

11. Curious, because there has been more debate over them than over anything else in this passage of colonial history, including the nature of the polity the colonists found in Virginia. A fundamental question is whether Smith made the whole thing up (see, for example, the discussion in Bradley 1910); but recent scholarship tends to take Smith at his word (e.g., Barbour 1986, 1:lviii; but see also Rountree 1989:121). For a more detailed discussion of this point, see Williamson 1992:372n.

12. In other words, Smith was taken to a "temple," or quioccasan, for this ceremony. Powhatan, to judge from his appearance, took the part of chief priest or quiyoughcosough. The quioccasan and the quiyoughcosough are discussed in detail in chapter 4.

13. The "country of Capahowosick" is an area near present-day Gloucester, Virginia. The village is marked on Smith's map, but nowhere does he identify it as a "king's house."

14. The conventional anthropological kin designations are M = mother, F = father, Z = sister, B = brother, D = daughter, S = son. A succession of letters indicates degrees of relationship: MBD = mother's daughter's brother.

15. The reason the Chickahominy could be independent, situated though they were in the heart of this polity, may be that they were a large tribe. In their talleys of population, Smith and Strachey both indicate that this was a tribe almost as large as the Pamunkey, with between 200 and 300 able men (Smith

1986 [1612]:146; Strachey 1953 [1612]:69; the larger estimate is Strachey's). Smith estimates the number of men among the Pamunkey at 300 (1986 [1612]:147, [1624]:104), a figure with which Strachey agrees (1953 [1612]:69). Evidently, the Chickahominy as a fighting force could resist any military pressure Powhatan, through the Pamunkey, might exert.

2. "Civilizing" the Powhatan

Stages in the development of the argument of this chapter were presented in papers at the 1992 meeting of the American Ethnological Society, the 1993 meeting of the Southern Anthropological Society (Williamson 1993), and the 1999 meeting of the American Society for Ethnohistory.

1. In many regards, the substance of this chapter is very similar to the points made by Kupperman (2000), although our emphases differ.

2. See, for example, the vigorous attack on Smith in A. Brown (1890:1006–1008); cf. Arber 1910:cxv–cxviii; Barbour 1964, 1986; Vaughan 1973, 1975; Dabney 1971; Oberg 1999.

3. Barbour's edition of these (1986) is at once the most recent and the most comprehensive and is best consulted for details concerning editing, publication, and the like.

4. "Spelman . . . became one of a small group of teenagers on both sides, including Pocahontas and another English boy named Thomas Savage, who served as emissaries and interpreters in Virginia" (Kupperman 2000:77).

5. This embassy presents a mystery. Hamor wrote his account to counteract the scurrilous stories about Virginia circulating in London. In other words, he intended it to be published and to be widely read. He mentions Lady Dale, then living in England (Hamor 1615:25). At the same time, he gives minute particulars of his visit to Powhatan for the purpose of furnishing Sir Thomas with a (second) wife. Hamor's exact words to

Powhatan, so he writes, were, "your brother [Dale] (by your fauour) would gladly make [her] his neerest companion, wife and bedfellow" (1615:37–42). Rowse, in his introduction to the Virginia State Library facsimile reprint of Hamor's *Discourse* (1957), does not comment on this passage.

6. Lewis and Loomie evidently find Don Luis's volte-face perplexing, as they write, "From the first, Don Luis provides an interesting study in psychology" (1953:44). Psychology is not the issue, of course. Rather, as Mallios argues, Don Luis and his people took exception to the Jesuits trading with every tribe but theirs. The Spanish not only seemed ungenerous, but they were upsetting, or threatening to upset, the economic and political equilibrium in the area (Mallios 1998). See also Gleach (1997), who, however, offers only slight evidence for the motivation of the Indian raiders.

7. The full passage reads:

> Their Priests (whom the [*sic*] call *Quiokosoughs*) are no other but such as our English Witches are. They liue naked in bodie, as if their shame of their sinne deserued no couering: Their names are as naked as their bodie: they esteeme it a vertue to lie, deceiue and steale as their master the diuell teacheth them. Much more might be said of their miserable condition, but I refer the particular narration of these things to some other season. If this bee their life, what thinke you shall become of them after death? but to be partakers with the diuell and his angels in hell for euermore. . . . The seruice of their God is answerable to their life, being performed with great feare and attention, and many strange dumb shewes vsed in the same, stretching forth their limbes and straining their bodie, much like to the counterfeit women in *England* who faine themselues bewitched, or possessed of some euill spirit. They stand in great awe of their *Quiokosoughs* or Priests, which are a generation of vipers euen of Sathans owne brood. The manner of their life is much like to the popish Hermits of our age; for they liue alone in the woods, in houses sequestred from the common course of men, neither may any man bee suffered to come into their house or to speake with them, but when this Priest doth call him. (Whitaker 1613:24–26)

The association between papistry and the Devil's work is so obvious as to need no exegesis.

8. Potter (1993:17; 1989:153) agrees with Haynes (1984:100) that this was more probably four-fifths of what the lesser werowances collected from their immediate subjects rather than four-fifths from those subjects themselves. Either way, Strachey's point about Powhatan's greed remains effective. I discuss this point again in chapter 3.

9. The considerable history associated with the notion of the divine right of kings in England, though of great interest, is not essential to the argument being advanced here. Sources I have consulted include Davies (1938), Elton (1965), Figgis (1965), Kantorowitz (1957), McIlwain (1918), and Sharpe (1989).

10. I base this summary on comments in Sharpe (1989:14), although they are themselves ambiguous.

11. The notion that heavenly bodies—stars, planets, the sun, and the moon—had influence on the earth and the people on it was a common idea (see, e.g., Yates 1964), although not shared by all. For example, Shakespeare has Cassius say, "The fault, dear Brutus, is not in our stars,/But in ourselves, that we are underlings" (*Julius Caesar* I, ii).

12. It may be going too far to argue that James I thought of himself as a divine king like the Shilluk *reth* or the Natchez Great Sun. Nevertheless, certain facts are suggestive. I have mentioned the relevant political opinions—that he owned the land and everything in it, that reciprocity between king and subject was impossible, and that a king was above and beyond the sphere of normal social life. Concerning the last, other facts may be pertinent: his dirtiness—according to Willson (1956), he never bathed and only occasionally washed his hands; his drunkenness; and his homosexuality. While failure to bathe is not a necessary attribute of divine kingship, nevertheless divinity may be manifest in a lack of order as well as in extreme order. Drunkenness may be evidence of a personality disorder, or it may be a symbol of the extra-social (de Heusch 1972). As for the king's homosexuality, this is perhaps better called bisexu-

ality (although we must remember that these classifications are much more recent), since he not only had three children but is reported to have taken great interest in comely women. These interests may be taken as peculiar to his personality or as a conscious attempt on his part to become genderless and therefore without definition—universal and cosmic, like God.

13. The king had not been reading Dumézil. On the contrary, his advice confirms Dumézil's argument. Even in the 17th century, the idea of dual sovereignty expresses itself in this radical political theorist.

14. This discussion might appear to be a reiteration of Sheehan's argument (1980) that the colonists initially took the Virginians to be, and described them as, "noble savages." But Sheehan does not draw any parallels to other contemporary descriptions of monarchs, either in the Old World or in the New. My point is not that that Jamestown writers were putting a positive spin on the native institutions—that much is obvious—but rather to identify the sources of the rhetorical terms they chose to use and suggest the reasons for and the consequences of making those choices.

15. She may have been unusually prescient. In the winter of 1610 she was shot dead in the woods and her town destroyed, in revenge for her having lured a party of Englishmen to a feast so as to massacre them (Strachey 1953 [1612]:64).

16. Strachey has an entry in his word list: "*a Chayne of Copper with long linckes*—Tapaantaminais" (1953 [1612]:179). Copper, and Powhatan words for copper, are discussed more fully in the penultimate chapter.

17. Barbour (1986, 1:102n) writes, "Italian *biscione*, 'great snake.'" Evidently, this was a battle formation.

18. Terms like "noble" and "gentle" are very difficult to define. I have relied here on Laslett's discussion of status in England during this period (1971:27–38).

19. Regarding "*pegatwek-Apyan*," compare Strachey's entries

"*Poketawes*—Wheat" and "*Pekatawes*—Beanes;" and "*Apones* —Bread" (1953 [1612]:196, 175).

20. "Cates" is not a misprint for "cakes." According to the *Concise Oxford English Dictionary*, "cate" is an archaic term, usually found in the plural, meaning "choice food." Compare cater, caterer.

21. "Rank" as used here should not be taken to imply "class." Ranked but classless societies are frequent in anthropological literature; English society at this time was likewise ranked but without class (Underdown 1985:20; Wrightson 1982:65).

22. Girouard provides a plenitude of examples of the "axis of honour" in English houses, although the idea seems to have become explicit only after the Restoration. The highest accolade was to be received in a room not only farthest from the common room but also the smallest in the series, one therefore suitable only for a tiny, intimate group (1978:144–146).

3. Kings and Councilors in Tidewater Virginia

1. Needham (1970) presents a catalog of shortcomings in Hocart's argument, with none of which can I disagree. But it is, as he says, "a novel theory of the origin of government" (1970:lxii). I agree with him, too, that although the argument cannot be tested in a scientifically accepted way, we may nevertheless "form reasoned opinions on it [and] . . . refer its contentions to social facts" (1970:lxiii).

2. Gleach's analysis (1997) likewise represents as complementary the relationship between these statuses: he regards the werowance as a peace chief and his subordinate (Gleach does not use the word "cockarouse") as a war chief. The balance of this chapter presents an alternative interpretation together with relevant evidence.

3. In the captions on John White's paintings of the Carolina Algonkian chiefs, the word is written "Herowan" (Cat. 50:Indian Elder of Chief), "Heround" (Cat. 38:Village of Secotan), and

"Cherounes," to which White adds "or chiefe personages" (Cat. 41:Indian Charnel House).

4. Specifically, Abnaki *wirawighi*, " '[I] am rich' "; Natick *wenau-wetu*, " 'rich' "; Massachusetts dialect, "*a winnaytue*, that is a rich man, or a man of estimation' "; Delaware (Munsee) *wayawew*, " 'chief,' " and East Cree *weyotisiw*, " 'he is of in-fluence' " (Barbour 1972:46).

5. Specifically, Abnaki *[ne]kakikiman*, " '[I] give him advice' "; Natick *kogkohkoowaii*, " 'he gives counsel (to him)' "; Dela-ware (Munsee) *kihkay*, " 'chief' " (Barbour 1972:34). Siebert (1975) does not discuss this word. Some confusion about this term arises from Strachey's referring to the "chief men" among the Powhatan as "cronoccoes" or "cronockoes" (1953 [1612]:58, 67), as in the phrase "his *Cronoccoes*, 1. [?] Councellors, and Priests" and in his word list giving "crenepo," "cucheneppo," and "cutssenepo," all of which he translates as "woman," pre-sumably on the basis of Smith, who himself got it from Hak-luyt (Barbour 1972:35). Barbour rejects the translation on the ground that the suffix is masculine and suggests that "crenepo and cronockoes may both be distortions of a word mean-ing 'chief men' [i.e., cockarouse]," while Strachey's words "cutssenepo" and "cucheneppo" may refer to a sequestered menstruating woman (1972:35). Geary, however, finds noth-ing dubious about "crenepos" meaning "woman" and suggests that it comes from stems meaning "forbid" and "die," so that "the meaning might be 'she who hinders death" [1991:886–887].

6. " 'Swoon'; a variant spelling" (Barbour 1986, 1:175n).

7. In the colonists' discussions of justice among the Powhatan, we can discern two applications of law: one to do with of-fences against society generally, capital offences; and the other against persons, corporal offences. What constituted a capi-tal offence is a little unclear. Spelman states that murder, theft, and being found in flagrante delicto with another man's

wife were all punishable by death (1910 [1612]:cviii–cxi), but Whitaker says that only murder was so treated, and adultery and "other offences" were merely "seuerely punished" (1613:27). In the *Generall Historie*, Smith describes Powhatan punishing an errant wife by making her sit naked on a stone for nine days with only a minimum of food, adding, "yet he loved her exceedingly" (1986 [1624]:128). Elsewhere Smith reports that a woman must obtain the permission of her husband before having intimate relations ("dishonesty") with other men (Smith 1986 [1612]:160). Presumably "playing the whore" meant sexual congress without such permission. Spelman (1910 [1612]:cviii) also reports a chief punishing his wife physically, although in that case it was for beating Spelman, not for sleeping with him. Whether punishing a wife for infidelity should be classed with authorizing beating, flaying, disemboweling, and the like for other kinds of offenses is questionable. Smith's report suggests, indeed, that a wronged man had some discretion in the punishment of his wife (and, perhaps, of the corespondent as well), while discussions of more public punishments convey that these were carried out according to "custom."

8. It is not certain that the Powhatan enslaved anyone or—if they did—for what reason.

9. Colleagues familiar with Polynesia and parts of Africa will, of course, instantly cite the resplendent obesity of the monarchs there as a counter to this statement. But the principle is still valid. Those kings are as obliged to be fat as !Kung and Nambikuara headmen are to be thin. Either way, they symbolize (and so effect) prosperity: the large king metaphorically, the thin one metonymically.

10. I use "chief" and "king" interchangeably in this discussion, since I agree with Hocart that "there is, of course, no fundamental distinction between headman and king: both are merely varieties of the principal" (1970a:86).

11. Compared to copper, pearls, and furs, a stone hatchet blade must seem an anticlimax until one realizes that there is no native stone in Tidewater Virginia. All these ax blades must have come by trade from elsewhere. Probably they were traded from the mountains to the west (where the people were inimical) and through a good many hands. They may, like *kula* valuables, have increased in value with each trade, but on that point there is no evidence. At the least, we can suppose that the difficulty of obtaining these pieces, their consequent rarity, and their utility as tools all contributed to their value.

12. Powhatan's actions on this occasion are very different from those Spelman describes in another account of trading: "Captaine Ratclyff came w*it*h a shipp w*it*h xxiiij or xxv men to Orohpikes, and leauing his shipp there came by barge w*it*h sixteen men *to* yᵉ Powhatan to Powmunkey where he very curtuously in shew received them. . . . The next day the Powhatan w*it*h a company of Saluages came to Capt: Ratclyff, and caried our English to their storehouse where their corne was to traffique w*it*h them, giueing them pieces of copper and beades and other things" (1910 [1613]:civ; editors' italics). The thing ended badly for the English, though. They suspected the Indians of cheating them — they may have been — and both parties departed in disgust. Later the Indians killed all but two of the English.

13. The distinction between psychology and anthropology proceeds from the discussion in Hanson 1975.

14. I take this speech to be a reasonable representation of what Powhatan said and thus an expression of a native point of view, even though one can make an argument that Smith is putting words into Powhatan's mouth. Although there is no way to prove absolutely that this speech was Powhatan's and represents the native point of view, evidence and anthropological common sense persuade me that it is.

15. The distinction between "commodity" and "gift" economies is based on the argument in Gregory 1982. Gregory's original

argument has elicited discussion and disagreement (e.g., the collections edited by Appadurai [1986] and Parry and Bloch [1989]); nevertheless, I find his distinction useful. Mallios (1998) considers in detail the consequences of the meeting between the two economies in Virginia.

16. Although Spelman says that others planted and harvested Powhatan's garden, Smith says Powhatan did some planting himself; in fact, that Powhatan was a producer as well as a collector of other people's products. "For the King himselfe will make his owne robes, shooes, bowes, arrowes, pots; plant, hunt, or doe any thing so well as the rest" (Smith 1986 [1624]:151). Both Smith and Spelman refer to Powhatan in these passages, but we do not know whether the statements about Powhatan apply to his subordinate werowances. If both men are right, it suggests that Powhatan, at least, had two kinds of garden, one that he and his family worked for their use; the other, described by Spelman, was for some special purpose such as entertaining visitors or maintaining priests.

17. Both these offerings were presented within a short time during the latter part of Smith's stay in Virginia (the exact dates are obscure), when relations between himself and Powhatan were extremely tense. According to the account, the first gift was Powhatan's effort to explain away an attempt to murder Smith in Powhatan's house. When the attempt failed, Powhatan wished by this means to reestablish something like friendly relations. Or so the account reports the "ancient Orator" as saying (Smith 1986 [1612]:249). The second prestation followed a skirmish between the English and a band of about 300 men whom Powhatan had organized to bring about Smith's end. That failed also, and, according to the account, the Indians were so alarmed when they heard his ship depart in the night — they took it that he was going for reinforcements — that they sent their ambassador with this gift in the morning (Smith 1986 [1624]:254–255).

These stories, written by three of Smith's supporters, are but two of a number of such narratives that were intended to demonstrate his services to the colony—in this case, his increasing domination of the Indians and their attempts to come to peaceful terms with him. (Apparently he always received these envoys graciously no matter how badly the Indians had treated him before.) Thus there is some question how accurate these accounts may be. Although in the initial situation the English may have seen a threat where there was none, and panicked, it is more difficult to dismiss as mistaken their characterization of the second encounter. Nevertheless, the accounts may exaggerate the Indians' fear of Smith and his men and misunderstand (deliberately or not) the nature of the embassies sent him after these encounters.

18. The English are almost completely reticent about intimate relations between themselves and the Indians. With one exception that I know of, we have no evidence at all that anything of that kind occurred; although to suppose that it did not is naive, to say the least. Smith praises Pocahontas for, among other things, being the first Virginia Indian to have "a childe *in mariage* by an Englishman" (1986 [1624]:260; emphasis added).

19. Beverley describes the three kinds of beads current in the early 18th century, which according to him were in use in 1607 also. These include white and purple "peak," or wampum, made from conch shell. The purple was twice as valuable as the white, and both were more valuable than other kinds of beads. Another sort made from conch were "runtees." Unlike the peak, which was slender and tubular, like "*English Buglas*" or bugle-beads, runtees were either plump ovoids drilled the long way or disks more than an inch in diameter drilled "edgeways." Both peak and runtees had carefully smoothed surfaces. Roanoke was the least valuable kind of bead. It was made by breaking cockleshells roughly into small pieces and drilling

them for stringing without smoothing the edges (Beverley 1947 [1705]:227–228).

20. It is interesting that the Powhatan identified none of the English as a religious, even though the colony usually had at least one minister. This may have been because among the Powhatan, the shaman lived apart from everyone else, unlike the English minister.

4. "Priests" and "Conjurors"

1. As modern anthropologists, we are more inclined to regret omissions in colonial documents than to wonder why any particular information is included. Moreover, a constant easy answer to the question "why this?" in regard to any information about divinities and their service is that the colonists wished to make Protestants of the Powhatan and took it as axiomatic that understanding the Indians' own "errors" was the first step to correcting them. Nevertheless, it seems equally plain that they did not get the whole story from the Powhatan—some of them admit this—and so the question still remains: why this information rather than something else? It is interesting, then, that Percy, among all the early colonists, tells us most about sun worship. Although we cannot know why he does so, still the fact that he was brother to the "wizard earl" of Northumberland, who was a friend of such occultists as Raleigh, Dee, and Harriot and imprisoned by James I for witchcraft, is suggestive. The occultists took astrology seriously. They considered that the heavenly bodies were powers that affected events on earth, and among those powers they ranked the sun the most important (Stevens 1900:20, 86, 93–94, 109; French 1972:98–99, 101–102, 171–172). It is tempting, then, to see in Percy's comments an interest in Powhatan cosmology that differed from that held by his orthodox Protestant companions. See next note also.

2. This phrase, "great powers . . . by whose vertues and Influences, . . .

seasons," also reads like the doctrine of the Occultists (e.g., Yates 1979). Strachey may have been of their number (if Yates [1979:127] is correct about Shakespeare, it seems almost inevitable that he was), or he may simply have borrowed their rhetoric to describe a religion he found as alien as theirs.

3. The description of the virtues and powers of Ahone, the creator, make him sound something like the Great Hare. None of the variations on the name of the Hare—Michabo, Manibozho, Nanibojouo, Missibizi, Michabo, and Messou (Brinton 1896:197) resembles Ahone, however, so assuming an identity between them is questionable.

4. For "god" he gives the term *rawottneind* (186), which as Barbour says, "seems to be badly distorted, with a hint of the element 'manito'" (1972:39). Curiously, Siebert (1975) does not discuss any Powhatan words pertaining to religion.

5. The Algonkian term for "spirit," *manito*, is missing almost entirely from these reports. The two examples that I know of are in Harriot (1972 [1590]:25) and Spelman (1910 [1613]:cv).

6. "Manitou, the impersonal force that permeated the world, observable in anything marvelous, beautiful, or dangerous" (Bragdon 1996:184).

7. Plate 21 in Harriot purports to show such an image. Hulton casts doubt on its authenticity, however (1984:Fig. 25, 191).

8. Most of the engravings in Harriot's *Breife and True Report* are de Bry's work, but some, like these two, are by Gysbert van Veen (Hulton 1984:18).

9. Gleach argues, persuasively, that this was not a "divination" (his term) but rather a species of ritual that included "creations or renewals of cultural relations, rituals that maintain the world, processes that require the participation of supernatural forces to achieve or maintain significant effects." "The details of this ritual demonstrate that the Powhatans were redefining the world to include the English colony" (Gleach 1997:114-115). Note, however, that despite the explanation he gives, Smith

calls this a "conjuration," not a "divination," suggesting that even at that time the most striking thing about it was the invocation of and communication with spiritual beings.

10. Rountree has criticized, on the basis of this passage, my argument regarding the relative status of quiyoughcosough and werowance (Williamson 1979). The matter merits attention because I use the same argument in this book. An important point is the celibate status of the quiyoughcosough. Rountree disputes this (and therefore my entire argument) because Tomocomo, whom she takes to be a quiyoughcosough, was married to one of Powhatan's daughters. She reads this passage to mean that "priests" and "sacred persons" are the same thing. The werowance was also, however, a sacred person with sacerdotal responsibilities. In addition, we have no other evidence at all that a quiyoughcosough ever married, which would make this man anomalous to a degree. I think it more likely, then, that Purchas's meaning is that a gathering of priests, or of sacred persons, or both, called upon Oke to appear, and that Tomocomo said he was one of the sacred persons. This would not make him a quiyoughcosough. Another possibility is that he was making himself important for Purchas's benefit.

11. Beverley (1947 [1705]:202) mentions this also.

12. "Antic: Absurd from fantastic incongruity; grotesque, bizarre, uncouthly ludicrous: a. in gesture." The word in this sense was in use in English as early as 1590, when Marlowe used it in *Edward II*. Both he and Drayton use it in connection with satyrs, giving us a good idea of its meaning to them and, incidentally, how the Powhatan shamans appeared to the colonists. "Antic" is derived from Italian *antico*, "orig. applied to fantastic representations of human, animal, and floral forms, incongruously running into one another, found in exhuming some ancient remains (as the Baths of Titus) in Rome, whence extended to anything similarly incongruous or bizarre" (*OED* s.v. "antic").

13. Siebert (1975) does not discuss this word.

14. The substance of this paragraph comes from Davies (1970:chapters 1 and 2).

15. But compare Smith's descriptions of the "conjuration" performed on him when he was a prisoner—seven men in a circle, putting down grains of corn and little sticks, singing and groaning for ten hours at a stretch—with, for instance, his or Strachey's description of curing or with Harriot's description of the "flyer" of the Outer Banks.

5. Dual Sovereignty in Tidewater Virginia

1. Clayton, on the contrary, says that the priest was subordinate to both the king and the war captain (1965 [1687]:22, 21). Since Beverley's account follows Clayton's by almost 20 years, and he reports virtually the same situation as that existing in 1607 and before (Harriot [1972 (1590):26] reports the same relationship between shaman and chief among the Carolina Algonkians in 1585), we cannot put the difference down to cultural change. This is another of those singular aberrant commentaries on Powhatan life.

2. This discussion proceeds from conversations with Rafael Alvarado, then at the University of Virginia, on the nature of Maya kingship; I am happy to acknowledge his influence.

3. In the margin next to the word "Cakeres," Spelman, who acquired a good mastery of Powhatan during his captivity, has written, "*Caukewis Manato Taukinge souke Quia uasack,*" a phrase that remains untranslated so far as I know. *Caukewis* would appear to be another spelling for *cakeres;* but neither form appears in Smith's or Strachey's word list, and Geary (1953, 1991) and Siebert (1975) do not discuss it. The translation of *taukinge souke* is likewise unknown to me, but there is the possibility that it, too, is one word since the second, *souke,* could be a standard Algonkian plural ending (i.e., "sok"). *Manato* is recognizable as *manito,* and it is one of the few—if not the

only—appearance of this Algonkian word in the Jamestown documents. *Qui uasack* would appear to be a version of *qui-youghcosough*, the middle "q" left out, possibly by a printer's error. Both of these identify the phrase as something to do with the spiritual, which is appropriate for the subject of the main text.

4. The substance of this argument is in Williamson (1979).

5. Barbour has reconstructed a history of the ethnographic report: "Apparently White was the source for the story, and while Smith printed it first, Percy jotted it down and told it to Strachey in Virginia (or Strachey saw it in Smith's work and wanted to favour Percy)" (1969:148-149n). Strachey's account (1953 [1612]:98-100) comes almost verbatim from Smith, but Strachey credits Percy with the information.

6. For other versions, see Purchas (1617:952), Barbour (1969, 1:147-149), Strachey (1953 [1612]:98-99), Beverley (1947 [1705]:207-209), Anonymous (1959 [1689]:234-236).

7. The juxtaposition of the Devil and the sucking of blood in this description must not go unremarked. At that time, it was known in Europe that one could identify a witch—one who had made an unholy pact with the Devil—by the "Devil's mark," one or more supernumerary teats on the body by which the witch suckled her (or his) familiar in exchange for favors performed (Sharpe 1997:73). I do not, though, consider this part of the description a falsification. For one thing, the "Devil's mark" was an extra teat, not a naturally occurring one; also, it was usually found in the private parts (Sharpe 1997:178). Rather, I regard this as one of our few examples of native informing. The English fastened on to it, and reported it, because it confirmed their suspicion—if it did not give rise to it—that the Powhatan served the Devil rather than God.

8. The category of "friends" in England at that time overlapped with, but was not coterminous with, that of "kin." Especially in the context of marriage and marriage contracts, a

woman asked her relatives as well as her acquaintances to be her "friends" and might make it a condition of marriage that her friends approved her choice of husband (O'Hara 1991).

9. The colonial documents provide virtually no information that allows us to determine Powhatan rules of exogamy. A case can be made for village exogamy (Williamson 1972:71–72). We are also told that on the Eastern Shore "in their mariages they observe a large distance, as well in affinitie as consanguinitie" (Smith 1986 [1624]:291), with the clear implication that the western shore Indians, that is, the Powhatan, do neither. But what construction to put on this comment, which is part of a diatribe about the Powhatan, is impossible to know.

10. The very useful suggestion to use "mundane" and "spiritual" rather than "profane" and "sacred" was made to me, many years ago, by Peter Rivière, to whom I am grateful. Mundane: in popular speech this means pedestrian, slow, ho-hum; but I use it in this analysis in its more literal sense, "worldly, of this world," material, sensible. It opposes "spiritual," which is none of the above.

11. Spelman describes a different ritual that sounds in some respects like the funeral of a chief, although he does not say that it was. According to his account, the body was left on a platform perhaps 12 feet high until nothing but the bones remained. At the time of deposition, the relatives of the deceased threw beads to the assembled crowd, who scrambled for them, sometimes accidentally breaking their limbs in the process. When only the dried skeleton was left, the relatives collected the bones, put them in a skin container, and hung this in the house, where the widow and children continued. When the house collapsed in due course, the bones were thereby buried (Spelman 1910 [1613]:cx). This is so much at odds with what Smith and Strachey say about burial of common Powhatan that I am tempted to call it a Potomac custom not observed among the Powhatan of the southern Tidewater. But the asso-

ciation of elevation and the spiritual informs this ritual as well. The flinging of beads, which recalls the conclusion of planting Powhatan's cornfields, probably had a similar meaning, too, namely, to reassert life in the face of death.

12. White's watercolor does not show the figures, only the pot boiling on the fire. Veen has dressed his woman in an otter skin loincloth, like a "flyer," whereas everything else we know about the women of this area has them dressed in a fringed skin from the waist to midthigh before and behind. Hulton concludes that the woman's dress in Plate 15 is "probably an error on the part of the engraver." He expresses doubts also about the fan the man is using on the fire, since it seems to be a Florida invention, not middle Atlantic (Hulton 1984:189.)

13. The contemporary meaning of "meat" was "food in general," not animal tissue, for which the term "flesh" was used. Hence "mays" could be called meat with no incongruity.

14. In fact, reports about the preservation of foodstuffs are mixed. Smith, for instance, says that although they plant a variety of foods and that these yield a pretty good harvest, nevertheless this does not last them very long, and "for neere 3 parts of the yeare, they only observe times and seasons, and live of what the Country naturally affordeth them from hand to mouth, etc." In another passage he amplifies this: "Powhatan their great king and some others that are provident, rost their fish and flesh upon hurdles . . . and keepe it till scarce times" (Smith 1986 [1612]:158-159, 163). On the other hand, Archer describes several Indians following the James River exploring party for six miles or more offering them dried oysters in exchange for English baubles (1910 [1607]:xlii). This was in June, suggesting that Smith's comments about Powhatan food preservation may not be accurate. He himself describes so many ways of drying and storing a variety of foods that he seems to give himself the lie (see Rountree 1998:3-4).

15. Strachey translates "*Pokoranse*" as "a minerall stone" (1953

[1612]:196). Barbour says that "the derivation of this word is uncertain" (1972:40); evidently Geary (1953) and Seibert (1975) agree, since neither discusses the word at all.

16. Rountree writes of this custom: "This act presumably deprived the men of their manhood in Powhatan society," and she explains in a note that wearing the hair long on the left and short or shaven on the right was a divinely ordained style for "real men" (1989:116; see Purchas 1617:954). She does not explain why the Powhatan thought it necessary to deprive a culprit of his manhood before execution, or why, if they did, cutting off the hair rather than the genitals would be considered sufficient.

17. So far as we can tell, this sacrifice was practiced on men only.

18. None of the Jamestown accounts identifies a special preparer of bodies, as were found, for example, among the Choctaw (Milfort 1959:124; Swanton 1931:173) and the Ninnimissinouk of southern New England (Bragdon 1996:215–216). Speculation is risky, but it does seem—given their great interest in the funereal—that the English would have remarked such a status had there been one among the Powhatan.

19. White's account of Cassen's end is the one exception to this of which I am aware. It belongs, with Tomocomo's implication that shamans married, Purchas's assertion that the Powhatan were "sodomites" (Purchas 1617:956), and Percy's statement that women performed these sacrifices, to a category of unique and therefore inexplicable statements about Powhatan life. They may all be true, in the sense that one shaman was married, one sacrificial victim was treated like a chief, some men were homosexual (or perhaps *berdaches*), on one occasion women flayed and defleshed a living victim. Ethnographers are familiar with the situation in the field: the informants state a rule and then explain why what appear to be patent failures to follow it are in fact no such thing. The exceptions do not therefore cause us to dismiss the rule but to understand how it works in people's lives. With the Powhatan, of course, that is

no longer possible; in the circumstances, the only thing to do is rely only on what the majority of reports tell us.

20. We know comparatively little about the sacrifice of human victims on pawcorances. No one says to whom they were made or what became of the body afterward. Presumably it was not left to decay, since the English would have commented on what must have struck them as a savage practice. The little evidence we have suggests that this fate was reserved to Powhatan victims, while immolation in fire was appropriate for captured enemies; perhaps the family of the victim were allowed to bury the body in the usual way. But the poverty of evidence makes analysis unfruitful.

21. Three colors only may seem unlikely for an American Indian culture, given the widespread recognition of four as the number of completion and the sacred. The opposition between white and red, however, is found throughout southeastern Indian cultures, although the color black is rarely mentioned either in the colonial documents or in recent analyses of color among these peoples (e.g., Lankford 1992; Hudson 1976).

The absence of blue among these cultures is puzzling, particularly in view of its great importance to the cultures of Mesoamerica. Nevertheless, the Jamestown documents include but scant references to blue. Percy describes the werowance of Quiyoughcohannock coming in state to welcome the English with his face covered with blue paint (1910 [1607]:lxv). Strachey provides a word for blue, *osaih*, and the word *vnetagwushomon*, which he translates as "blew beades" (1953 [1612]:177). Possibly he includes the second because of Smith's story about Powahtan's coveting some strings of blue beads Smith had (Smith 1986 [1608]:71), whose value to the paramount was, so Smith says, that they were the color of the sky (see Kupperman 2000:175); this, though plausible, remains speculation on Smith's part. Hantman (personal communication 1991) suggests that the antimony mines the Powhatan controlled may have been a source of blue pigment, suggesting its importance to them. Harriot, commenting on the horticulture of the Carolina Algonkians, says that they raised white, red, yellow, and blue corn (1972 [1590]:13; see Beverley 1947 [1705]:144). Several of John White's watercolors of the Carolinians show blue items; for example, the "Indian Woman" (Cat. 51) wears a necklace of black and blue beads and an earring also of blue beads, and the "chiefe Herowan" (Cat. 50) also wears black or dark blue beads in his left ear. The "idol" shown in the mortuary house (Cat. 41) seems to be blue, with a yellow headdress. Hulton and Quinn, though, describe it as black (1964:94), and possibly the Algonkians themselves made no distinction between the hues. But the sources themselves are not more forthcoming.

References to yellow are similarly hard to find. Strachey, again, provides a word for this, *oussawaik*, which seems to be a legitimate Algonkian word (Siebert 1975:409; he does not discuss Strachey's word for "blue"); Strachey mentions also that men sometimes painted "their bodies . . . yellow," after which they apply oil and bird feathers, "which makes a wonderous shew" (1953 [1612]:73). But otherwise we find yellow mentioned only as a particular color of corn. Thus we are left with the white-red-black triad familiar from cultures all over the world (Turner 1967; Needham 1981).

22. Lest this conclusion be dismissed as a mere statement of what must be obvious, I remind the reader that among the Carolina Algonkians copper seems not to have been so marked, since women of all social levels wore it quite as frequently as men.

23. The "Gentleman from Elvas," writing about the depredations of Governor de Soto in Florida, observes the same of the pearls there: "Some pearls, spoiled by fire and of little value, were found there [i.e., in the temple]. The Indians bore them through in order to string them for beads, . . . and they esteem them greatly" (Elvas 1993:57, cf. 84).

24. There is some ambiguity about what went into the abdomen of a deceased chief. Smith says that it was just copper and that the exterior of the body was hung with chains of pearls, beads, and copper. But Strachey says that a mixture of copper and beads filled the hollow. In a sense, the difference is nugatory, since a valuable is a valuable. On the other hand, the logic of colors outlined here suggests that copper and not shells or pearls was more suitable for the interior of a deceased werowance. But resolution seems unlikely.

References

Amussen, Susan Dwyer. 1988. *An Ordered Society: Gender and Class in Early Modern England.* Basil Blackwell.

Andrews, Kenneth R. 1984. *Trade, Plunder and Settlement: Maritime Enterprise and the Genesis of the British Empire, 1480–1630.* Cambridge University Press.

Anonymous. 1931. "Relation de la Louisiane." In *Source Material for the Social and Ceremonial Life of the Choctaw Indians,* edited by John R. Swanton. Smithsonian Institution, Bureau of American Ethnology Bulletin 103, 243–258.

Anonymous. 1959 [1689]. "An Account of the Indians in Virginia." Edited by Stanley Pargellis. *William and Mary Quarterly* 16 228–243.

Appadurai, Arjun, ed. 1986. *The Social Life of Things: Commodities in Cultural Perspective.* Cambridge University Press.

Arber, E. 1910. Introduction to *Travels and Works of Captain John Smith,* edited by Edward Arber and A. G. Bradley. 2 vols. John Grant.

Archer, Gabriel. 1910 [1607]. "A relayton of the Discovery of our River, from *Iames Forte* into the Maine: made by Captaine *Christofer Newport:* and sincerely writen and observed by a gent: of yᵉ Colony." In *Travels and Works of Captain John Smith,* edited by Edward Arber and A. G. Bradley, 1:xl–lv. John Grant.

———. 1910 [1609]. "Letter from James Town, 31 August 1609." In *Travels and Works of Captain John Smith,* edited by Edward Arber and A. G. Bradley, 1:xciv–xcvii. John Grant.

Axtell, James. 1981. *The European and the Indian: Essays in the Ethnohistory of Colonial North America.* Oxford University Press.

———. 1988. *After Columbus: Essays in the Ethnohistory of Colonial North America.* Oxford University Press.

Bacon, Francis. n.d. *The Works of Lord Bacon, Moral and Historical.* Ward, Lock, and Co.

——. 1985 [1625]. *The Essayes or Counsels, Civill and Morall.* Edited and with an introduction and commentary by Michael Kiernan. Harvard University Press.

Balandier, Georges. 1970. *Political Anthropology.* Translated from the French by A. M. Sheridan Smith. Vintage Books.

Barbour, Philip L. 1964. *The Three Worlds of Captain John Smith.* Houghton Mifflin.

——. 1972. "The Earliest Reconnaissance of the Chesapeake Bay Area: Captain John Smith's Map and Indian Vocabulary, Part II." *Virginia Magazine of History and Biography* 80:21–51.

—— 1980 "The Riddle of the Powhatan 'Black Boyes.'" *Virginia Magazine of History and Biography* 88:148–154.

——., ed. 1969. *The Jamestown Voyages Under the First Charter 1606–1609.* 2 vols. The Hakluyt Society.

——., ed. 1986. *The Complete Works of Captain John Smith (1580–1631).* 3 vols. University of North Carolina Press.

Barker, Alex W. 1992. "Powhatan's Pursestrings: On the Meaning of Surplus in a Seventeenth Century Algonkian Chiefdom." In *Lords of the Southeast: Social Inequality and the Native Elites of Southeastern North America,* edited by Alex W. Barker and Timothy R. Pauketat, 61–80. Archaeological Papers of the AAA, No. 3.

Barker, Alex W., and Timothy R. Pauketat. 1992. "Introduction: Social Inequality and the Native Elites of Southeastern North America." In *Lords of the Southeast: Social Inequality and the Native Elites of Southeastern North America,* edited by Alex W. Barker and Timothy R. Pauketat, 1–10. Archaeological Papers of the AAA, No. 3.

Barth, Fredrik. 1965. *Political Leadership among Swat Pathans.* Athlone Press.

Beverley, Robert. 1947 [1705]. *The History and Present State of Virginia.* Edited and with an introduction by Louis B. Wright. University of North Carolina Press.

Biedma, Luys Hernández de. 1993. "Relation of the Island of Florida." Translated and edited by John E. Worth, with footnotes by John E. Worth and Charles Hudson. In *The De Soto Chronicles. The Expedition of Hernando de Soto to North America in 1539-1543,* edited by Lawrence A. Clayton, Vernon James Knight Jr., and Edward C. Moore, 221-246. University of Alabama Press.

Bland, Olivia. 1986. *The Royal Way of Death.* Constable.

Bossu, M. 1931 [1768]. "Nouveaux Voyages aux Indes Occidentales." Paris. In *Source Material for the Social and Ceremonial Life of the Choctaw Indians,* edited by John R. Swanton. Smithsonian Institution, Bureau of American Ethnology Bulletin 103, 258-264.

Bradley, A. G. 1910. Introduction to *Travels and Works of Captain John Smith,* edited by Edward Arber and A. G. Bradley. 2 vols. John Grant.

Bragdon, Kathleen J. 1996. *Native People of Southern New England, 1500-1650.* University of Oklahoma Press.

Brenner, Robert. 1972. "The Social Basis of English Commercial Expansion, 1550-1650." *Journal of Economic History* 32, no. 1:361-384.

———. 1993. *Merchants and Revolution.* Princeton University Press.

Brinton, Daniel G. 1896. *The Myths of the New World: A Treatise on the Symbolism and Mythology of the Red Race of America.* 3rd ed., rev. David McKay.

Brown, Alexander. 1890. *The Genesis of the United States.* Houghton Mifflin.

Brown, James A. 1975. "Spiro Art and Its Mortuary Contexts." In *Death and the Afterlife in Pre-Columbian America,* edited by Elizabeth P. Benson, 1-32. Dumbarton Oaks Research Library and Collections.

Brown, Kathleen M. 1996. *Good Wives, Nasty Wenches, and Anxious Patriarchs: Gender, Race, and Power in Colonial Virginia.* University of North Carolina Press.

Bry, Theodor de. 1618. *Zehender Theil: Americae darinnen zubefinden: Erzlich zwo Schiffarten Herrn Amerigi Vesputii unter Koenig Ferdinando in Kastilien vollbracht.* Oppenheim.

Bucher, Bernadette. 1981. *Icon and Conquest: A Structural Analysis of the Illustrations of de Bry's* Great Voyages. Translated by Basia Miller Gulati. University of Chicago Press.

Bushnell, David I., Jr. 1931. "Monacan Sites in Virginia." In *Explorations and Field-Work of the Smithsonian Institution in 1930,* 211–216. Smithsonian Institution.

———. 1933. *Evidence of Indian Occupancy in Albemarle County, Virginia.* Smithsonian Miscellaneous Collections 89, no. 7. Smithsonian Institution.

———. 1940. "Virginia before Jamestown." *Essays in Historical Anthropology of North America.* Smithsonian Miscellaneous Collections, 125–158. Smithsonian Institution.

Carniero, Robert. 1970. "A Theory of the Origin of the State." *Science* 169:733–738.

Clastres, Pierre. 1977. *Society against the State: The Leader as Servant and the Humane Uses of Power among the Indians of the Americas.* Translated by Robert Hurley and Abe Stein. Urizen Books.

———. 1994. *Archeology of Violence.* Translated by Jeanine Herman. Semiotext(e).

Clayton, John. 1965 [1687]. "Letter" to Dr. Nehemiah Grew. In *The Reverend John Clayton. A Parson with a Scientific Mind. His Scientific Writings and Other Related Papers,* edited by Edmund Berkeley and Dorothy Smith Berkeley, 21–39. University Press of Virginia.

Cohen, Ronald, and Elman R. Service, eds. 1978. *Origins of the State: The Anthropology of Political Evolution.* Institute for the Study of Human Issues.

Coomaraswamy, Ananda K. 1942. *Spiritual Authority and Temporal Power in the Indian Theory of Government.* American Oriental Series 22.

Craven, Wesley Frank. 1932. *Dissolution of the Virginia Company: The Failure of a Colonial Experiment*. Oxford University Press.

———. 1957. *The Virginia Company of London, 1606–1624*. Virginia 350th Anniversary Celebration Corporation.

———. 1970. *The Southern Colonies in the Seventeenth Century, 1607–1689*. Louisiana State University Press.

Cronon, William. 1983. *Changes in the Land*. Hill and Wang.

Crosby, Alfred W. 1986. *Ecological Imperialism*. Cambridge University Press.

Culliford, S. G. 1965. *William Strachey, 1572–1621*. University Press of Virginia.

Cunningham, Clark E. 1973. "Order in the Atoni House." In *Right and Left*, edited by Rodney Needham, with a foreword by E. E. Evans-Pritchard, 204–238. University of Chicago Press.

Curry, Dennis C. 1999. *Feast of the Dead: Aboriginal Ossuaries in Maryland*. Archaeological Society of Maryland.

Dabney, Virginius. 1971. *Virginia, the New Dominion*. Doubleday.

Darnton, Robert. 1984. *The Great Cat Massacre*. Basic Books.

Davies, Godfrey. 1938. *The Early Stuarts, 1603–1660*. Oxford University Press.

Davies, Horton. 1970. *Worship and Theology in England from Cranmer to Hooker, 1534–1603*. Princeton University Press.

Davis, Richard Beale. 1955. *George Sandys, Poet-Adventurer*. Bodley Head.

Day, Gordon M. 1998. *In Search of New England's Native Past: Selected Essays by Gordon M. Day*. Edited by Michael K. Foster and William Cowan. University of Massachusetts Press.

Demarest, Arthur A. 1992. "Archaeology, Ideology, and Pre-Columbian Cultural Evolution: The Search for an Approach." In *Ideology and Pre-Columbian Civilizations*, edited by Arthur A. Demarest and Geoffrey W. Conrad, 1–13. School of American Research Press.

Densmore, Frances. 1929. *Chippewa Customs*. Smithsonian Institution, Bureau of American Ethnology Bulletin 86.

Dent, Richard J., Jr. 1995. *Chesapeake Prehistory*. Plenum Press.

Dietz, Brian. 1973. "England's Overseas Trade in the Reign of James I." In *The Reign of James VI and I*, edited by Alan G. R. Smith, 106–122. St Martin's Press.

Dole, Gertrude E. 1968. "Tribe as the Autonomous Unit." In *Essays on the Problem of Tribe*, edited by June Helm, 83–100. Proceedings of the 1967 Annual Meeting of the American Ethnological Society. University of Washington Press.

Dumézil, Georges. 1973. *The Destiny of a King*. Translated by Alf Hiltebeitel. University of Chicago Press.

———. 1988. *Mitra-Varuna. An Essay on Two Indo-European Representations of Sovereignty*. 2nd ed. Translated by Derek Coltman. Zone Books.

Dumont, Louis. 1972. *Homo Hierarchicus*. Paladin.

Earle, Carville V. 1979. "Environment, Disease, and Mortality in Early Virginia." In *The Chesapeake in the Seventeenth Century*, edited by Thad W. Tate and David L. Ammerman, 96–125. University of North Carolina Press.

Earle, Timothy. 1997. *How Chiefs Come to Power*. Stanford University Press.

———., ed. 1991. *Chiefdoms: Power, Economy, and Ideology*. Cambridge University Press.

Early, Ann M., 2000. "The Caddos of the Trans-Mississippi South." In *Indians of the Greater Southeast: Historical Archaeology and Ethnohistory*, edited by Bonnie G. McEwan, 122–141. University Press of Florida.

Elliott, J. H. 1970. *The Old World and the New 1492–1650*. Cambridge University Press.

———. 2000. *Europe Divided 1559–1598*. 2nd ed. Blackwell.

Elton, G. R. 1965. Introduction to *The Divine Right of Kings*, by J. N. Figgis. Harper and Row.

Elvas, Fidalgo de. 1993. "The Account by a Gentleman from Elvas." Translated and edited by James Alexander Robertson, with footnotes and updates to Robertson's notes by John H. Hann. (Originally published in 2 vols., 1932, 1933.) In *The De Soto Chronicles*, edited by Lawrence A. Clayton, Vernon James Knight Jr., and Edward C. Moore, 19–219. University of Alabama Press.

Emerson, Thomas E. 1989. "Water, Serpents, and the Underworld: An Exploration into Cahokian Symbolism." In *The Southeastern Ceremonial Complex: Artifacts and Analysis*, edited by Patricia Galloway, 45–92. University of Nebraska Press.

Evans-Pritchard, E. E. 1940. *The Nuer*. Oxford University Press.

———. 1956. *Nuer Religion*. Oxford University Press.

———. 1962. *Social Anthropology and Other Essays*. Free Press.

Fausz, J. Frederick. 1985. "Patterns of Anglo-Indian Aggression and Accommodation along the Mid-Atlantic Coast, 1584–1632." In *Cultures in Contact: The European Impact on Native Cultural Institutions in Eastern North America*, A.D. 1000–1800, edited by William W. Fitzhugh, 225–268. Smithsonian Institution Press.

Feeley-Harnick, Gillian. 1985. "Issues in Divine Kingship." *Annual Review of Anthropology* 14:273–313.

Feest, Christian F. 1966. "Powhatan: A Study in Political Organisation." *Wiener Völkerkundliche Mitteilungen*. 13 Jhg, N.F., Bd. 7, 69–83. Vienna.

———. 1969. "Virginia Algonkian 1570–1703: Ethnohistorie und historische Ethnographie." Ph.D. diss., University of Vienna.

———. 1978. "Virginia Algonquians." In *Handbook of North American Indians*, vol. 15, edited by Bruce Trigger, 253–270.

———. 1986. *Indians of Northeastern North America*. Iconography of Religions 10, no. 7. E. J. Brill.

Figgis, John Neville. 1965. *The Divine Right of Kings*. Introduction by G. R. Elton. Harper and Row.

Fincham, Kenneth. 1993. "Introduction." In *The Early Stuart Church, 1603–1642*, edited by Kenneth Fincham, 1–22. Stanford University Press.

Fogelson, Raymond D. 1977. "Cherokee Notions of Power." In *The Anthropology of Power: Ethnographic Studies from Asia, Oceania, and the New World,* edited by Raymond D. Fogelson Richard N. Adams, 185–194. Academic Press.

Fogelson, Raymond D., and Richard N. Adams, eds. 1977. *The Anthropology of Power: Ethnographic Studies from Asia, Oceania, and the New World.* Academic Press.

Fortes, M., and E. E. Evans-Pritchard. 1940. "Introduction." In *African Political Systems,* edited by M. Fortes and E. E. Evans-Pritchard, 1–23. Oxford University Press.

Frayn, Michael. 1974. *Constructions.* Wildwood House.

French, Peter J. 1972. *John Dee: The World of an Elizabethan Magus.* Routledge and Kegan Paul.

Fried, Morton H. 1967. *The Evolution of Political Society: An Essay in Political Anthropology.* Random House.

———. 1968. "On the Concepts of 'Tribe' and 'Tribal Society.'" In *Essays on the Problem of Tribe,* edited by June Helm, 3–20. Proceedings of the 1967 Annual Meeting of the American Ethnological Society. University of Washington Press.

———. 1978. "The State, the Chicken, and the Egg; or, What Came First?" In *Origins of the State: The Anthropology of Political Evolution,* edited by Ronald Cohen and Elman R. Service, 35–47. Institute for the Study of Human Issues.

Galloway, Patricia. 1989. "'The Chief Who Is Your Father:' Choctaw and French Views of the Diplomatic Relation." In *Powhatan's Mantle: Indians in the Colonial Southeast,* edited by Peter H. Wood, Gregory A. Waselkov, and M. Thomas Hatley, 254–278. University of Nebraska Press.

———. 1995. *Choctaw Genesis, 1500–1700.* University of Nebraska Press.

Gearing, Fred. 1962. *Priests and Warriors: Social Structures for Cherokee Politics in the 18th Century.* American Anthropological Association Memoir 93.

Geary, James A., Rev. 1953. "Strachey's Vocabulary of Indian Words used in Virginia, 1612." In *Historie of Travell into Virginia Britania*, by William Strachey. Edited by Louis B. Wright and Virginia Freund. Appendix B, 208-214. The Hakluyt Society.

———. 1991. "The Language of the Carolina Algonkian Tribes." In *The Roanoke Voyages 1584-1590*, edited by David Beers Quinn, vol. 2, Appendix 2, 873-900. Dover.

Gerard, William R. 1907. "Virginia's Indian Contributions to English." *American Anthropologist*, n.s., 9:87-112.

Gibson, Arrell M. 1971. *The Chickasaws*. University of Oklahoma Press.

Gilbert, William Harlen, Jr. 1943. "The Eastern Cherokees." *Anthropological Papers*, Nos. 19-23. Smithsonian Institution, Bureau of American Ethnology Bulletin 133, 169-413.

Girouard, Mark. 1978. *Life in the English Country House*. Yale University Press.

Gittings, Clare. 1984. *Death, Burial and the Individual in Early Modern England*. Croom Helm.

Gleach, Frederic W. 1997. *Powhatan's World and Colonial Virginia: A Conflict of Cultures*. University of Nebraska Press.

Gledhill, John. 1994. *Power and Its Disguises*. Pluto Press.

Gowing, Laura. 1996. *Domestic Dangers: Women, Words, and Sex in Early Modern London*. Oxford University Press.

Greenblatt, Stephen. 1991. *Marvelous Possessions: The Wonder of the New World*. University of Chicago Press.

Gregory, C. 1982. *Gifts and Commodities*. Academic Press.

Haas, Jonathan. 1982. *The Evolution of the Prehistoric State*. Columbia University Press.

Hakluyt, Richard [the elder]. 1935 [1578]. "Notes on Colonisation." In *The Original Writings and Correspondence of the Two Richard Hakluyts*, edited and with an introduction and notes by E. G. R. Taylor, 116-122. The Hakluyt Society.

———. 1935 [1585]. "Pamphlet for the Virginia Enterprise." In

The Original Writings and Correspondence of the Two Richard Hakluyts, edited and with an introduction and notes by E. G. R. Taylor, 327–338. The Hakluyt Society.

Hakluyt, Richard [the younger]. 1935 [1584]. "Discourse of Western Planting." In *The Original Writings and Correspondence of the Two Richard Hakluyts*, edited and with an introduction and notes by E. G. R. Taylor, 211–326. The Hakluyt Society.

———. 1962 [1589]. *Voyages.* 8 vols. Dutton.

Hall, Robert L. 1989. "The Cultural Background of Mississippian Symbolism." In *The Southeastern Ceremonial Complex: Artifacts and Analysis*, edited by Patricia Galloway, 239–278. University of Nebraska Press.

Hallpike, C. R. 1977. *Bloodshed and Vengeance in the Papuan Highlands.* Oxford University Press.

Hamor, Ralph. 1957 [1615]. *A Trve Discovrse of the Present Estate of Virginia, and the successe of the affaires there till the 18 of Iune, 1614.* Reprinted from the London edition, 1615, with an introduction by A. L. Rowse. Virginia State Library.

Hanson, F. Allan. 1975. *Meaning in Culture.* Routledge and Kegan Paul.

Hantman, Jeffrey L. 1990. "Between Powhatan and Quirank: Reconstruction Monacan Culture and History in the Context of Jamestown." *American Anthropologist* 92, no. 3:676–690.

Harringon, M. R. 1921. *Religion and Ceremonies of the Lenape.* Indian Notes and Monographs, Museum of the American Indian, Heye Foundation.

Harriot, Thomas. 1972 [1590]. *A Briefe and True Report of the New Found Land of Virginia.* With a new introduction by Paul Hulton. Dover.

Haynes, John H., Jr. 1984. "The Seasons of Tsenacommacoh and the Rise of Wahunsenacawh: Structure and Ecology in Social Evolution." Master's thesis, University of Virginia, Charlottesville.

Helm, June, ed. 1968. *Essays on the Problem of Tribe.* Proceedings of the 1967 Annual Meeting of the American Ethnological Society. University of Washington Press.

Hertz, Robert. 1960. "A Contribution to the Study of the Collective Representation of Death." In *Death and the Right Hand*. Translated Rodney and Claudia Needham, with an introduction by E. E. Evans-Pritchard, 27–86. Cohen and West.

Heusch, Luc de. 1972. *Le roi ivre ou l'origine de l'état*. Gallimard.

———. 1985. *Sacrifice in Africa: A Structuralist Approach*. Translated by Linda O'Brien and Alice Morton. Indiana University Press.

———. 1987. *Ecrits sur la royauté sacrée*. Institut de Sociology. Editions de l'Université de Bruxelles.

Hewitt, J. N. B. 1902. "Orenda and a Definition of Religion." *American Anthropologist*, n.s., 4, no. 3:33–46.

Hill, Christopher. 1980. *The Century of Revolution 1603–1714*. 2nd ed. W. W. Norton.

Hocart, A. M. 1970a. *Kings and Councillors. An Essay in the Comparative Anatomy of Human Society*. Edited and with an introduction by Rodney Needham and with a foreword by E. E. Evans-Pritchard. University of Chicago Press.

———. 1970b. *The Life-Giving Myth and Other Essays*. Edited by Rodney Needham. Methuen.

Hodgen, Margaret T. 1964. *Early Anthropology in the Sixteenth and Seventeenth Centuries*. University of Pennsylvania Press.

Huber, Peter B. 1980. "The Anggor Bowman: Ritual and Society in Melanesia." *American Ethnologist* 7, no. 1:43–57.

Hubert, Henri, and Marcel Mauss. 1964. *Sacrifice: Its Nature and Function*. Translated by W. D. Halls, with a foreword by E. E. Evans-Pritchard. Cohen and West.

Hudson, Charles. 1976. *The Southeastern Indians*. University of Tennessee Press.

Hulton, Paul. 1972. Introduction to *A Briefe and True Report of the New Found Land of Virginia*, by Thomas Harriot. Dover.

———. 1984. *America 1585: The Complete Drawings of John White*. University of North Carolina Press and the British Museum.

Hulton, Paul, and David Beers Quinn. 1964. *The American Drawings of John White 1577–1590*. 2 vols. Trustees of the British Museum and the University of North Carolina Press.

James I, King of England. 1918 [1598]. "The Trew Law of Free Monarchies: or the Reciprock and Mvtvall Dvetie betwixt a Free King and his Naturall Subjects." In *The Political Works of James I*. Edited and with an introduction by Charles Howard McIlwain, 53–70. Harvard University Press.

———. 1918 [1599]. "Basilikon Doron, or His Maiesties Instrvctions to his Dearest Sonne, Henry the Prince." In *The Political Works of James I*. Edited and with an introduction by Charles Howard McIlwain, 3–52. Harvard University Press.

———. 1918 [1605]. "A Speech in the Parliament Hovse, as Neere the Very Words as Covld be Gethered at the Instant." In *The Political Works of James I*. Edited and with an introduction by Charles Howard McIlwain, 282–289. Harvard University Press.

Jefferson, Thomas. 1832. *Notes on the State of Virginia*. Lilly and Wait.

Jones, Howard Mumford. 1946. *The Colonial Impulse. An Analysis of the "Promotion" Literature of Colonization*. Proceedings of the American Philosophical Society 90.

Kantorowicz, Ernst H. 1957. *The King's Two Bodies: A Study in Mediaeval Political Theology*. Princeton University Press.

Kingsbury, Susan Myra, ed. 1906–1936. *Records of the Virginia Company of London: The Court Book, from the Manuscript in the Library of Congress*. 4 vols. Government Printing Office.

Kinietz, Vernon, and Erminie W. Voegelin. 1939. *Shawnese Traditions. C. C. Trowbridge's Account*. Occasional Contributions from the Museum of Anthropology of the University of Michigan, No. 9.

Knight, Vernon James, Jr. 1989. "Symbolism of Mississippian

Mounds." In *Powhatan's Mantle: Indians in the Colonial South-east,* edited by Peter H. Wood, Gregory A. Waselkov, and M. Thomas Hatley, 279–291. University of Nebraska Press.

———. 1990. "Social Organization and the Evolution of Hierarchy in Southeastern Chiefdoms." *Journal of Anthropological Research* 46, no. 1:1–23.

Kroeber, A. L. 1939. *Cultural and Natural Areas of Native North America.* University of California Publications in American Archaeology and Ethnology 38.

Kupperman, Karen Ordahl. 1980. *Settling with the Indians.* Rowman and Littlefield.

———. 1984. *Roanoke: The Abandoned Colony.* Rowman and Allanheld.

———. 2000. *Indians and English: Facing Off in Early America.* Cornell University Press.

Landes, Ruth. 1971. *The Ojibwa Woman.* W. W. Norton.

Lankford, George E. 1992. "Red and White: Some Reflections on a Southeastern Metaphor." *Southern Folklore* 50, no. 1:53–80.

Laslett, Peter. 1971. *The World We Have Lost.* 2nd ed. Charles Scribner's Sons.

Lawson, John. 1967 [1709]. *A New Voyage to Carolina.* Edited and with an introduction and notes by Hugh Talmage Lefler. University of North Carolina Press.

Leach, E. R. 1965. *Political Systems of Highland Burma.* Athlone Press.

———. 1961. *Rethinking Anthropology.* Athlone Press.

Leland, Charles G. 1992. *Algonquin Legends.* 1884. Reprint. Dover.

Lévi-Strauss, Claude. 1966. *The Savage Mind.* University of Chicago Press.

———. 1967. "The Social and Psychological Aspects of Chieftainship in a Primitive Tribe: The Nambikuara of Northwestern Mato Grosso." In *Comparative Political Systems,* edited by Ronald Cohen and John Middleton, 45–62. Natural History Press.

Lewis, Clifford M., S.J., and Albert J. Loomie, S.J. 1953. *The Spanish Jesuit Mission in Virginia 1570–1572*. University of North Carolina Press for the Virginia Historical Society.

Litten, Julian. 1991. *The English Way of Death: The Common Funeral since 1450*. Robert Hale.

London Company of Virginia. 1910 [1606]. "Instructions by way of advice, for the intended Voyage to Virginia." In *Travels and Works of Captain John Smith*, edited by Edward Arber and A. G. Bradley, 1:xxxiii–xxxvii. John Grant.

Lowie, Robert H. 1967. "Some Aspects of Political Organization among the American Aborigines." In *Comparative Political Systems*, edited by Ronald Cohen and John Middleton, 63–87. Natural History Press.

Lurie, Nancy Oestreich. 1959. "Indian Cultural Adjustment to European Civilization." In *Seventeenth-Century America: Essays in Colonial History*, edited by James Morton Smith, 33–60. University of North Carolina Press.

MacCaffrey, Wallace T. 1992. *Elizabeth I: War and Politics*. Princeton University Press.

Macfarlane, Alan. 1986. *Marriage and Love in England: Modes of Reproduction 1300–1840*. Basil Blackwell.

Mackenzie, W. J. M. 1969. *Politics and Social Science*. Penguin Books.

Mallios, Seth. 1998. "In the Hands of 'Indian Givers:' Exchange and Violence at Ajacan, Roanoke, and Jamestown." Ph.D. thesis, University of Virginia.

Marshall, Lorna. 1967. "!Kung Bushman Bands." In *Comparative Political Systems*, edited by Ronald Cohen and John Middleton, 15–43. Natural History Press.

Mauss, Marcel. 1990. *The Gift: The Form and Reason for Exchange in Archaic Societies*. Translated by W. D. Halls, with a foreword by Mary Douglas. W. W. Norton.

McCartney, Martha W. 1989. "Cockacoeske, Queen of Pamunkey: Diplomat and Suzeraine." In *Powhatan's Mantle: Indians in the Colonial Southeast,* edited by Peter H. Wood, Gregory A. Waselkov, and M. Thomas Hatley, 172–195. University of Nebraska Press.

McCary, Ben C., and Norman F. Barka. 1977. "The John Smith and Zuniga Maps in the Light of Recent Archaeological Investigations along the Chickahominy River." *Archaeology of Eastern North America* 5:73–86.

McFarlane, Anthony. 1994. *The British in the Americas 1480–1815.* Longman.

McIlwain, Charles Howard. 1918. Introduction to *The Political Works of James I,* edited by C. H. McIlwain. Harvard University Press.

McMillan, Alan D. 1988. *Native Peoples and Cultures of Canada.* Douglas and McIntyre.

Medawar, P. B. 1967. *The Art of the Soluble.* Penguin Books.

Milanich, Jerald T., 2000. "The Timucua Indians of Northern Florida and Southern Georgia." In *Indians of the Greater Southeast: Historical Archaeology and Ethnohistory,* edited by Bonnie G. McEwan, 1–25. University Press of Florida.

Milfort, Louis LeClerc. 1959. *Memoirs or a Quick Glance at My Varioius Travels and my Sojourn in the Creek Nation.* Translated and edited by Ben C. McCary. Beehive Press.

Miller, Christopher L., and George R. Hamell. 1986. "A New Perspective on Indian-White Contact: Cultural Symbols and Colonial Trade." *Journal of American History* 73, no. 2:311–328.

Montaigne, Michel de. 1958. *Essays.* Translated and with an introduction by J. M. Cohen. Penguin Books.

Mook, Maurice A. 1943. "The Anthropological Position of the Indian Tribes of Tidewater Virginia." *William and Mary College Quarterly* 23:27–40.

———. 1944. "The Aboriginal Population of Tidewater Virginia." *American Anthropologist,* n.s., 46:193–208.

Mooney, James. 1907. "The Powhatan Confederacy, Past and Present." *American Anthropologist,* n.s., 9:129–152.

Morgan, Lewis Henry. 1996. *League of the Iroquois.* Introduction by William N. Fenton. 1851. Reprint. Citadel Press.

Neale, J. E. 1971. *Queen Elizabeth I.* Penguin Books.
Needham, Rodney. 1970. Introduction to *Kings and Councillors,* by A. M. Hocart. Edited by Rodney Needham. University of Chicago Press.
———. 1979. *Symbolic Classification.* Goodyear.
———. 1980. *Reconnaissances.* University of Toronto Press.
———. 1981. *Circumstantial Deliveries.* University of California Press.
———. 1985. *Exemplars.* University of California Press.

Oberg, Michael Leroy. 1999. *Dominion and Civility.* Cornell University Press.
O'Hara, Diana. 1991. " 'Ruled by my friends': Aspects of Marriage in the Diocese of Canterbury, c. 1540–1570." *Continuity and Change* 6, no. 1:9–41.
Oxford English Dictionary. 1989. Oxford University Press.

Pagden, Anthony. 1995. *Lords of All the World: Ideologies of Empire in Spain, Britain, and France, c. 1500–c. 1800.* Yale University Press.
Parry, J., and M. Bloch, eds. 1989. *Money and the Morality of Exchange.* Cambridge University Press.
Patterson, Annabel. 1984. *Censorship and Interpretation.* University of Wisconsin Press.
Percy, George. 1910 [1607]. "Observations gathered out of 'A Discourse of the Plantation of the Southerne Colonie in Virginia by the English. 1606:' Written by that Honorable Gentleman, Master George Percy." In *Travels and Works of Captain John Smith,* edited by Edward Arber and A. G. Bradley, 1:lvii–lxxiii. John Grant.
———. 1922 [1612]. "A Trewe Relacyon of the Procedeinges and

Ocurrentes of Momente wch have hapned in Virginia. from the Tyme Sr Thomas Gates was shippwrackte uppon the Bermudes an° 1609 untill my depture outt of the Country wch was in 1612." *Tyler's Quarterly Magazine* 3:260–282.

Peters, Christine. 1997. "Single Women in Early Modern England: Attitudes and Expectations." *Continuity and Change* 12, no. 3:325–345.

Pocock, J. G. A. 1967. *The Ancient Constitution and the Feudal Law: A Study of English Historical Thought in the Seventeenth Century.* W. W. Norton.

Potter, Stephen R. 1989. "Early English Effects on Virginia Algonquian Exchange and Tribute in the Tidewater Potomac." In *Powhatan's Mantle: Indians in the Colonial Southeast,* edited by Peter H. Wood, Gregory Waselkov, and M. Thomas Hatley, 151–172. University of Nebraska Press.

———. 1993. *Commoners, Tribute, and Chiefs: The Development of Algonquian Culture in the Potomac Valley.* University Press of Virginia.

Powers, William K. 1977. *Oglala Religion.* University of Nebraska Press.

Purchas, Samuel. 1617. *Purchas his Pilgrimage, or Relations of the World and the Religions observed in al ages and Places discouered, from the Creation vnto this Present.* 3rd ed. H. Featherstone.

———., ed. 1906 [1625]. *Hakluytus Posthumus, or Purchas His Pilgrimes. Contayning a History of the World in Sea Voyages and Lande Travells by Englishmen and others.* 20 vols. James MacLehose and Sons.

Quinn, David Beers. 1985. *Set Fair for Roanoke: Voyages and Colonies, 1584–1606.* University of North Carolina Press.

———., ed. 1991. *The Roanoke Voyages 1584–1590.* 2 vols. Dover.

Rabb, Theodore K. 1967. *Enterprise and Empire: Merchant and Gentry Investment in the Expansion of England, 1575–1630.* Harvard University Press.

Radcliffe-Brown, A. R. 1940. "Preface." In *African Political Systems*, edited by M. Fortes and E. E. Evans-Pritchard, xi–xxiii. Oxford University Press.

Rangel, Rodrigo. 1993. "Account of the Northern Conquest and Discovery of Hernando de Soto." Translated and edited by John E. Worth, with footnotes by John E. Worth and Charles Hudson. In *The De Soto Chronicles: The Expedition of Hernando de Soto to North America in 1539–1543*, edited by Lawrence A. Clayton, Vernon James Knight Jr., and Edward C. Moore, 247–306. University of Alabama Press.

Rountree, Helen. 1989. *The Powhatan Indians of Virginia: Their Traditional Culture.* University of Oklahoma Press.

———. 1990. *Pocahontas's People: The Powhatan Indians of Virginia through Four Centuries.* University of Oklahoma Press.

———. 1998. "Powhatan Indian Women: The People Captain John Smith Barely Saw." *Ethnohistory* 45, no. 1:1–29.

———., ed. 1993. *Powhatan Foreign Relations 1500–1722.* University Press of Virginia.

Rowse, A. L. 1957. Introduction to *A Trve Discovrse of the Present Estate of Virginia, and the successe of the affaires there till the 18 of Iune, 1614,* by Ralph Hamor. Virginia State Library.

Russell, Howard S. 1980. *Indian New England before the Mayflower.* University Press of New England.

Sahlins, Marshall. 1972. *Stone Age Economics.* Aldine de Gruyter.

———. 1976. *Culture and Practical Reason.* University of Chicago Press.

———. 1981. *Historical Metaphors and Mythical Realities: Structure in the Early History of the Sandwich Island Kingdom.* University of Michigan Press.

Salmon, Vivian. 1992. "Thomas Harriot (1560–1621) and the English Origins of Algonkian Linguistics." *Historiographia Linguistica* 19, no. 1:25–56.

Sandys, Edwin. 1605. *A Relation of the State of Religion: and with what Hopes and Pollicies it hath beene framed, and is maintained in the severall states of these westerne parts of the world.* Printed for Simon Waterson.

Sharpe, James. 1997. *Instruments of Darkness: Witchcraft in Early Modern England.* University of Pennsylvania Press.

Sharpe, Kevin. 1989. *Politics and Ideas in Early Stuart England.* Pinter.

Sheehan, Bernard. 1980. *Savagism and Civility: Indians and Englishmen in Colonial Virginia.* Cambridge University Press.

Siebert, Frank T., Jr. 1975. "Resurrecting Virginia Algonquian from the Dead: The Reconstituted and Historical Phonology of Powhatan." In *Studies in Southeastern Indian Languages,* edited by James M. Crawford, 285–453. University of Georgia Press.

Simmons, William S. 1986. *Spirit of the New England Tribes: Indian History and Folklore, 1620–1984.* University Press of New England.

Smith, John. 1910 [1612]. *A Map of Virginia. With a description of the Countrey, the commodities, people, government and religion.* In *Travels and Works of Captain John Smith,* edited by Edward Arber and A. G. Bradley, 1:41–173. John Grant.

———. 1986 [1608]. *A True Relation of such occurrences and accidents of noate as hath hapned in Virginia since the first planting of that Collony, which is now resident in the South part thereof, till the last returne from thence.* In *The Complete Works of Captain John Smith (1580–1631),* edited by Philip L. Barbour, 1:21–117. University of North Carolina Press.

———. 1986 [1612]. *A Map of Virginia. With a description of the Countrey, the commodities, people, government and religion.* In *The Complete Works of Captain John Smith (1580–1631),* edited by Philip L. Barbour, 1:119–370. University of North Carolina Press.

———. 1986 [1624]. *The Generall Historie of Virginia, New-England, and the Summer Isles.* In *The Complete Works of Captain John Smith (1580–1631),* edited by Philip L. Barbour, 2:26–488. University of North Carolina Press.

———. 1986 [1630]. *The True Travels, Adventures, and Observations of Captaine John Smith.* In *The Complete Works of Captain John Smith (1580–1631),* edited by Philip L. Barbour, 3:137–251. University of North Carolina Press.

Smuts, R. Malcolm. 1987. *Court Culture and the Origins of a Royalist Tradition in Early Stuart England.* University of Pennsylvania Press.

Speck, Frank G. 1924. "The Ethnic Position of the Southeastern Algonkian." *American Anthropologist* 26:184–200.

———. 1928. *Chapters on the Ethnology of the Powhatan Tribes of Virginia.* Indian Notes and Monographs 1, no. 5. Heye Foundation, Museum of the American Indian.

Spelman, Henry. 1910 [1613]. "Relation of Virginea." In *Travels and Works of Captain John Smith,* edited by Edward Arber and A. G. Bradley, 1:ci–cxiv. John Grant.

Stevens, Henry. 1900. *As to Thomas Hariot Virginia's First Historian, or, Thomas Hariot, the Mathematician, the Philospher, and the Scholar.* Privately printed.

Stone, Lawrence. 1965. *The Crisis of the Aristocracy 1558–1641.* Oxford University Press.

———. 1979. *The Family, Sex and Marriage in England 1500–1800.* Abridged ed. Harper.

Strachey, William. 1906 [1610]. "A true repertory of the wracke, and redemption of Sir Thomas Gates Knight; upon, and from the Ilands of the Bermudas: his comming to Virginia, and the estate of that Colonies then, and after, under the government of the Lord La Warre, July 15. 1610." In *Hakluytus Posthumus or Purchas His Pilgrimes. Contayning a History of the World in Sea Voyages and Lande Travells by Englishmen and others,* edited by Samuel Purchas, 19:5–69. James MacLehose and Sons.

———. 1953 [1612]. *The Historie of Travell into Virginia Britania,* edited by Louis B. Wright and Virginia Freund. The Hakluyt Society.

Swanton, John R. 1911. *Indian Tribes of the Lower Mississippi Valley and Adjacent Coast of the Gulf of Mexico*. Smithsonian Institution, Bureau of American Ethnology Bulletin 43.

———. 1928. "Sun Worship in the Southeast." *American Anthropologist*, n.s., 30:206–213.

———. 1929. *Myths and Tales of the Southeastern Indians*. Smithsonian Institution, Bureau of American Ethnology Bulletin 88.

———. 1931. *Source Material for the Social and Ceremonial Life of the Choctaw Indians*. Smithsonian Institution, Bureau of American Ethnology Bulletin 103.

———. 1935. "Notes on the Cultural Province of the Southeast." *American Anthropologist* 37:373–385.

———. 1952. *Indian Tribes of North America*. Smithsonian Institution, Bureau of American Ethnology Bulletin 145.

———. 1987. *The Indians of the Southeastern United States*. Reprint of Bureau of American Ethnology Bulletin 137 (1946). Smithsonian Institution Press.

———. 1998. *Early History of the Creek Indians and Their Neighbors*. Foreword by Jerald T. Milanich. University Press of Florida.

———. 2000. *Creek Religion and Medicine*. Introduction by James T. Carson. University of Nebraska Press.

Tawney, R. H. 1987. *Religion and the Rise of Capitalism*. Penguin Books.

Taylor, E. G. R. 1934. *Late Tudor and Early Stuart Geography 1583–1650*. Methuen.

———., ed. 1935. *The Original Writings and Correspondence of the Two Richard Hakluyts*. Introduction and notes by E. G. R. Taylor. The Hakluyt Society.

Tedlock, Dennis, trans. 1985. *Popol Vuh*. With commentary based on the ancient knowledge of the modern Quiché Maya. Simon and Schuster.

Thomas, Keith. 1971. *Religion and the Decline of Magic*. Weidenfeld and Nicolson.

Timberlake, Henry. 1948. *Memoirs, 1756–1765*. With annotation, introduction, and index by Samuel Cole Williams. Continental Book Company.

Tooker, Elisabeth. 1991. *An Ethnography of the Huron Indians, 1615–1649.* Smithsonian Institution, Bureau of American Ethnology Bulletin 190.

———., ed. 1979. *Native North American Spirituality of the Eastern Woodlands.* Paulist Press.

Turner, E. Randolph. 1985. "Socio-Political Organization within the Powhatan Chiefdom and the Effects of European Contact, A.D. 1607–1646." In *Cultures in Contact: The European Impact on Native Cultural Institutions in Eastern North America, A.D. 1000–1800,* edited by William W. Fitzhugh, 193–224. Smithsonian Institution Press.

Turner, Victor. 1967. *The Forest of Symbols.* Cornell University Press.

Underdown, David. 1985. *Revel, Riot, and Rebellion: Popular Politics and Culture in England 1603–1660.* Oxford University Press.

Vaughan, Alden T. 1973. "The Evolution of Virginia History: Early Historians of the First Colony." In *Perspectives on Early American History: Essays in Honor of Richard B. Morris,* edited by A. T. Vaughan and G. A. Billias, 9–39. Harper and Row.

———. 1975. *American Genesis: Captain John Smith and the Founding of Virginia.* Little, Brown.

Voegelin, C. F. 1970. "The Shawnee Female Deity." *Yale University Publications in Anthropology,* No. 10. 1936. Reprint. HRAF Press.

Wagner, Roy. 1975. *The Invention of Culture.* Prentice-Hall.

Walam Olum, or Red Score: The Migration Legend of the Lenni Lenape or Delaware Indians. 1954. Indiana Historical Society.

Walker, James R. 1991. *Lakota Belief and Ritual.* Edited by Raymond J. DeMallie and Elaine A. Jahner. University of Nebraska Press.

Waselkov, Gregory A. 1989a. "Indian Maps of the Colonial South-east." In *Powhatan's Mantle: Indians in the Colonial Southeast,* edited by Peter H. Wood, Gregory Waselkov, and M. Thomas Hatley, 292–343. University of Nebraska Press.

———. 1989b. Introduction to "Part Two: Politics and Economics." In *Powhatan's Mantle: Indians in the Colonial Southeast,* edited by Peter H. Wood, Gregory Waselkov, and M. Thomas Hatley, 129–133. University of Nebraska Press.

Whitaker, Alexander. 1613. *Good Newes from Virginia. Sent to the Covnsell and Company of Virginia, resident in England.* Scholars' Facsimiles and Reprints.

White, William. 1969 [1614]. Fragments. In *The Jamestown Voyages Under the First Charter 1606–1609,* edited by Philip Barbour, 1:147–150. The Hakluyt Society.

Williamson, Margaret Holmes. 1972. "Examination and Re-analysis of the Early Sources Relating to the Powhatan Confederacy of Tidewater Virginia in the Seventeenth Century." B.Litt. thesis, University of Oxford.

———. 1979. "Powhatan Hair." *Man,* n.s., 14, no. 3:392–413.

———. 1992. "Pocahontas and Captain John Smith: Examining an Historical Myth." *History and Anthropology* 5, nos. 3–4:365–402.

———. 1993. " 'Civilising' the Powhatan." Paper presented at the Annual Meeting of the Southern Anthropological Society, Atlanta.

Willoughby, Charles C. 1935. "Michabo the Great Hare: A Patron of the Hopewell Mound Settlement." *American Anthropologist,* n.s., 37:280–286.

Willson, D. Harris. 1956. *King James VI and I.* Jonathan Cape.

Wingfield, Edward Maria. 1910 [1608]. "A Discourse of virginia." In *Travels and Works of Captain John Smith,* edited by Edward Arber and A. G. Bradley, 1:lxxiv–xci. John Grant.

Wissler, Clark. 1938. *The American Indian.* 3rd ed. Oxford University Press.

Wolf, Eric R. 1997. *Europe and the People without History*. 2nd ed. University of California Press.

———— 1999. *Envisioning Power: Ideologies of Dominance and Crisis*. University of California Press.

Wright, Louis B., and Virginia Freund. 1953. Introduction to *The Historie of Travell into Virginia Britania*, by William Strachey. Edited by Louis B. Wright and Virginia Freund. The Hakluyt Society.

Wrightson, Keith. 1982. *English Society 1580–1680*. Hutchinson.

Yates, Frances A. 1964. *Giordano Bruno and the Hermetic Tradition*. University of Chicago Press.

————. 1969. *Theatre of the World*. University of Chicago Press.

————. 1972. *The Rosicrucian Enlightenment*. Shambhala Publications.

————. 1975. *Astraea: The Imperial Theme in the Sixteenth Century*. Routledge and Kegan Paul.

————. 1979. *The Occult Philosophy in the Elizabethan Age*. Routledge and Kegan Paul.

Zuckerman, Michael. 1995. "Identity in British America: Unease in Eden." In *Colonial Identity in the Atlantic World, 1500–1800*, edited by Nicholas Canny and Anthony Pagden, 115–157. Princeton University Press.

Index

Accohannock (Powhatan Indian tribe), 55, 71

Accomac (Powhatan Indian tribe), 55, 70, 71

adultery, among Powhatan. *See* Powhatan Indians: and law

Ahone (Powhatan divinity). *See* religion, Powhatan Indian: divinities of

Algonkian Indians: of North Carolina, 49, 61, 79, 81, 180, 181–182, 184–185, 193, 197, 230, 231, 248, 250, 289 n.21 n.22; of New England, 45–46, 173, 175, 177, 193, 218, 250, 257

Alvarado, Rafael, 283 n.2

Amidas, Captain Philip, 25

Anglicans. *See* Church of England

Appomattox, Powhatan Indian tribe, 39, 59, 62, 63, 65, 70, 112, 122, 124, 168, 249

Archer, Captain Gabriel, 74, 76

Argyll, Captain Samuel, 39–40, 77

Aristotle, 92

Arrohattock (Powhatan Indian tribe), 52, 56, 59, 62, 113, 122, 124, 139, 154, 167–168, 231

authority: categorical associations of, in Powhatan culture, 206, 217, 221, 224, 227, 228, 229–230, 234, 241, 247, 248, 252–253; as complement to power, 13–15, 106, 168, 192, 201, 254–255, 258. *See also* dual sovereignty; politics

Barlowe, Captain Arthur, 25, 79, 81

beads, 41, 43, 153, 154, 156, 157, 158, 160, 161, 162, 212, 234, 242, 249, 251–252, 253, 285–286 n.11; as currency, 45; as decoration, 111, 115, 118, 166, 224, 248; manufacture of, 279 n.19. *See also* pearls; wampum

Bead-Spitter (Southeastern Indian mythic figure), 43, 157

Beverley, Major Robert, 81–82, 89, 180–181, 185

bias, cultural, 90, 261 n.2

black. *See* colors: black; symbolic oppositions, Powhatan Indian

Bry, Theodor de, 79–80

burial. *See* funerals: Powhatan Indian customs for

Caddo Indians, 45

cannibalism, 38, 240

Capahowosick, 66, 67, 146, 171, 269 n.13

Catholics, 16–17, 20–21, 80, 194, 195, 196. *See also* Protestants; Spain

celeritas, 14, 171, 185, 193, 200, 248, 253. *See also* symbolic oppositions, Powhatan Indian

center-periphery opposition. *See* symbolic oppositions, Powhatan Indian

"charnel" houses. See *quioccasan;* Southeastern Indians: mortuary structures of

Cherokee Indians, 44, 45

Chesapeake Bay, 25, 29, 32–33, 55; Eastern Shore of, 33, 34, 40, 54, 55, 71, 285 n.9

Chesapeake Indians, 64

Chickahominy Indians, 35, 52, 55–56, 61, 71, 136, 198, 269 n.15

Chickasaw Indians, 44, 45

chief, social status of, 5, 13, 148–152

chiefs, Carolina Algonkian, 49, 133, 134, 138

chiefs, Powhatan Indian, 41, 82, 103, 252–253; power of, 8–9, 15, 95; rule of succession among, 107–108. *See also* "kings," Powhatan Indian; *werowance*

Chiskiak (Powhatan Indian tribe), 59, 61, 62, 63, 83

Choctaw Indians, 44, 45, 182

Chowan Indians, 54

Christianity. *See* Catholics; Church of England; Protestants

Church of England, 16, 107, 194

circles, 173, 166, 181, 188–189, 190, 225, 226, 241. *See also* symbolic oppositions, Powhatan Indian civil: defined, 92, 93; Powhatan Indians as, 74, 85, 94, 95, 109, 111, 114, 122, 125. *See also* savage

Clayton, Rev. John, 83

cockarouse (Powhatan councilor), 55, 133–138, 165–172, 192; etymology of term, 137, 165–166; power of, 168, 170; relation of to *werowance*, 136, 168, 215; as war leader, 134, 136, 166, 169–170

codpiece, deplored by James I, 110

colors, 288 n.21; black, 66, 180, 183, 185, 223, 249–251; blue, 111, 288 n.21; red, 41, 44, 111, 115, 117, 118, 122, 159, 165, 180, 183, 213, 233, 248–249; white, 43, 44, 115, 117, 118, 180, 183, 207, 248, 251–252; yellow, 289 n.21. *See also* color symbolism; symbolic oppositions, Powhatan Indian

color symbolism, 247–254. *See also* colors

command, 88, 95, 98. *See also* obedience

conjuror: in Renaissance English thought, 196–197; as subordinate to priest, 196–197; term for *quiyoughcosough*, 192–193. *See also quiyoughcosough*

Conoy Indians, 41, 54

contradictions, in Jamestown accounts, 130, 255

copper, 28, 41, 53, 55, 61, 111, 113, 114, 139, 153, 154, 156, 160, 161, 162, 165, 166, 224, 236, 241–242, 247, 248–249, 250, 252, 253, 273 n.16

corn (maize), 35, 37, 66, 139, 146, 153, 154, 156–158, 164, 171, 208, 213, 217, 226, 231, 289 n.21. *See also* Powhatan Indians: culinary practices of, subsistence among

councilor. See *cockarouse*

counsel: in English political theory, 99; among Powhatan, 166

Creek Indians, 44

culture areas, 42–46

Dale, Sir Thomas, 39, 56; and marriage proposal to Pocahontas's sister, 78, 158, 162, 270 n.5

death-life opposition. *See* symbolic oppositions, Powhatan Indian

Dee, John, 25

deer, 62, 122, 123, 156, 164, 174, 208, 231, 235, 239, 243, 245

Delaware Indians, 180

De la Warr, Lord, 36, 39

despot, 101. *See also* tyrant

Devil, 173, 178, 196, 197, 199, 208, 236, 239, 250, 271 n.7, 284 n.7. See also Oke; sacrifice, among Powhatan

Discourse of Western Planting (Richard Hakluyt the Younger), 17–25

divination, Powhatan, 281 n.9. *See also* religion, Powhatan Indian; Smith, Captain John: "conjuration" over

Don Luis de Velasco (Powhatan werowance), 70, 83, 136, 143, 144, 271 n.6

dual sovereignty, 4, 6, 13, 98, 229; in native North America, 44–46, 256–257, 258; possibly universal, 14; in Powhatan Indian culture, 138, 144, 172, 217, 226–227, 248, 254–255, 257–260. *See also* dyarchy, in Powhatan Indian culture

dyarchy, in Powhatan Indian culture, 202, 204, 206, 258, 260. *See also* dual sovereignty

east-west opposition. *See* symbolic oppositions, Powhatan Indian

efficacy. *See* power: as equivalent to efficacy

Elizabeth I (queen of England), 15, 17, 21–22, 23, 109, 121, 125, 126

England: colonial enterprises of, 17; desire to trade with Indians, 19–20, 22, 28, 36; economic problems of, 23; funerals, in seventeenth century, 241; and hostilities toward Spain, 20, 24; interest of, in productivity of Virginia, 22; as Protestant nation, 16, 194–195; and sincerity of missionary efforts, 18–19, 20, 22

ethnographic imagination, 3

ethnography, 74, 87, 130; interpretations vs. reports in, 89–90. *See also* native voice

evidence, value of, 8

execution, among Powhatan, 139–140, 142, 216, 237–238. *See also* sacrifice

feather cloaks, 114, 166, 213

female-male opposition. *See* Powhatan Indians: gender definitions among; symbolic oppositions, Powhatan Indian

fire, 140, 181, 182, 183, 188, 219, 222, 225, 228, 229-230, 234, 238, 239, 240, 243, 249, 250, 253, 254
Fortune, R. F., 87
fractal, 228
funerals: English, 241; Powhatan Indian customs for, 208, 222, 223, 285 n.11

gardening. *See* Powhatan Indians: subsistence among
Gates, Sir Thomas, 36, 38, 39, 75
gifts, among Powhatan Indians, 148, 155, 160-161, 171. *See also* hierarchy; Mauss, Marcel
God, Christian, 177-178
gold, 28, 111
gravitas, 14, 171, 185, 193, 200, 248, 253. *See also* symbolic oppositions, Powhatan Indian
Great Hare (Powhatan divinity): Algonkian, 174-175, 281 n.3. *See* religion, Powhatan Indian: divinities of

Hakluyt, Richard, the younger, 17, 262 n.7. See also *Discourse of Western Planting*
Hamor, Ralph, 78, 158, 162
Harriot, Thomas, 25, 75, 79, 80-81, 82, 87
hat, symbolism of, 117-118
hatchets, 153, 154, 181, 242, 247, 249, 277 n.11
Heraclitus, 246
Hertz, Robert, and theory of mummification, 244-245
hierarchy, 126, 256; in aboriginal Virginia, 129, 146-147, 166-167, 192, 200, 202, 228, 254; defined, 15; dialectical, 145, 170-171, 172, 205, 254-255; in England, 98, 129, 197; exchange, relation to, 149-150, 151, 155-156, 161; of gender, 258; power, relation to, 15; as syntagmatic relationship, 215, 221
high-low opposition. *See* symbolic oppositions, Powhatan Indian
Horned Serpent, Great, 174-175
hunting. *See* Powhatan Indians: subsistence among
Huron Indians, 176

huskanaw (Powhatan initiation ritual), 75, 79, 170, 207-209, 225, 248, 250, 251, 252; etymology of, 207
Hyrcania, 121, 126

Indians, American. *See specific area or tribe*
Iopassus (Iapazaws; Potomac werowance), 39, 234
iron, 249
irony, 100, 110, 144
Iroquois Indians, 263 n.12

James I (king of England), 15, 16, 56, 60, 73, 98, 99-102, 103, 105, 107, 109, 117, 121, 125, 157, 272 n.12
James River, 31, 40, 63, 71; first English exploration of, 29, 56, 62, 74, 122; Indian tribes along, 52
Jamestown, 31, 63, 66; early accounts from, 73-83, 88, 89, 91; settlement of, 28-29. *See also* Virginia, colony of
joint stock company, 26-27. *See also* Virginia Company of London
junior-senior opposition. *See* symbolic oppositions, Powhatan Indian
justice, among Powhatan. See *werowance*: as judge; Powhatan, paramount chief: as judge; Powhatan Indians: and law

Kecoughtan (Powhatan Indian tribe), 49, 50, 52, 64, 65, 124, 146, 179, 225-226
kings, European, 73, 98, 106; appearance of, 109-110; divine right (doctrine) of, 99-100; generosity of, 118-119, 121; as God's instruments on earth, 96, 98, 99, 100, 105, 107; and relation to the law, 99-101, 102, 103; and relation to subjects, 73, 99, 100-101; rights of, 100-101, 103; rules of succession for, 108-109; sources of authority of, 98, 100, 101, 102, 108, 194; as symbols of realm, 109-110, 120-121; will of, 101, 102, 103. *See also* monarch; spatial symbolism, European; tyrant
kings, Hocartian, 99, 121, 131-132, 142
"kings," Powhatan Indian, 41, 212. *See also* chiefs, Powhatan Indian; *werowance*

Tappahannock (Powhatan Indian tribe, on Rappahannock River), 64

temples. See *quioccasan*

theft, 35–36, 191

Timucua Indians, 44, 45, 182

tobacco, 22, 41, 122, 174, 188, 222, 226, 234, 236, 240, 242, 243, 262 n.6

Tockwogh Indians, 34, 41, 54

tombs. *See* Powhatan Indians: funeral customs of

Tomocomo, 79, 176, 177, 189, 282 n.10

total social phenomenon, 6, 150–151, 152

tribe, definition of, 48

tribes, Powhatan, 53–59; character of, 47–53; inherited and conquered, 59–60, 61–63; relations among, 59–64; and relations to the paramount, Powhatan, 59–60, 61, 62, 64. *See also specific tribal names*

Tsenacommacoh, 1

Turkey, 110

Tuscarora Indians, 268 n.5

Tutelo Indians, 40

typology, 3–4, 6

tyrant, 88, 110, 142, 214; defined, 101–102, 106; as scourge of God, 101–102. *See also* kings, European

Uttamussack, 54, 58, 59, 153, 171, 181, 182, 185, 186, 188, 198, 204, 205, 236

Veen, Gysbert van, 80, 184, 199, 200

Virginia, colony of: likened to Mediterranean, 22; perceived as paradise, 31, 75, 85; reasons for founding, 16–17, 25–26, 27. See also *Discourse of Western Planting;* Jamestown

Virginia, London Company of, 27, 28–29, 36, 263 n.8 n.9

Wahunsonacock. *See* Powhatan (paramount chief of Powhatan Indians)

wakan, 176

wampum, 45. *See also* beads

warfare, Powhatan Indian, 41, 52–53, 55, 202–203, 219, 220; manner of conduct during, 35, 52, 143; between Powhatan

Indians and neighbors, 41, 143; between Powhatan Indian tribes, 61, 64; and prisoners of war, 142, 144–146, 147, 167, 168; as related to sacrifice, 142, 147, 237; role of werowance in, 52, 61, 134, 143; as source of prestige, 35, 53, 147

Weanock (Powhatan Indian tribe), 52, 55, 61, 62, 63, 64, 122

werowance (*wiroans;* Powhatan Indian chief), 49, 72, 132–165, 170–172, 183, 192, 208, 223; afterlife of, 172, 204, 253; appearance of, 111, 113, 248; authority of, 138, 159, 170, 171; change in status of, through time, 133, 170; dance style of, 225; etymology of term, 137; generosity of, 148, 155, 171; houses of, 125; as judge, 138, 164, 170; kinship among, 65, 68–71, 136; life-giving, 137, 161, 163–164, 171, 242, 245; as likened to Eurasian monarch, 104, 110–127; marriage of, 161–163; mummification of, 172, 181, 219, 241–242, 254, 290 n.24; name of, how related to territory, 56–57, 104; polygynous, 161; power of, 96–98; as prisoner of war, 67, 146; as provider of shamans for tribe, 164–165; ranked, 136; relation of, to *cockarouse* (councilor), 168, 170–172, 215; relation of, to *quiyoughcosough* (shaman), 202–205, 283 n.1; rule of succession among, 41, 67; spiritual or sacerdotal status of, 66, 164, 171–172, 189, 204, 224, 245; as symbol of tribe, 159; as total social phenomenon, 151–152, 165; trading activities of, 156; as war leader, 133, 134, 142–145, 147, 249; wealth of, 137, 153–154; welcome of, when visiting, 124, 158–159, 227. *See also* chiefs, Powhatan Indian; "kings," Powhatan Indian; monarch; Powhatan (paramount chief of Powhatan Indians); symbolic oppositions, Powhatan Indian

Werowocomoco (Powhatan Indian tribe or village), 34, 35, 54, 57, 59, 67, 71, 154

West, Master Francis, 37, 38, 77

west-east opposition. *See* symbolic oppositions, Powhatan Indian

wet-dry opposition. *See* symbolic oppositions, Powhatan Indian
Whitaker, Rev. Alexander, 76, 79, 90
White, John, 79, 80, 180, 184, 200, 248, 252
White, William, 75, 79, 207, 225, 236
white. *See* colors: white; symbolic oppositions, Powhatan Indian
whore, playing the, 217, 276 n.7
wighsacan, 233
wild-settled opposition. *See* symbolic
oppositions, Powhatan Indian
Wingfield, Edward Maria, 31, 62, 63–64,
122

witch, European, 178–179, 196, 197, 271 n.7,
284 n.7
women: English, 209–212, 213, 214, 216, 285
n.8; Powhatan Indian, 67–68, 113–114,
115, 116, 117, 118, 122, 144, 145, 159, 161,
162, 163, 168, 171, 208, 209–217, 223, 225,
228, 230, 248, 249, 250, 254, 275 n.5; as
Powhatan Indian chiefs (*werowanqua*),
65, 108, 112–113, 123, 124, 136, 168, 210,
249

Youghtanund (Powhatan Indian tribe), 59,
61, 62, 182